Space-Time of the Bororo of Brazil

Space-Time

of the

Bororo of Brazil

STEPHEN MICHAEL FABIAN

University Press of Florida

Gainesville Tallahassee Tampa Boca Raton
Pensacola Orlando Miami Jacksonville

Library of Congress Cataloging in Publication Data

Fabian, Stephen Michael.
    Space-time of the Bororo of Brazil / Stephen Michael Fabian.
        p.   cm.
    Includes bibliographical references and index.
    ISBN 0–8130–1104–3
    1. Bororo Indians—Astronomy.   2. Bororo Indians—Religion and
mythology.   3. Bororo Indians—Social life and customs.   4. Space
and time.   5. Cosmology.   I. Title.
F2520.1.B75F34   1992   91–23287
305.898'4081—dc20   CIP

This book was approved for publication by the University of Florida
editorial committee.

The University Press of Florida is the scholarly publishing agency for the
State University System of Florida, comprised of Florida A&M University,
Florida Atlantic University, Florida International University, Florida State
University, University of Central Florida, University of Florida, University
of North Florida, University of South Florida, and University of West
Florida.

University Press of Florida, 15 N.W. 15th Street, Gainesville, FL 32611

All photographs by Stephen Fabian and Surabela Blatt-Fabian

To Surabela—

my wife, companion, best friend, and inspiration

CONTENTS

Illustrations

Preface

Few Bororo not living at the Catholic mission of Meruri are literate, and of course the Bororo language has no indigenous writing system. Several early collections of vocabularies and brief grammatical descriptions exist (e.g., Magalhães 1919; Von den Steinen 1940 [1894]), but the Salesian fathers were the first to give systematic treatment to this material (see especially Colbacchini 1925; Colbacchini and Albisetti 1942). Later Salesian work published in the *Enciclopédia Bororo* (hereafter *EB*) uses a complex system of diacritical marks to designate Bororo pronunciation. In this text, the transcription of Bororo words is simplified; vowels and consonants generally resemble those of Portuguese, with the following notable exceptions:

> g, t, and d are always hard, as in English "go," "to," "do,";
>
> there is no shift in the pronunciation of word-final -e or -o as occurs in common Brazilian speech;
>
> Bororo words are stressed on the penultimate syllable;
>
> č as used by the *Enciclopédia Bororo* to express the sound "tch" has been replaced in this text by an x.

In addition to the works already cited, readers with a specific interest in the Bororo language are directed to recent work by the Summer Institute of Linguistics, specifically that of T. Crowell and J. Crowell (n.d.).

Those Portuguese words that have no discrete English gloss and that commonly occur in the anthropological literature, such as babaçu and cerrado, are not italicized; all other Portuguese and Bororo terms that are not used as proper nouns are italicized throughout the text.

This work could not have been done but for the contributions of many people, and to all of them—whether specifically named below or not—I express my deepest appreciation. Of course full responsibility for the work must rest with me alone.

Dr. Anthony F. Aveni (Colgate University) and Dr. R. Tom

Zuidema (University of Illinois) have been the most influential in the cultivation of my theoretical position on space-time. Furthermore, in their relationships with me as academic advisors, fellow fieldworkers, and personal mentors, they have provided much more than technical and scholarly guidance over the years. Dr. Terence Turner (University of Chicago), Dr. Donald Lathrap, Dr. F. K. Lehman, Dr. James Kaler, and Dr. D. Seigler (all University of Illinois) provided valuable technical assistance, and Dr. Claire R. Farrer (California State, Chico) has time and again shared her considerable expertise and enthusiasm. My sincere appreciation is also due the Sky Publishing Corporation, for their kind permission to reproduce the "SC001 Constellation Chart."

In Brazil many organizations and individuals contributed their advice and support: the Fulbright Commission, particularly Sr. Marco Antonio da Rocha and Mr. Harold M. Midkiff, which funded fifteen months of research and was instrumental in gaining the necessary official permission for my project from the Brazilian government; the Brazilian government agencies CNPq and FUNAI; the Salesian Mission of Brazil, particularly Padre Gonçalo Ochoa C. and Mestre Mario Bordignon of the Meruri mission, Padre J. Winkler, and Padre Angelo Venturelli; the Museu Paulista and the University of São Paulo; Dra. Thekla Hartmann, Dra. Renate Viertler, and Dra. Sylvia Caiuby Novães (all of the University of São Paulo); Professor Marcio D'Olne Campos (University of Campinas); the Associação Brasileira de Antropologia; the Associação Alumni; and the Summer Institute of Linguistics. Generous hospitality was always extended to my wife and me by the Nunes da Cunha and Gluck families, for which we are exceedingly grateful.

Adequate appreciation can hardly be extended to our hosts and the subjects of this study, the Bororo themselves, to whom our presence was not only a curiosity but probably at times a frustrating nuisance. Both my wife and I wish to express our gratitude for the invitation and welcome extended by the residents of Garças village, who became our neighbors, mentors, and relatives during the course of our stay, and to the Bororo at Meruri, from whom we also received a warm reception. To all of the Bororo we wish continued fervor in practicing and maintaining *boe erore*, and hope that our relationship with them, as well as this work, helps inspire appreciation for the true richness of their culture.

For the strong support and encouragement extended by my own and my wife's families I would like to express my most heartfelt gratitude. Their belief in my abilities helped this project grow, as their nurturing continues to help us. And although my father is deceased, his courageous life and simple teachings are constant lights of guidance and inspiration along my way.

Finally and most importantly I wish to thank my wife, Surabela: as stalwart companion, insightful colleague, and competent editor she has particularly enriched the research experience upon which this work is based, as well as its written presentation.

One

The Bororo and Indigenous Space-Time

Researchers living and working among America's native peoples are coming to perceive the considerable extent to which the sky is a daily—and nightly—influence on traditional society and culture. This is not a simple task. Outside of indigenous times and areas the world has grown increasingly urbanized and industrialized: the skies are often smog-blanketed and otherwise obscured by towering edifices and the beaming, flashing, glaring lights that transform much of a city's night into artificial day. The rhythms of our modern world have changed, with seasonality and the observed coursing of celestial entities less crucial than business hours, banking hours, the flux of the stock exchange, and tax deadlines. Researchers interested in indigenous perceptions of the cosmos must rid themselves of the blinders imposed by their own culture and the ignorance it spawns in so many areas of knowledge of primary importance to the native.

It has generally been easier to put aside such blinders with those high cultures that have left impressive testimony to their development, such as the grandiose pyramids, complex ceremonial centers, and intricate codices of Mesoamerica, and the stunning architecture, climbing roads and waterways, and magnificent artisanry of the Andes. Indeed, work in Mesoamerica and the Andes has shown these areas to have possessed highly developed and sophisticated astronomies that were integrated into all facets of indigenous life.[1]

Early ethnographic works on lowland South American cultures, however, were more likely to characterize these cultures as undeveloped in this regard. For example, the noted Brazilian anthropologist Herbert Baldus (1940) described native Brazilian cultures as lacking the observation and accurate definition of days, months, and years (considered to be "unnecessary abstractions for [such] cultures"), lacking computational ability and numeric nomenclature, and also lacking systematic astronomical observa-

1

tions. Consequently, native Brazilian time reckoning—a major concomitant of celestial observation—was considered an essentially incidental and ad hoc endeavor. In contrast, Williamson in his *Living the Sky* speaks clearly and forcefully about native North Americans' celestial attention: "Their connections to the rhythms of the cosmos were both strong and visibly evident. . . . Astronomy pervaded their lives—ritual, hunting, and farming were all affected by the heavens" (1984: 5–6). In spite of some of the attitudes expressed in the earlier ethnographic literature, native lowland South Americans, like their northern relatives, were well attuned to the sky and the "rhythms of the cosmos," as attested to by a growing number of works on these native peoples.[2] The authors of these studies have made the effort to put aside their own cultural biases and world views in an effort to better apprehend, delineate, and analyze the native view.

From a very limited, ethnocentric perspective, Baldus's depiction of native Brazilian cultures was not incorrect. After all, the definitions he used for days, months, and years were those of Western science, i.e., based upon theories of a heliocentric solar system, the revolution of the earth around the sun, the rotation of the earth upon its axis, and the revolution of the moon about the earth. Furthermore, lowland South American cultures often do have a limited set of numerals, including perhaps discrete terms for "one" and "two," and then generally opposing these to "many"; numbers may also be named by an unwieldy set of terms related to counting upon the fingers and toes. In these systems mathematical computation beyond simple tally-counting is virtually nonexistent. And in comparison to contemporary Western astronomical observations that can determine sun risings and settings, the occurrence of the full moon, and the "official" beginning of the seasons all to the exactitude of seconds, those of the native Brazilians could be construed as crude and unsystematic, apparently nothing more than "unsystematic abstractions."

However, the very concepts that underlie Baldus's perspective are themselves relatively recent developments of Western astronomical cosmology, particularly "recent" with respect to the earliest reports of native Brazilians during the sixteenth and seventeenth centuries, having been advanced by Copernicus only during the Western Renaissance (A.D. 1400–1600). Even the Mesoamerican and Andean cultures, which Baldus compares favorably to the West with respect to their computational abilities, shared little of a theoretical nature with the West in their basic tenets of cosmology.

2

In a vein similar to that of Baldus, Leach expresses the opinion that all "primitive" time measurements are not precise, as they are not based on mathematical calculations or exact observations (1954:110). This belies the fact, however, that indigenous peoples do make exact observations of their environment. The book *Animal Myths and Metaphors in South America* (Urton 1985; Fabian 1987b) is replete with examples of the ability of native South Americans to make precise, detailed observations of the world around them. It is illogical and inconsistent to suppose that the ability and practice of consistent, keen observations necessary to detail the nest structure of a specific bee or the pheromonal activity of various fauna would not be applied elsewhere, particularly to the sky.

From the sky come such gifts as solar light and heat, and life-nurturing rain, gifts that, while essential to sustaining life, may also become perilous to it when bestowed overabundantly. The sky and the astronomical bodies that course along it are therefore curiously and attentively observed. In an outdoor, wilderness environment the sky is an ever-dominant feature. Even simple observation reveals the daily presence of the sun, the star-studded nights, and the variable moon that regularly waxes and wanes while occupying the sky both at night, and, less prominently, during the day. Furthermore, all of these appear to move, on any specific day or night, progressing from east to west. Slightly more attentive sky gazing will reveal the sun's yearly peregrination between fixed northern and southern extremes, and the moon's monthly wanderings within more or less the same limits, while among the relatively fixed patterns of stars can be observed the wanderings of a certain few, the "planets" (a term that comes from the Greek for "wanderer").

Studying a people's astronomy can help us better understand their temporal and spatial organizations, including such diverse concerns as calendar and social structure, while helping us to make detailed cross-cultural comparisons, and through them, enriched analyses. In this regard astronomy has much to offer, since all peoples construct their astronomical systems based upon the same set of elements: sun, moon, and stars (among which are often classed the planets). As Zuidema has so cogently argued, "On this primitive set of concepts peoples have built astronomical, cosmological, and calendar systems with as much variation as they have with kinship systems. We should be able to analyze the former systems, therefore, with the same rigorous and theoretical detail as the latter. . . . Kinship and astronomy (in their broadest sense) complement each other, and provide equal opportunities, in a nonevolutionary way, of studying human variation in using limited sets of variables for the general purpose of classification" (1981:29, 31). Astronomical observations can also be and are directly related by native peoples to social organization, as a model for both the structure and process of society.

Regular celestial motions, the apparent paths of the sky's major components, are well-known, prominent natural features to the native. The stationary and dynamic patterns in the heavens can and do influence the activities, organization, and relations of the people who observe them. Seasonal variations are readily related to the sun's regular annual motion, while the meteorological changes of the seasons are accompanied by other obvious environmental transformations: blooming flowers, ripening fruit, falling leaves, the return of fish to spawning grounds, animal migrations, the birth and growth of a new generation of wildlife. Whether or not native peoples observe all of these phenomena in cause-effect relationships, they do perceive them as interrelated, all rhythms within a cosmic dance of life. Partly from a natural affinity to these rhythms, and partly out of necessity, native peoples are highly attuned to the patterns and flows of their environment, leading their lives in such a way as to best synchronize themselves within it.

The Bororo of Mato Grosso, Brazil

One such native people are the Bororo Indians of central Brazil. Tall, robust, and muscular, the Bororo once controlled a large area of South America definable as directly south of the Amazon drainage system, west from the Araguaia River, north of the tributaries of the Rio Paraná, and east from the Paraguay River, centering upon the Rio São Lourenço and its affluents (the Salesian missionaries estimate the indigenous area of the Bororo to have extended from about 14° to 19° south latitude, and 51° to 59° west longitude; see Colbacchini and Albisetti [1942], map facing p. 28, and *EB*I:283). The Bororo once certainly extended west of the Paraguay, as well, and in the anthropological literature are divided into Eastern and Western Bororo, the provenience of the latter largely unknown. As the Western Bororo are no longer known to exist as an identifiable people, it is appropriate to leave off the no longer functional "Eastern" designation of the surviving Bororo.

(The Bororo are indifferent to this point: they refer to themselves as Boe in their native language.)

Bororo lands are typically tropical savannah, characterized by broad grasslands, scattered forests, lush riverine settings, and swamps (including the vast Pantanal of Brazil). It is a region of great seasonal extremes: during the half-year of rains all is lush greenness, a wealth of waterways crisscross the terrain, grasslands can become marshes, and paths may be treacherous with mud; during the dry season much of the area is a parched brown, all but the major springs and rivers run dry, and sand rather than mud is prevalent. Topographically the region is a broad plateau sloping gradually from east to west, with occasional mesa-like formations punctuating the landscape. In this variegated geography a rich assortment of both flora and fauna were once available to the Bororo, who traditionally hunt, fish, and gather the wild produce of the region and cultivate corn (three varieties have been identified by the Salesians, e.g., *EBI*:754–55), "sweet" manioc, and an assortment of other crops. Through these various subsistence strategies, which included shifting residence from stable villages to trekking camps during the year, the Bororo were able to support large village populations—a village diagram provided by João Barbosa de Faría (Rondon 1948, part 3) from the first quarter of this century illustrates 140 houses, all identified by the name of the corresponding social unit—with intricate social institutions and an elaborate ritual complex.

Unfortunately, as is common in the experience of America's natives, contact with the incoming and encroaching neo-Brazilian communities unalterably changed the Bororo life-style, their environment, and their relationship with it. Possibly gold and gem hunters exploring around what is today the capital city of the state of Mato Grosso, Cuiabá (from a Bororo word for the local waterway), were the first Euro-Brazilians to contact the Bororo, in the eighteenth century (cf. Hemming 1978: 405). Disease and escalated warfare ravaged the Bororo for the next century and a half. Turn-of-the-century estimates reckoned from 5,000 to 10,000 Bororo in traditional villages (Cook 1908:61), with 1,000 alone along the São Lourenço River (*EBI*:293); fifty years later all known Bororo barely totaled 1,000 (ibid.). Population decline continued through the 1960s, with Hartmann (1964) and Crocker (1979) estimating the total population at 500. Today there are about 700 culturally viable Bororo scattered among nine villages (see table 1.1). The recent trend toward increased numbers is due at least in part to

Table 1.1
Bororo Villages and Population Estimates

Reserve	Village	Estimated population
Gomes	Gomes Carneiro	128
Carneiro	Piebaga	34
Tadarimana	Tadarimana	48
	Paulista	15
	Pobore	10
Meruri	Meruri	260
	Garças	100
Perigara	Perigara	86
Sangradouro	Sangradouro	25
	Total	706

Source: Bordignon Enawureu 1987:38.

improved medical facilities accessible for childbirth, resulting in a reduced infant mortality rate. Increasing Brazilian population in the area and the concomitant shift in exploiting the environment drastically affects the natural resource base and Bororo access to it. Fences, plantation-style farming, controlled pasturage for domesticated herd animals, industry, even commercial fishing are factors limiting Bororo use of their native region, while such problems as continued declining numbers, loss of self-identity, malnutrition, and alcoholism are among the subsidiary effects.

Today Bororo still hunt, fish, and gather the wild produce available to them as best they can, although these activities are hampered by reduced area of access and reduced concentration of game and other wild foodstuffs. The result has been a greater emphasis on agriculture, and the native set of crops has been significantly altered by additions from Brazilian culture. Even then, however, there are some increased difficulties: with limited land resources there is the problem of overuse and soil depletion, and fewer people in the village often means insufficient numbers to carry on intensive agriculture and maintain the social and ritual complexes of a traditional life-style. In an effort at self-support some communities are drawn into cash cropping, a system of production that may have drastic consequences upon the maintenance of tradition (Fabian 1983). Some Bororo have also taken to working part-time or seasonally outside their villages for wages, or to spending a large amount of time, resources, and energy in making tourist articles for barter or sale in order to afford those commodities that have become necessities to contemporary village life, including Western-style clothing (traditionally, men essentially wore only a penis sheath fashioned of palm and women a belt of bark-cloth about the loins); hunting, fishing, and farming equipment; and tobacco, coffee, sugar, wheat and manioc flour, and thread.

In east and central Brazil the Bororo and Gê peoples are known for their rather complex social organizations, characterized by groups localized along the circumference of their predominantly circular villages and within the village plaza; cardinal orientations of these villages; considerable technical and aesthetic mastery of palm and feather working; and a subsistence of well-developed horticulture complemented by fishing and hunting-gathering. The theme of space-time and its relation to the principles of social organization has not been well investigated yet in this area in spite of such promising data as the importance of east-west directionality in village orientation, and the relationship of social groups with specific seasons, day- or nighttime, and particular celestial objects (e.g., as reported by Nimuendajú for the Eastern Timbira, 1946:84). Zuidema anticipated this direction of inquiry (1964:21–22, 244–45) by suggesting apparent similarities between the Inca and the Bororo in village organization, dual organization of social structures, spatial location of the social groups, and nature and significance of the central religio-ceremonial precinct. Furthermore, the published literature reveals a rather large, tantalizing body of astronomical information for the Bororo (Fabian 1982) which, even prior to my fieldwork, suggested a depth of interest in the sky meriting further attention.

For the period of my field stay among the Bororo (January–October 1983) I was primarily interested in their existing astronomy and calendar—which I broadly interpret as any system of time reckoning—and in examining how these are expressed in social and spatial organization and in myth and ritual. After securing research support from the Fulbright Commission, and the permission required from FUNAI (Fundação Nacional do Indio, which controls all projects among Brazil's native peoples), my wife and I traveled to the state of Mato Grosso and began visiting the few remaining Bororo villages.

Although Crocker (1985:28) maps five Bororo villages along the traditional Bororo heartland of the Rio São Lourenço and its tributary the Rio Vermelho, his data are based on research carried out during the 1960s. Several of the villages he includes are today defunct (e.g., Pobojari and Jarudori), while Garças village has been

Fig. 1.1. Location of Garças village

formed, some 40 kilometers from the Meruri mission (see figure 1.1). As an indication of the continuing rapid pace of change in the Bororo heartland, Hanbury-Tenison (1973), after his brief visit to the village of Gomes Carneiro (Corrego Grande), listed the overall Bororo situation as "in poor conditions" and in "permanent contact" with FUNAI/Mission (1973:255; see also pp. 139–42, 260). Yet merely a decade earlier this same village provided the most traditional location of the Bororo (Crocker 1985).[3]

Ironically, the safest haven for the Bororo today was historically one of their most dangerous threats: the Catholic Salesian mission known as Meruri, in Mato Grosso State. At the turn of this century the missionaries were actively repressive of Bororo tradition. Since the reexamination of Catholic doctrine that occurred during the ecumenical council of Vatican II of the 1960s, however, missionaries have become strongly supportive of native cultural expression. Although continuing to proselytize the Bororo, the missionaries at Meruri now teach elements of Bororo culture and language in their mission school and encourage native performances, self-reliance, and Bororo unification. Meruri mission reserve lands are also the site of Garças village—the name is taken from a tributary of the Araguaia River where the population of this village was initially settled—which is an amalgam of survivors from defunct communities who are self-avowedly intent upon maintaining as much of their tradition as possible. After my wife and I visited the Bororo villages of Tadarimana and Corrego Grande—where we were well received but not encouraged to stay—we focused upon Garças village as providing the best potential setting for our interests. Since conditions for our staying in the village were favorable to us and the villagers, Garças village became the ethnographic context from which much of the data for this study was obtained.

As my intention was to experience Bororo culture as much as possible from the "inside," my wife and I assisted in the building of a native-style house as our residence and attempted to live in a manner similar to that of our neighbors. These efforts enabled us to establish better rapport with our hosts and they with us. Since Bororo society is structured along significant male-female divisions, my wife and I often had complementary versions of shared experiences or could offer descriptions of those experiences not shared. As a couple I believe we were more readily received than if I had entered into the village alone, and my wife's presence was more crucial to the project than at first I had anticipated. Her companionship and participation in daily and ceremonial activities, and the depth in village relationships that her affinity with some of the women initiated for us, were factors that made feasible and enriched the fieldwork situation. Although she had not entered the village with a research goal, she found herself naturally drawn to the women's craft of palm working, in which she became apprenticed to two of the most expert of the village's few remaining weavers and upon which she wrote the paper for her master's degree in anthropology (Blatt-Fabian 1985).

Garças village was well acquainted with a money economy, and some of the villagers had worked with professional anthropologists in the past. Detailed information on the central topics of my research, therefore, was often necessarily a purchased commodity. Despite hours in the men's house (where much of a man's time is spent while in the village) and my participation in fishing, hunting, gardening, and gathering forays and ceremonial performances, there was reticence among the men and they did not impart information freely. Much data gathering had to be done through the context of formal, paid interviews. These were often carried out in Portuguese, although some informants gave information both in Bororo and Portuguese; at other times it was necessary to work with a third party as interpreter. In general, my principal informants were men of middle age and older who were considered culturally knowledgeable in the village, and who occasionally demonstrated this knowledge through their key roles in traditional ritual and ceremony. This demonstration of the depth of cultural knowledge of my informants and the respect for them exhibited by the villagers, as well as my ability to verify portions of information through other informants and published materials, leave me confident as to the veracity and reliability of my field data. Fortunately, my wife, who had never been identified as an official investigator, was never required to pay money for what she was told or taught, and her discussions with the women constituted another rich source of information, as well as verification of my own data. Our personal experience in both secular and ceremonial activities was of incalculable value in approaching perception from the native perspective and was useful as a further check on the reliability of informants and their statements.

The Bororo as a society have had considerable contact with anthropologists and have been prominent in the literature at least since Karl von den Steinen's visit among them in the 1880s (1940/1894). Although some of his observations and conclusions have been criticized by later researchers (e.g., *EBI*:240, 627, 668), von den Steinen's observations of Bororo social complexity and ideological richness, belied by their relatively simple technology, have been borne out and elaborated upon by a century of later scholars and publications.[4] Principal among more recent Bororo studies are several works by the Salesian missionaries, based on direct contact since the turn of the century. Of great significance is the *Enciclopédia Bororo* (three volumes to date), which presents an unparalleled wealth of ethnographic data.[5]

10

As a people who have tenaciously struggled to preserve their culture despite influences from a long history of neo-Brazilian contact, and who occupy a prominent place in anthropological interest, the Bororo are a likely choice for ethnographic research and cross-cultural comparisons. Furthermore, they present certain cultural attributes that make them particularly suitable for a study of indigenous Brazilian space-time concepts: their propensity for circular village organization with a paradigmatic cardinal orientation; the localizing of social groups along the circumference of the village as well as within the central men's house; and the wealth of data—in both quantity and quality—already available in the published literature, including details of their astronomical observations and concepts of the cosmos.

Theoretical Intent

Early works on native South Americans, such as that of Baldus cited previously, tended to describe indigenous time systems primarily from the perspective of what they were not, or what they lacked in comparison with contemporary Western concepts of time. Such depictions obviously distort and denigrate the native systems, which deserve a fuller, positively oriented description, placing the native beliefs and practices with respect to time within their customary and highly integrated setting in native culture and society.[6]

Although not developed as such, certain data included in Baldus's paper begin to illustrate important elements of what native Brazilian time constructs are. For example, it is reported that in Brazil "seasons can be characterized by the maturation of a fruit . . . by the abundance of fish, by cold or heat, by rain or by dryness, and such characteristics can be put in relation to celestial phenomena as, for example, the appearance of the Pleiades" (Baldus 1940:90; unless otherwise noted, all translations are my own). The cognition of a variety of seasonal characteristics in relation to themselves and to celestial phenomena indicates a prominent trait of native calendrics: the recognition and use of *layers* in time-related observations. This system makes use of multiple, observable environmental phenomena that occur more or less contemporaneously. Leach has labeled such phenomena "synchronous natural events" (1954:116), although in essence he refers to only two synchronous events, whereas I am concerned with the observations of multiple contemporaneous environmental phenomena. Taken together, the layering of these many different observations will yield precise information, even though any single observation may itself be imprecise in nature (see Aaboe and de Solla Price, 1964). Although a single major property such as heavy rains may be emphasized, it is the observation of a host of related characteristics that creates the layered effect resulting in precise temporal cognition. This principle is fundamental to native time reckoning.

Baldus (1940:91) provides a clue for another feature of native Brazilian time reckoning by relating that a series of months, designated by particular environmental occurrences such as maturing fruits or flowering trees—with an undetermined relationship to lunar observations—is used to divide the year. Besides implying the need for a more detailed examination of native moon watching and beliefs, this information suggests the significance of *sequences* in native reckoning (of a temporal or other nature): non-numerical sequencing can be and is used as effectively as counting (i.e., numerical sequencing) to divide, order, or reckon a specific interval in time and space by native South Americans.

A crucial factor in attempting to comprehend native systems of time is an awareness of the relevance of space and spatial concepts to time constructs. Without developing the idea, Baldus (1940:93) reports that the Tapirapé word *mõ* or *mũ* (*longe* in Portuguese) is used to designate great distances in time as well as space. Had Baldus given more attention to the relationship of space to time, he might have avoided the error of limiting the recognition of "midnight" to peoples in possession and use of clocks (1940:92). Actually the middle of the night can be quite accurately determined by stellar observation: a star located diametrically opposite the sun and rising as the sun sets will reach the meridian (its highest point in the sky) as the sun reaches the lower meridian, the nonobservable phenomenon marking the middle of the night; that same star will later be setting at sunrise. Whether or not any theoretical relationship is made between sun and star, the empirical observations are sufficient basis for precise time reckoning. In fact, the observation of a star's (or the sun's or moon's) movement through space to designate the passage of time is completely analogous to reading time from the face of a (nondigital) clock, where the movements of the hands of the clock in space are used to measure time; for the practiced stargazer the one technique is as accurate as the other.

I define the salient theorems of the Bororo space-time system as (1) time being less a measured quantity than it is a perceived composite of diachronic layers, and, as such, (2) being reckoned more as synchronic sequences based upon detailed environmental observations than as a function of numerical computation. Furthermore, (3) time is both functionally and conceptually related to space—so much so that all features of Bororo space-time are encompassed within a single paradigm. It can be briefly stated as:

> for any reckoning process beginning at a point within a domain of bounded space (geographical, temporal, or cosmic), once the boundary of the domain is reached, there is a return to the point of origin in that domain.

The different but analogous—and often overlapping—domains comprise spatiotemporal layers, whose boundaries define the sequences demarcating lines of process. It is this interplay of linear processes with the recursivity of return to origin that not only characterizes Bororo space-time but defines the progression and cyclicity fundamental to all human spatiotemporal perception. A study of Bororo space-time reveals the pervasive nature of the complementarity of structure and process in Bororo cosmology, and the static and dynamic aspects of being that are held by them to comprise all of life.

Calendar, for the Bororo, serves not only to order and reckon the passage of time and its related activities but as a map and definition of temporal space it is conjoined with geographic and cosmic spaces and applied in such a way as to integrate more fully the Bororo as humans with each other and with the various dimensions and domains of their world. The Bororo socialize their theory of space-time via their village and its localized social groups and their interrelations. While observed natural processes are replicated within society, explanations consistent with Bororo social theory are projected onto those processes.

The village arrangement, moreover, shares elements with what Goody (1977) defines as lists, formulas, and tables and, like these constructs, is used to store and communicate precise and systematic knowledge. Goody, however, limits these features to literate systems, whereas the Bororo data would suggest otherwise. This latter point supports Zuidema's challenge to Goody's claim, which he demonstrated (1982a) by detailing how the nonliterate Incas achieved, stored, and communicated sophisticated precise and systematic knowledge, also using constructs essentially similar to lists, formulas, and tables as defined by Goody.

Underlying all Bororo formulations of space-time are accurate and detailed observations of the sky and of the various regular features that animate it. The positions, movements, and relationships of such celestial entities as the sun, moon, and stars and their routes in the sky have been influential to the Bororo in their formulation of an elaborate social theory and practice. Their interest in and attention to these features go far beyond the haphazard or superficial and are inspired by a cognizance of the interrelatedness of all elements of the cosmos and the fundamental significance of the wonders of the sky to this interrelatedness.

The Book's Structure

Since one of my major objectives is to encourage a fuller awareness of the significant differences between the indigenous Brazilian and Western time-reckoning systems and the viability and appreciation of native systems on their own merits, the work is patterned somewhat along native lines. I begin with a myth rich in cultural detail whose hero is named Toribugu, a version from Garças village of the key myth used in Lévi-Strauss's *Mythologiques* series. Besides introducing relevant themes, it gives a meaningful view of the Bororo by the Bororo themselves. A preliminary analysis of the myth is also given in chapter 2, and the myth's interpretation is returned to from another perspective later in the work.

Chapter 3 orients us within Bororo concepts of space by defining their village organization, one of their principal diagnostic traits and one that links them to the entire cosmos as they perceive it. The next two chapters orient us in the Bororo perception of time, as it is noted socially in marked stages of the life cycle and as it is reckoned throughout the day, night, month, and year. While chapters 3 through 5 are organized by the separation of specific details of space and time, it soon becomes evident that the domains are intimately linked, comprising one comprehensive space-time.

Emphasis is given in chapter 6 to the Sun and Moon, mythical heroes and celestial bodies of great importance to the Bororo, and through whom space and time merge. Their characters and relevance are illustrated through examples taken from a large corpus of Sun and Moon myths.

Other significant Bororo-perceived celestial phenomena are discussed in chapter 8 and detailed in an extensive table compiled from both textual and informant sources given in Appendix A. It is in this chapter that certain theories concerning Bororo time concepts are further developed, and an additional analysis of the structure of time in the initial myth of Toribugu given in chapter 2 is undertaken. In the final chapters the role of the village in the relationships of space, time, nature, and society is elucidated, and the inherent integration of structural and processual elements of Bororo society and culture is made evident. The Sun and Moon are depicted as mediators between society and nature, space and time, and structure and process, while the synchronization of these domains—as celebrated within a rite involving the Pleiades star group—is discussed. Bororo observation of celestial dispositions and movements is shown to contribute significantly to their social structure and processes, as well as providing them with a basis for a fundamental orientation within space and time.

Two

The Dynamics of Personal and Societal Growth: The Myth of Toribugu

While I was living in Garças village I collected a version of the myth of Toribugu (also called Jerigigiatugo), another version of which appears as the "key myth" in Lévi-Strauss's *Introduction to a Science of Mythology (Mythologiques)* series. This coincidence is not accidental: the myth's richness of cultural detail makes it interesting and important for non-Bororo and Bororo alike: a version of it was the first myth recounted to me (unsolicited) by a Bororo elder residing at the Meruri mission, even prior to our establishing residency in Garças village. The myth's significance stems from its treatment of major cultural themes: the incest taboo and marriage rules; the maturation of the (male) individual; cultural growth; conflict between child and adult, offspring and parents, and consanguines and affines; the crucial role of nonconsanguineal relatives such as ritual sponsors. More pertinent for the purposes of this work, the Toribugu myth is apparently "complete," not part of any identifiable series of myths and therefore analyzable as it stands; it also includes some important astronomical observations. Other versions are readily available in published texts (including Bororo, Portuguese, and English renditions) and include some prior analysis (Colbacchini 1925:231–36; Colbacchini and Albisetti 1942:225–29, 343–37; *EBII*:303–59, #14; and Wilbert and Simoneau 1983:198–210, #104 and #105).

This version was collected in its entirety on 27 April 1983 from a cultural chief of the Paiwoe clan. (In the myth text, clan affiliations are bracketed following a person's name; the nature of Bororo clans is given fuller treatment in chapter 3. Appendix C lists by their Bororo, English, Portuguese, and Latin names plant and animal species mentioned in the myth.)

Api Ikiga: Branch of the Sucupira Tree[1]

One day there was a dance, *reruya*, known as *iparereru* or *jure*.[2] At this time the Bororo were without real body decorations, using

The nonfunerary jure dance.

only such poor things as leaves and the like. While the youths were dancing, Toribugu [Paiwoe][3] was also dancing in their midst, and it was only he who was well decorated. When the dance finished, his mother, Toriatugo [Paiwoe Xebegiwu], went to forage in the forest and asked her son, "Why don't you go with me? Maybe there's a jaguar or some other danger." When his mother arrived in the forest, she found a wild potato called *oko*.[4] While she was digging it up from the ground, Toribugu saw his mother's genitals, and exclaimed, "Ola!" His mother asked him, "What happened?" to which he only responded, "Nothing." She continued digging and took out more, and Toribugu again saw her genitals and exclaimed "Ola!" after which his mother again asked him what happened, and his response was the same as before: "Nothing." The mother had faith in her son.[5] It happened a third time the same as before. Then the mother rose up, embraced her son, lay with him, and "did a good service there." As Toribugu lay with his mother, some of the resin and down of his decoration, called *kogo pariri iwoi*, stuck to his mother's belt without their knowing it.

When they arrived at their house in the village, Toriatugo's husband Kiarewari [Baadajeba Xebegiwu] saw the decorations stuck to his wife; without saying anything he ordered another dance, the *iparereru* again. He observed all the youths, but only Toribugu had real body decorations. As the group danced the father of Toribugu decided that it was only he—Toribugu—who had those decorations [of the type stuck to his wife's waist]. Kiarewari said to himself, nodding, "So, yes, it's no one else, only really you two." Kiarewari said, "My son, prepare the babaçu refreshment, *metotodawu,* for the men." Toribugu answered "O.K.," and went to his "grandmother," Kikoroda. He said, "Imarugo, Father told me to make the babaçu refreshment for the men." She thought for a moment and then said, "You should hunt a large spider, *iyera-gadu,* and the squirrel, *koda koda.* [*Awu-tu ewugeje.*]"[6] Toribugu answered, "Yes."

He hunted them, then rode on top of the spider over a marsh to the foot of the babaçu. He climbed up [either himself, or transformed into the squirrel, or the squirrel itself] until he reached the nuts of the babaçu, where he nibbled at the stem of the bunch of nuts. When he spat out part of the stem into the lagoon, the piranha came and the water rose but then lowered again. He bit the stem and spat it out again, and again the water rose and the piranha came, up to the height of the fronds of the palm, then descended again. He chewed it a third time and spat it out, and again the piranha came with the rising water, over the fronds; he escaped up a shoot [shoots grow vertically from the top center of the palm], and when the water descended again he cut through the bunch of nuts. He crossed the water again on the spider and arrived at the other side, where he stood up and became human once again. Then he took out the palm hearts from young babaçu plants on that side of the lagoon. He arrived in the village and made the refreshment. Finished, he grabbed his father's arm and said: "Here is your babaçu, refreshment." Kiarewari exclaimed in surprise [to himself], with his hand on his heart, "How could he have done it?!"[7] The father thought, "What shall I do?" Then he remembered. "My son, my son, now you will hunt *adugo,* the jaguar, for me."

"Yes," was the son's reply.

Toribugu went again to the old woman. "Imarugo, Imarugo, Father told me to go hunt a jaguar for him now." She said, "Hmm, go to the forest and look for a large, yet soft tree, *powari gagurerewu i,* that also has vines." The instructions were to cut down the tree and leave it on the ground with all the leaves on top of it, himself staying quiet and away from it. Then he would have to say a special phrase to make the tree turn into a jaguar.[8]

Toribugu did as he was told and said, *"Adugo do aki"* three times. He threw off the leaves and found a (dead) jaguar, not wood, underneath. So Toribugu already had the jaguar. He carried it to the village and gave it to his father, saying, "Here is your jaguar."[9]

The father said again [with incredulity], "How did he do it?" Then he spoke. "My son, go hunt *aigo*, the puma, for me." Toribugu said, "Yes" and went to his grandmother again. "Imarugo, now Father wants me to hunt a puma."

She said, "Yes, go look for the hardwood, *kudo i*, cut it down, arrange the leaves over it, sit away from it to the side, and say '*Aigo do aki*, you are a puma,' just like this."[10]

Toribugu did everything just as she said to: found and cut down the tree, put the leaves over it, sat quietly to the side, then stood and said: "*Aigo do aki*, become a puma." Taking the leaves off as he said it, he saw a puma, already dead. He carried it to the village and gave it to his father saying, "Father, here is your puma."

The father said to himself, "How did he do it?" Then he thought and remembered, "Ah yes," and said aloud, "My son."

"Ho?"

"Go hunt *aroe exeba*, the harpy eagle."

Toribugu went to the old woman again. "Imarugo, Father said for me to go hunt the harpy eagle now."

She thought, "Why is the father sending him to do all this? Perhaps he has a motive for doing this." She said, "Go find the leaves that appear similar to the tail of the *parigogo*, cut them, arrange them so, then put other leaves on top."[11]

He did as he was instructed, then said over the leaves, "*Padarogwa rewure, padarogwa rewure*," and it became a real harpy eagle. He carried it to the village to give to his father, and said, "Father, my father, here is the harpy eagle."[12]

The father said, "How did he do it?" Then he remembered. "I know, he won't escape now," he thought.

"My son, my son."

"Ho?"

"Go hunt the *kurugugwa*, eagle."[13]

"Yes."

He went to the old woman. "Imarugo, Father told me to hunt the *kurugugwa*, eagle."

She told him to look for leaves of the same type as before but of a smaller variety, and to prepare them in the same way.[14] He found them, cut them, put other leaves on top, and waited. He got up and said, "*Kurugugwa do aki*, become the *kurugugwa*." And he already saw the actual *kurugugwa*. He took it to the village and gave it to his father. "My father, my father, here is the *kurugugwa*."

His father thought to himself, "Hmm, what shall I do with him?" He thought and thought, then he remembered. "My son, my son."

"Ho?"

"Go hunt the *bapo*, large rattle, for me."

Toribugu went to the old woman again. She again thought about what could be happening with all of these requests. She told him to find the large grasshopper, *mamore*, and also told him how to ask a tree to grow with him.[15]

He went to the place of the *bapo*, rattle, which was in the midst of its guardian *aroe*, spirits: the lord [*dono* in Portuguese] of the rattle was *aiyere aroe*. The others included: *aroe koe*, *aroe joware*, *aroe bakarai*, *aroe bokomo-doge*, *aroe buregodure-wuge*, and *aroe paiku-doge*.[16] Toribugu walked among them stealthily and grabbed the *bapo*, but then it rattled "juuu" and those warriors awoke. "Hmm, hmm, give a look around and surround the intruder." They did this and caught Toribugu in the middle. He saw a small tree about chest height, a jatobá, and asked of it, "Grandfather, Iedaga, grow with me." Toribugu turned into [or sat upon] the large grasshopper, and in this way the tree grew tall and thick with him on it. The warriors united at the foot of the tree and shot arrows to kill him, but he was protected by the grasshopper [either by having become one or by shielding himself upon/behind it], into which the arrows stuck. Because of this the grasshopper was left with many holes in its body, which it still has today.[17]

Night fell, with the guardian *aroe* still waiting for him. After midnight Toribugu began to call out the names of stars as they rose, by whistling.[18]

"*Kiye* [*kiege*] *barege erudu*, the birds/animals/stars are rising."[19]

The *aroe* replied, "Hmm, hmm, hmm."

Next Toribugu announced, "*Okoge joku rutu*, the eye of the dourado fish rises."[20]

The *aroe* again responded.

Somewhat later Toribugu whistled, "*Bokodori jari paru kajeje-wuge erudu.*" This time fewer voices answered him from below, as some of the *aroe* had fallen asleep.[21]

He whistled again, "*Tugiga kiwu rutu.*"[22]

Fewer *aroe* answered him.

He whistled again, "*Tuwagowu rutu.*"[23]

The *aroe* commented, "Hmm, hmm, hmm," but only a few.

Next, "*Jekurireu rutu.*"[24] But none of the *aroe* spoke.

It was getting lighter. Toribugu whistled again, "*Barogwa tabowu rutu,"* when it was already dawning. [Akiri-doge, the Pleiades, were added in at this point in the sequence as an afterthought when my informant reviewed in his mind and on his fingers which names he had given.][25]

When it was dawn, *"Barogwa kudodu* rises," but everyone was quiet.[26] So then Toribugu asked of the jatobá, "Iedaga, Grandfather, let me down," to let him down on the far side of the surrounding warriors. And that is how it happened, the tree left him on the ground [by bending over]; the tree rose up again, but it did not return exactly right, that is why some of them are formed thus [i.e. curved, leaning]. Once on the ground Toribugu began to run, but the rattle again made its sound, awakening the warriors. These said, "Hmm, hmm, give a look around and surround him!"

But Toribugu had really run, and he safely reached the village where he gave the rattle to his father.

Kiarewari exclaimed, "What? How did he do it?" And then he remembered. "Now I know, he won't escape this time. My son, my son."

"Ho?"

"Go hunt for the *xibae,* the red macaw; but I'll go with you."

Toribugu went to the old woman and told her what his father had said. She was almost crying when she heard it [because she thought Kiarewari wanted to kill his son] and wondered how to help Toribugu. Then she gave him something, a *tuberigara.* She said, "This you can put in the stone; with it you won't fall."[27]

"O.K."

Toribugu went with his father to the place where there were nests.

His father said, "Here, here; but wait, I'll look for a log for you to climb up on." He went and returned with a length of wood, *ejerigiga,* a dry wood, but he was only fooling his son.[28] He leaned the length of tree against the rock cliff for Toribugu to climb to the macaw nest. Toribugu climbed up and entered the macaw nest [a hole in the eroded cliff side], but there was no macaw there, only an egg [or eggs]. He took it [them] and called out, "Father, there are no macaws, only an egg[s]." So he tossed the egg[s] down to his father who said, "O.K., you can come down."

Toribugu left the nest, but when he put his foot onto the wood, his father kicked out the bottom [so that the trunk fell]. Toribugu put the *tuberigara* in/on the rock and it kept him from falling. Then he climbed to the top of the cliff using vines that were hanging down the side.

21

His father was watching, and he said, "Ah, because of this [that's why] there is that type of vine in the hills [and not in the cerrado where there is only a smaller variety]."[29]

Then he spoke again. "You will have to travel far to find us, since we will be going on ahead of you. But you'll get lost and never find us."[30]

Toribugu was left alone. He walked on the mountain without finding a place to descend. He began to think he was lost and that he really was going to die. Then he remembered his cotton adornments, cut a cord of it off, stretched it out, cut a straight stick, and made a bow that would serve to shoot with. He saw a type of grass [*boe yabutu iworeu*] and made arrows from it. With these he hunted the small *kukaga*, lizard, killed many, and gathered them all together. He tied them all onto his body adornments, weighted down by the creatures. He went walking in this way, and the lizards began to rot. He laid down amidst that awful smell. A vulture arrived, left, then came again and left again, then many came, sitting close to him. One pecked his side, but he moved, and they moved away a short distance. They came back, and one pecked him again, but again he moved, and they drew back. The same thing happened a third time. Then a beautiful vulture, *xiwaje*, pecked him, and he remained still, until the vulture pecked his hindquarters. Suddenly Toribugu grabbed the vulture and said, "Iedaga, Iedaga, descend with me to the ground. Pass close to the grass that is on the cerrado."[31]

The vulture replied, "Yes, let's go."

Toribugu sat on top of the vulture, which flew with him, and Toribugu asked him two more times to descend with him. [Finally] when they passed close to the grass he jumped off, landing on his feet in the grass. He grabbed one arm of the vulture and broke it, and then the other also. The vulture cried, "Iaii," and it is because of this that the vulture looks so beautiful and different.

Toribugu was on the ground again and he began walking. "Where are my people?"

He arrived at a foot path of the Bororo and followed it to a camp, but it was already empty. But there was a signal there; beneath some ashes he found some wild potatoes, *makaworewu* [which were good to eat]. He went on again, found another camp, but again it was empty although newer than the last. Again he found a wild potato in the ashes. He ate the *kiiri*, but again he could not keep it in him, it just came right out, due to the damage the vulture had done to his anus. He arrived at another encampment, this one very recently deserted, and thought that it was one where he and his people always stayed. He found another potato, *kudo*, and ate it but it also came right out. Walking further he again found another camp, and this time a potato, *pobodori*, still hot in the ashes. This one stayed in after he ate it.[32]

He went on and heard a song ahead, and then saw an old woman and a young boy. He changed into a small bird, *ino*, and sat on the basket of the old woman, who was his "grandmother." She spoke to the young boy, who was his younger brother. "Imedu, Imedu, take a look there [on my basket]."[33]

"There's nothing, only a small bird."

They continued walking and singing. Toribugu turned into another little bird, the *xururu*, and pulled on the walking stick [*uyodo/iwayga*] of the old woman, then flew off. She again asked the young boy to see what it was, but he saw nothing. Toribugu came behind them for the third time, but this time as a person, and he pulled on the basket.

"Imedu, what is it?"

The young boy really looked and saw his brother. "Imuga, my older brother has arrived!" Now she herself turned and saw him. She embraced him and cried and sat down with him on her lap.[34] Then Toribugu said, "Imuga, let's go. So they went on again and made a new camp. Here Toribugu told the old woman to stay [to make her shelter] somewhat further away from the others in the camp.[35] Then he suggested to his brother to tell others not to kill the *arao*, lizard, when they see it, but to say that he himself [the younger brother] would; then he instructed the old woman to do the same. He went ahead and turned into the *arao*. When his younger brother found him he yelled, "Don't shoot it, I'll shoot it for my mother!" Then the lizard ran towards the old woman, who recognizing that it was Toribugu said, "Don't kill it, I'll kill it for myself." She threw an old mat over the lizard, and he turned into a human once again. In this way Toribugu had entered the camp without being discovered.

Toribugu sent strong wind and heavy rain that ruined everything of the Bororo there and put out their fires so that they suffered. But where he was it was calm, without wind, and a big fire burned. The others saw this and wondered, "How could it be?"

The mother of Toribugu went to get some fire; she saw the back of him sitting there. She got a burning branch and returned to her husband Kiarewari and told him that she had recognized Toribugu. The father sent his younger son to fetch Toribugu to his house. The young boy said to Toribugu, "My brother, our father is calling for you in order to sing over you [in welcome]."

Toribugu said, "Tell our father that I'm not going there."

His little brother took the message to his father. The father shouted to bring him there for the singing. The little boy went but again Toribugu answered, "No, I'm not going. Tell our father that he can sing over you as if you were me."

The young boy went and said, "My father, my father, my brother said to sing over me, that I'm the same as him."

But the father said, "No," to bring Toribugu, that he wanted to sing over him. So the little boy went again to his older brother but received the same answer. He again delivered the message to his father, who this time did sing over Toribugu's younger brother.

Kiarewari then initiated a deer hunt. The Bororo went to hunt; Toribugu came behind, the last, with his younger brother, hunting and searching. Then Toribugu found some dry wood, *mana ikiga*, put it on his head, and turned into the *atubo* deer. He ran through the forest, but the wood was not strong enough, and the antlers were destroyed. He found another wood, *apegirerewu yi*, turned once again into a deer, but this wood also fell apart. He found another type, this time *api ikiga*, which he put on his head; then he turned into the *atubo* once again. He ran very hard, but this time the wood [as antlers] held firm.[36]

The Bororo were hunting in a circular formation called *bakure*. Toribugu told his younger brother to go and find their father and to report back to him. The young boy went along the hunting circle until he saw his father, then ran back and reported to his brother.[37]

"Go again and show me well where our father is."

The younger brother turned into the rodent *mea* this time to see their father and returned again with the information. Then Toribugu said, "Say thus: 'Don't shoot it [the deer], I will shoot it for my father.'" And Toribugu—as the deer—ran, while the Bororo shouted, "There's a deer!" But his younger brother, who was called Baipore, shouted, "Leave it for me!" Toribugu arrived in front of his father and Kiarewari tried to dodge to avoid the deer but he could not. The deer pierced him on its antlers and threw him into the marsh. Piranha in the lagoon came together and there was the sound "juuuu" as they fell upon Kiarewari. Only the liver and lungs of the man floated to the surface, where they became the water plant *anobo*, like in the legend of Ari.[38]

Toribugu spoke. "That's how it is done, how I do it." He was speaking badly to his father, whom he had killed.

He gathered up his father's things in the village.[39] He really turned into his father; everyone thought it was his father returning. To his younger brother he said, "Sit right in front of me, let me know if anyone recognizes me." Then his father's two wives arrived. They recognized him as his father, gave him a bath, fanned him, picked lice from him, treated him like their husband. All the while his younger brother was sitting before him. Then the wives found the sign of something strange on his head that made them suspicious. The little boy gave a signal that the women had noticed something, and Toribugu stood up and killed the two women.[40]

This occurred at the end of the rainy season, like the time we're in now [narration on 27 April].[41]

In Colbacchini (1925) and in Colbacchini and Albisetti (1942), the myth is presented as "The Legend of Jerigigiatugo or Toribugu: About the Origin of Wind and Rain." The initial episode begins with Toribugu's mother, Korogo in these versions, and other women gathering palm leaves for the making of *ba*, penis sheaths, to be presented to boys during their initiation ceremonies. One rendering, however, states that the palm collection was for the making of mats. Jerigigiatugo sees his mother in the forest and rapes her. His father, Bokwadorireu, sees feathers on his wife's belt and becomes suspicious. He then calls for the *iparereru* dance. After two dances he sees that his son is the only participant with the suspect type of feather ornamentation. Bokwadorireu therefore begins to order his son on a series of quests hoping that Jerigigiatugo will be killed. The three quests have as their objective noise-making artifacts that must be taken from the watery abode of the *aroe* spirits: the *bapo* or large rattle, the *bapo rogu* or small rattle, and the *buttore* or ankle rattle. Upon the advice of his "grandmother" (*avó* in Portuguese, and *imarugo* in Bororo), Jerigigiatugo gains the aid of the *piodudu* (hummingbird), the *metugu* (dove), and the *mamori* (giant grasshopper) for the successful completion of these tasks. His father then orders the macaw hunt during which he knocks the pole out from under Jerigigiatugo, who saves himself by means of his grandmother's magical staff. Jerigigiatugo climbs to the cliff's top, kills lizards, and faints when overcome by the stench of their rotting carcasses. Vultures and other avian scavengers descend upon him, eat the lizards and his buttocks, then carry him to the base of the cliff for water.

25

Once back down upon the ground, Jerigigiatugo "returns to himself as if awakening from a long dream." Although he eats fruit he is unable to hold anything within him due to his missing anus. Remembering a legend he had heard from his grandmother he fashions the missing part from a wild potato, *pobodori*, and is then able to retain food. Then he walks for days in search of his people, finally seeing the staff marks and footprints he can identify as belonging to his grandmother and younger brother. After teasing his relatives through a series of appearances as different animals (including at least two lizards and five birds), he finally appears in his own human form. The earliest version (1925) ends here, with Jerigigiatugo saying, "'I no longer want to live with the Orarimugu [a designation for the Bororo] who have ill-treated me, and in order to have my revenge on them and my father, I shall send them wind, cold, and rain.' Then he took his grandmother into a beautiful and distant land and returned to punish the Indians as he said he would" (translation taken from Lévi-Strauss 1969:37). The 1942 version continues with more detail: upon Jerigigiatugo's arrival in the village a furious storm puts out all of the fires except that of his grandmother, where the villagers then come to renew their own. This includes Kiareware, the second wife of Bokwadorireu. She recognizes her husband's son and reports his presence to her husband, who takes his *bapo*, rattle, and performs the appropriate welcoming ceremony.

Jerigigiatugo does not, however, forget "the bad that his father had done him" and sends his younger brother to ask his father to call for a deer hunt. During the hunt he is advised of his father's whereabouts by his younger brother, who becomes a *mea*, rodent, to do so. Using the *api* plant as an aid, Jerigigiatugo turns into a deer, attacks his father, impales him, and throws him into a lagoon where the piranha devour him. "Only the lungs came to the surface and were transformed into a plant whose leaves resemble a lung." Returning then to the village, Jerigigiatugo also avenges himself upon his father's two wives.

In the *Enciclopédia Bororo* version it is explained that Toribugu's mother is dead and his father, Kiare Ware, has another wife who is of the same clan as Toribugu's mother. Meanwhile, Toribugu's younger brother is being raised by their maternal grandmother. The wife of Kiare Ware decorates Toribugu for a festival, but the *Enciclopédia* notes (II:309) that since he was already an adult, Toribugu should not have accepted this distinction. The two then engage in sexual intercourse. Kiare Ware notices traces of decoration on his wife and has his suspicions confirmed after calling for

26

two dances and identifying the telltale decoration on his son. He then sends Toribugu after unspecified numbers and types of animals hoping that his son will be killed, but in each case Toribugu is saved by his grandmother's advice. Following this, Toribugu is sent after the *bapo rogu*, small rattle, and babaçu palm nuts, and the *mamori* (grasshopper) aids him with the former while the *ieragadu*, spider, and *kodokodo*, squirrel, with the latter, again on the advice of his grandmother. The hunt for macaw fledglings follows, with events the same as those recounted in the earlier Salesian versions.

Once Toribugu has been carried by the vultures to the base of the cliff after they have eaten the lizards and his anus, he attempts to locate the moved village. Finding food remains in the ashes of his grandmother's fires as he follows the group, Toribugu is able to repair his anus with the *pobodori*, tuber, and finally hears the mourning wail his grandmother is singing for him. After initial appearances as a bird and lizard, Toribugu finally reveals himself in human form to his grandmother and his younger brother. Suggesting that his grandmother place her house some distance from the village circle, Toribugu is able to enter it unnoticed as a lizard. A thunderstorm then puts out all of the village fires except for that of his grandmother, attracting the villagers to her house. The wife of Kiare Ware recognizes her husband's son, and her husband sings over Toribugu to welcome him. The remainder of the myth is essentially the same as in other versions: the deer hunt, Toribugu as a deer using the sucupira branch as antlers and killing his father, his father's lungs floating to the surface of the piranha-infested lagoon into which he was tossed, and Toribugu reentering the village in imitation of his father and killing his father's wife.

Variations among the myth versions are relatively minor and in most cases easily reconciled. For example, as each Bororo possesses several names, the number of which can be added to over the course of a life, the different names of the principal figures are not generally a problem, especially when the clan affiliations denoted by the names remain consistent. The question of whether Toribugu's mother is his real mother or a stepmother is raised by the *Enciclopédia Bororo* version, but technically this question is insignificant since the stepmother is of the same clan as Toribugu, and the two are therefore traditionally barred from sexual relations by the incest taboo. An additional question concerns the old woman's relationship to Toribugu. The Bororo term *imarugo* that Toribugu uses in addressing her is a term that may be applied to one's mother's mother or father's mother, as well as to other secondary relatives (see note 6). Perhaps more significantly, the term *imarugo* is also used to address the woman who, along with the male *iedaga*, is crucial in one's name-giving ceremony, a ceremony that culturally marks the birth of a child. Unlike the *iorubodare,* or initiation sponsor, who must be from the opposite moiety, the *imarugo* and *iedaga* should preferentially be from the child's own clan. They are the Bororo equivalent of Christian godparents. Since the old woman consistently serves as "guardian" for Toribugu throughout the myth, the more appropriate designation for her rather than grandmother would be "godmother."

Although the words used in both Portuguese and Bororo accentuate the apparent youth of Toribugu, his involvement in an adult, sexual relationship calls his age into question. My informant specifically referred to Toribugu's adult status when the latter comes into inappropriate physical contact with his *imarugo* when he is reunited with her towards the end of the myth. Ambiguity of the hero's age and status may be significant for the overall inter-pretation of the myth and is discussed below.

Toribugu's quests are described with some variation, but the crucial feature, as far as his father is concerned, is their inherent danger. A key element in all versions is the challenge to take the "noise of culture" (rattles used in the performance of virtually all religious ceremonies) from the *aroe,* the natural, ancestral, and totemic spirits of Bororo culture. This feature can be compared with elements from a set of myths to which the Toribugu myth is related, which concern the theme of the "bird-nester," a youth who, like Toribugu, is deserted by a relative while hunting macaw fledglings. Among the Gê, the hero of this myth returns after a suc-cessful encounter with a jaguar, bringing the secrets of hunting (the bow and arrow) and cooking (fire) back to the village. The Bororo hero brings back ritually significant artifacts which, like the prizes of the Gê hero, are key elements in relating society to nature. Furthermore, Toribugu returns as the master of wind and rains, and by extension fire, as the storm he sends extinguishes all flames save that of his *imarugo* (in whose house he abides), from which all other village fires are rekindled.

A Preliminary Analysis

At least two scholars have previously made analytical forays into the myth of Toribugu or Jerigigiatugo. As stated earlier, this myth is used by Lévi-Strauss as the first or key myth in his *Mythologiques* series. Lévi-Strauss attempts to demonstrate that the Toribugu myth "belongs to a set of myths that explain the origin of the *cooking of food* (although this theme is, to all intents and purposes, absent from it); that cooking is conceived of in native thought as a form of mediation; and finally, that this particular aspect remains concealed in the Bororo myth, because the latter is in fact an inversion, or reversal, of myths originating in neighboring communities" (1969:64).

As the Toribugu tale is the key myth in his work, Lévi-Strauss refers to it throughout the four-volume series in a variety of associations; unfortunately, specific details of the myth are analyzed only as needed, with little attempt at any systematic treatment. Lévi-Strauss examines the Toribugu and other myths within related, cross-cultural sets in order to approach their underlying structure and through this attempts to gain a closer glimpse of native thought.

Oosten is more concerned with examining the Toribugu and other Bororo myths in order to "discover their meaning for the participants" of the specific culture to which they pertain (1981:204). In his analysis Oosten draws heavily upon the work of Crocker and concentrates specifically on the social coding of the myth. He begins by criticizing Lévi-Strauss's analysis of Bororo myths, contending that the French scholar's "'alliance' theory of kinship informs much of his myth analysis" (1981:200), and he suggests that this preoccupation results in either the misinterpretation of details of Bororo mythology and/or an emphasis on the interpretation of details of myth and culture that are not ethnographically warranted. Oosten interprets the Toribugu myth and two others that also appear in *The Raw and the Cooked* (Lévi-Strauss, 1969) to be concerned with an opposition of alliance and filiation, concluding that "the myths offer an explanation for the genesis of the tensions" between matrilineal and patrilineal relations in Bororo culture and the ambiguous position of men with respect to them (1981:212).

In his own defense, Lévi-Strauss has claimed that "a myth may well contradict the ethnographic reality to which it is supposed to refer, and the distortion nevertheless forms part of its structure" (1969:45). He examines the Toribugu myth with respect to several cultural codes (e.g., astronomical, alimentary, social) and is concerned with the myth as an element within intersecting sets of native American myths in general. In contrast, Oosten approaches his analysis from a specific facet of the social code and limits his examination of it to its cultural context.

In my interpretation of the Toribugu myth I emphasize its contextual setting within Bororo culture and also pay attention to the broader central Brazilian context with which it is so clearly related. Beginning with the assumption that the myth's social code can inform us of other dimensions of Bororo culture, my principal concern in analyzing the myth is the nature of indigenous concepts of space and time that are revealed within it.

Both space and time are major themes within, and organizers of, the Toribugu myth, in both social and natural dimensions. Social time is marked by the specific social relations depicted therein, including those of the hero with his mother, with his father, with his grand/godmother, and with his younger brother. As all of these relationships stress generational differences (the half-generation relation between older and younger siblings can be skewed in Bororo society to full generational proportions), a sense of social time is inherent in all of them; by the changes in these relationships that occur during the myth, the processual elements of social time are highlighted.

In the case of Toribugu and his mother, the course of the relationship proceeds from the original dominance over Toribugu by his mother, through a brief phase of equivalence when the two are both physically and socially contiguous during intercourse, to Toribugu's dominance over his mother, graphically illustrated when he kills her at the end of the myth. Toribugu's relationship with his father begins with the original dominance of father over son; then Toribugu slays his father and briefly assumes his identity, thus becoming both equal to and dominant over him. Bororo society attempts to protect itself against these conflicts between parents and offspring by such rules as that of moiety exogamy and the incest taboo, thereby prohibiting mother-son sexual relations; and matrilineal descent and uxorilocality (residence with the wife's social group), thereby reducing father-son competition.

In relation to his grand/godmother Toribugu also moves from a position of inferiority when he continually seeks her help to one of superiority upon his return from the wilderness, at which time he has the power of bodily transformation and instructs his *imarugo* as to the placement of her dwelling and how to receive him. In Toribugu's relationship with his younger brother the elder brother's dominance can be assumed throughout the myth, although it is only emphasized at the end, when Toribugu is dominant in all of his relationships.

The nature of these social relations illustrates areas of social conflict in Bororo culture: the nature of Bororo matrilineality in clan affiliation, exogamous marriage prescriptions, father-son authority, and intergenerational tensions. Possible conflict stemming from the Bororo descent system, which emphasizes a dichotomy in familial relations of consanguineal ties to the mother's clan and moiety but affinal ties to the father's, is partially alleviated through the *aroe maiwu* of the funeral service. The institution of the *aroe maiwu*, the "new soul," is enacted through the choosing of a man to represent the deceased (whether male or female). This man must be from the moiety opposite that of the deceased, and he becomes the ritual "son" of the deceased's parents (either real or substitute parents, in the latter case mother's sister and her husband). This relationship is seriously maintained and observed throughout the lives of those involved through the appropriate use of terms of address between the nuclear "family" members, the use of special proper names, and the performance of services such as food preparation and exchange. These ritual family ties proliferate throughout Bororo society, even though they are an inverse to normal kinship patterns in which children pertain to the clan of their mother. In these replacement families, the "son" is not only from a clan other than that of his "mother," he is specifically from the opposite moiety and due to traditional marriage rules is likely to be a member of the clan of his ritual "father."[42]

Father-son tensions and the conflict of generation-based authority is illustrated in Toribugu's relationship with his father, even though in actuality the father-son relationship may be characterized by considerable mutual affection (cf. Crocker 1979:284). In this case the myth's presentation of the father-son relationship is in some contradiction to the observed relationship, but the myth may be using father-son tensions to represent intermoiety tensions (father and son belong to opposite moieties), which are mediated and resolved through a complex alliance system. While the father in Bororo culture may honor responsibilities such as food supply and assistance in the manufacture of certain artifacts for his son, it is the *iedaga*, a boy's mother's-brother and name-giver (whose positive relationship is represented in the myth by the female counterpart to the *iedaga*, the *imarugo*), and his *iorubo-dare*, initiation sponsor, who have particular responsibility for a boy's education (these relationships are further discussed in chapter 4). The generation-based authority can only be resolved with the passing of time and the rise in importance of younger men as that of their elders declines.

The social growth and maturation of the hero, illustrative of the development of the Bororo male in general, is the emphasis of the Toribugu myth when viewed from the perspective of social time.[43] As a youth, Toribugu is manipulated by his father and finally separated from his family and village and left to die. Essentially, all Bororo boys must "die" in order to be culturally reborn as adults privy to a complex set of rights and responsibilities. Their social death is marked by a period of separation from the village during which they undergo rigorous training and trials and receive instruction in the details necessary for adult male life. Appropriately, this period of sociocultural death and rebirth for male initiates culminates during funeral services. At this time the boys return to the village, their figurative unrecognizability, stemming from the change undergone in their person, amplified through camouflage with which they are adorned. Once identified by their mothers, they remain with their families only briefly before moving from their natal households to the communal men's house.

While suspended at the macaw's nest, Toribugu is a metaphorical fledgling (a theme made much clearer in Gê bird-nester myths). His isolation from the village, arduous trials, and the maturation and growth he experiences while in the wilderness, as well as his reappearance as a powerful adult, are analogous to the stages of male initiation. Upon his return he is "camouflaged" as different animals and is at first unrecognized, until upon recognition he addresses his *imarugo* as "mother." Even the title of the version of the myth presented at the beginning of this chapter emphasizes the theme of Toribugu's social growth and maturation. "The branch of the sucupira" refers not only to the type of wood used by Toribugu to implement his transformation and revenge upon his father but carries a deeper significance related to the wood's principal characteristics. The sucupira is noted among the Bororo and other central Brazilian groups as the epitome of strength and hardness. Since traditional Bororo beliefs about the maturation of infants and children concern their growing degree of "hardness," the branch of the sucupira is used metaphorically to express the fact of the hero's transformation not only into the antlered *atubo* deer, but into a strong, "hard" adult. Toribugu's growth is likewise representative of the male Bororo's transition from child to adult.

Along with the social growth of Toribugu as an individual, and by extension that of all Bororo males, cultural growth is also described in the myth. It derives from the successes of Toribugu's perilous adventures in response to his father's orders, as a result of

Ceremony for a hunter who has just killed a feline.

which he presents certain dead animals, noise-making artifacts, and the power over wind and rain (or its converse, the control of fire). The animals, which are all powerful predators, pertain to a set named *marege mori-xe* (detailed by Crocker 1985:191, 280–90), and are those specifically required in the system of retribution (*mori*) that is part of all funerary observances (see Fabian 1985). One of the *aroe maiwu*'s most important responsibilities is to hunt and kill an animal of this category and present it to his new nuclear family (the family of the deceased). It is particularly appropriate that Toribugu presents them to his father, a man of the opposite moiety, since this would be the normal relationship between *aroe maiwu* and the deceased (that is, of opposite moieties). The hero's efforts may therefore represent the initial observance of this rite, and with its addition to Bororo culture, the enrichment of observed ritual; his presentation may also establish another vehicle to mediate matrilineally derived tensions, the *aroe maiwu* being related to his new (ritual) parents patrilineally. The Toribugu myth perhaps takes the *aroe maiwu* relationship to its furthest ironic extension: just as the *aroe maiwu* becomes the deceased whom he represents, Toribugu becomes his father after first presenting him with the appropriate *aroe maiwu* offerings or gifts and then kills him.

By supplying the rattles of the *aroe* to the village, Toribugu allows for the proliferation of Bororo ceremony, as no significant ritual can occur without the use of these rattles. In essence, the myth chronicles individual and, by extension, group social maturation as well as cultural growth and relates the two. The relationship between the two is further emphasized in Bororo culture and society in that it is generally only initiated men who enact and perform the elaborate ritual repertoire.

While the hero grows and changes in observable social time, social and other environmental specifics make explicit references to natural time. Both day and night time are significant: the former as context for most of the action, the latter for specific occurrences such as the star sequence (related to the quest for the rattle). Seasonal time is also evident, through the availability of certain foods (the tubers that Toribugu finds while tracking the people of his village are available only during the dry season), the wind and rain that Toribugu calls down upon the village after his return, and the residence pattern and activities of the people. Initially the myth places actions in the village, for which my informant used the Portuguese word *aldeia*. The locations at which Toribugu later encounters traces of his people while tracking them are in contrast only "camps" (*campamentos*) and indicate trekking activity, which the Bororo and other cerrado-dwellers engage in principally during the dry season. Corroboration between residence pattern and available foodstuffs identifies the dry trekking season and opposes it to the full village occupancy found at the beginning of the myth, as illustrated by the large group dance, which is characteristic of the rainy season.

As is already evident, direct relationships exist between space and time: the "when" of activities is closely linked to the "where." Spatially, action in the myth alternates between "cultural" space and "natural" space. The village is the essential domain of human culture: it is where the *jure* or *iparereru* dance at the beginning of the myth is performed, and where products obtained from outside the village are "cultured" or rendered usable for village inhabitants. Toribugu continually moves between social, cultural space and the surrounding wilderness in his quests for animals, food/drink, and artifacts. The latter come specifically from the abode of the *aroe*, who inhabit an ambiguous space between "culture" and "nature," for they are "nature" spirits as well as ancestral and totemic beings from whom the social groups (clans, subclans, and name groups) of Bororo society are derived.

Whereas natural products are "cultured" within the village, Bororo boys (and Toribugu) must leave the village to be immersed

34

in the wilderness before becoming fully "cultured," social adults. This distinction is indicative of the Bororo perception of their environment, for although they conceive of a concentric distinction between the domains of "culture" and "nature," they are also quite aware of their interrelation: the potential for growth and fruition of each is perceived to lie within the other. A boy must suffer in the wilderness to become a man in society, and it is the fruits of the wilderness in hunted game and other natural resources that sustain society. On the other hand, the Bororo also say that what are today seen as forests were once really Bororo villages, a reference to the proliferation of vegetal growth in the abandoned but fecund cultural space of villages.

The Bororo themselves have also made unsolicited references to the relation of time and space elements in the Toribugu myth. The informant who related the myth, upon finishing his narration, commented that it had occurred at about the time we were currently in, that is, the end of the rainy season, 27 April. Unfortunately, since the myth encompasses a passage of time, it is not clear to which event of the myth he was referring. Speaking in a separate interview another informant commented that the wind and rain sent by Toribugu "in order to put out the fires and to kill his father" occurred during *butaokau*, the rainy season. He continued by saying that Toribugu stayed (with the village) through the following *jorukau*, dry season, and killed his father in the next *butaokau*. From these references the action in the myth seems to transpire over the course of a year, a theme that will be returned to when the myth is reexamined in chapter 7. While this temporal sequence may not necessarily be completely evident from the text of the myth itself, what is significant is that the Bororo are cognizant of temporal sequences in their mythology and may use the format of myths precisely for the purpose of preserving valuable time-sequenced knowledge. They also connect their myths to actual seasons or natural time periods.

Lévi-Strauss interprets the Toribugu myth to be about the cooking of food, suggesting cooking as a form of mediation in native thought. My own interpretation of the myth holds it to be a description of the maturation of the hero, his social growth, and by extension the transition of all Bororo males from child to adult. The myth also describes the process of social and cultural development of Bororo society, including the addition of instruments to their culture, the dead animals significant for retribution in the cult of the dead, and the control of fire.

"Fire" forms a link between the myth's theme as I interpret it and Lévi-Strauss's analysis. As the agent of cooking food, fire mediates the transformation of certain natural and wild products into a culturally usable state as food. Fire is also used to mediate the transition of Bororo males from boys to men, from a "wild" and socially immature state to one of cultured adulthood, in the final stage of male initiation when boys are figuratively (and almost literally) "cooked" by a bonfire and so fully transformed.[44] It is interesting that while Lévi-Strauss has interpreted this myth from the comparative context of similar myths in cultures other than Bororo, and my interpretation was applied specifically within the context of Bororo culture, we have reached similar conclusions about the myth.

A single interpretation of this or any other myth cannot claim to give its "meaning" since the very nature of native narrative lies in its richness and multivocality. These "layers" or levels of meaning and understanding are significant insights into the workings of native thought and can be used and manipulated in strategic ways by members of the culture for desired ends, and as a way of gaining deeper insight and broader perspective on their own culture.

Three

Village Organization and Spatial Orientation

Bororo social relations, as introduced in the Toribugu myth, are controlled by cultural rules that ascribe to the paradigmatic structuring of the social groups localized within the Bororo village.

An ideal Eastern Bororo village is located where access to principal resources is enhanced. Such a setting includes a river as water source and fishing site; perhaps a smaller spring may also be available. A variety of plant species must be accessible, with palm stands of particular importance: the babaçu, buriti, and to a lesser extent, the acuri providing materials for housing (walls and roof), for woven articles (baskets, mats, trays, fans, etc.; see Blatt-Fabian 1985), and for food and drink (palm hearts, nuts, and juice or sap). There must also be reasonably large tracts of fertile forest areas, which the Bororo clear for agriculture in necessary preference over the common cerrado soils, which are sandy and less fertile. Village access to the major ecological zones ensures a higher potential yield of faunal and floral resources.[1]

All known and described villages of indigenous character are of circular or slightly elliptical form (cf. Rondon and Barbosa de Faría for a diagram of the latter type), although photographs included in Colbacchini (1925:7,9) illustrate a square or quadrangular village at the Rio Bareira. The river was also the site of the Meruri mission, however, which later arranged the Bororo houses into either a single line or L-shape in an effort to break the native orientation and related belief systems. Thus, missionary influence in the quadrangular arrangement of the houses is also suspect. The village circumference is composed of family houses that are rectangular in shape, with their longer sides tangent to the circumference and opening onto the plaza via a main door. There is usually a back or side door as well. These houses are ordered according to a paradigmatic plan for localizing social units on the village circumference (discussed in detail below).

At village center stands the men's house (*baimanagejewu* or *baito*, "house in the plaza/center"), also rectangular and several

Garças village as seen from the author's house. Groups of men are
ceremonially active in the western plaza during funerary proceedings.
View is toward the southeast.

times larger than the family dwellings. To what extent neo-Brazilian influence has affected the type and means of construction of
the Bororo house is unknown, as primary contact with the neo-
Brazilians (*barae*, in Bororo, *baraedu*, singular) has occurred in some
areas for nearly two centuries.[2] The *Enciclopédia Bororo* illustrates as
the typical indigenous Bororo dwelling a simple A-frame house
lacking closure on the short sides, whose walls are also the roof,
which slants to the ground (*EBI*:448, 449). Although this house
type is nowhere in common use in a Bororo village today, it serves
as temporary shelter at distant garden sites.

   While contemporary Bororo villagers clear of vegetation essentially all of the ground space between the family dwellings and
men's house, it is possible that in larger villages in the past paths led
through the growth of vegetation connecting the dwellings with the
men's house and central dance plazas similar to the pattern still maintained in contemporary Kraho villages.[3] In Bororo villages, areas to
the west and east of the men's house are used for the performance of
ceremonies, and of these, the western plaza (*bororo*, or *arigao bororo*)
is ceremonially the more prominent. Some informants expressed the
idea that the eastern plaza was used for joyous ceremonies, while the
western plaza was for those of sorrow. During my stay in Garças village only one organized village event was held in the eastern plaza,
the roasting of a cow for a feast. In comparison, a naming ceremony,
celebrations of the killing of feline predators, and a large number of
funerary services took place in the western plaza.

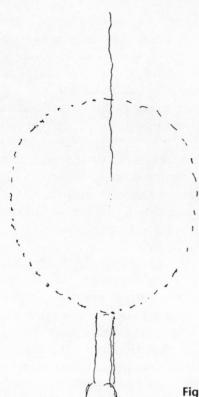

Fig. 3.1.   Culture chief's ideological
sketch of a Bororo village

Two other features of the village not commonly described in the literature but very significant to the Bororo are the *aije rea* and *aije muga*. The *aije rea*, or "path of the *aije* " (the *aije* is a powerful, aquatic *aroe*, spirit), extends from the *boe paru* or *ba paru*, the "base" or western area of the village circumference, westward to the *aije muga*, the plaza of the *aige*. (An excellent aerial photograph of a Bororo village complete with *aije rea* and *aije muga* appears in *EBI*:429.) One informant in Garças called the main village plaza *ipare wororo kurireu*, and the *aije muga*, *ipare wororo biagareu* (the "greater" and "lesser" plazas, respectively). Although the *aije rea* and *aije muga* technically function only during funerals, the funerary period is the most significant among Bororo ceremonies and may extend for a large part of the year. One elder, when asked to trace an outline of the village, supplied the design given in figure 3.1, illustrating the significance of the *aije rea* and *aije muga* as standard village features. In addition to the *aije rea*, other primary and secondary paths connect the village with the surrounding terrain.

Some lead to favored hunting, fishing, and gathering areas, others to water sources. A *mano rea*, path of the *mano* (a large wheel constructed of sections of the *mano* plant—a swamp dweller—and carried in races analogous to the log races of the Gê; see *EBI*: 154 for an illustration), is traditionally another prominent feature.

Although the village is circular, it stresses a directional orientation along an east-west axis that runs through the *aije rea* and connects the *aije muga* with the village. This axis bisects the entire village and the central men's house, which is positioned lengthwise north to south, and localizes the moiety division common to all Bororo villages (cf. early Salesian works of Colbacchini that describe the men's house as running lengthwise east-west, along the major village axis, as opposed to being perpendicular to it; no villages today exhibit this north-south pattern). The northern moiety is called Exerae, the southern Tugarege. In his 1936 study, Lévi-Strauss noted a secondary axis and division running north-south and dividing the village of Kejara into upriver and downriver, or upper and lower components. Although this division remains unreported by other Bororo fieldworkers, there is evidence to suggest that it may once have been more significant than recent research has indicated (this topic is discussed in more detail below). Waterways in the Bororo area tend to course in a westerly direction, such as is true for the São Lourenço River and its major arteries, as the overall slope of the land is generally from east to west. This direction of flow parallels the primary axial orientation of the village and is cosmologically significant for the Bororo, related to the perceived movement of the sun, moon and stars.

In accord with the overall east to west slope of the terrain in their territory, the Bororo loosely designate the eastern portion of the village *xobugiwu* ("upper") and the western portion *xebegiwu* ("lower"), a nomenclature formally applied to distinguish the two clans of the Baadajebage to whose ranks are traced hereditary chiefs: Baadajebage Xobugiwuge is the easternmost clan of the Exerae moiety, and Baadajebage Xebegiwuge is that moiety's westernmost clan. An "upper," *xobugiwu*, and "lower," *xebegiwu*, distinction is maintained in subclan designations to express relative position within clan space, although no clans other than the Baadajebage are themselves formally designated as "upper" or "lower" clans. There is also an apparent lack of relationship between social ranking and the geographical/cosmological usage of "upper" and "lower."

Membership in Bororo clans is traced matrilineally, and postmarital residence is preferentially uxorilocal. The total number of

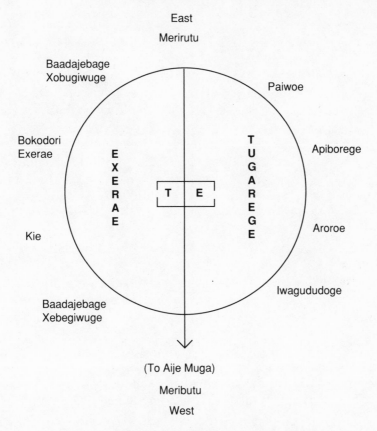

Fig. 3.2. Simplified scheme of a Bororo village

clans in a Bororo village is eight, and informants list them by beginning at the western end or "base" of the village. Each clan is fixed in space. As clans are composed of a number of localized sub-clans and smaller divisions (sub-subclans or lineages or name groups, the latter designation following Crocker's usage [1985] and preferred herein), some discrepancies in the placement of the sub-divisions do exist. The most simplified scheme lists the clans in the following order (see figure 3.2):

Exerae (beginning in the west):	*Tugarege* (beginning in the west):
Baadajebage Xebegiwuge	Iwagududoge
Kie	Aroroe
Bokodori Exerae	Apiborege
Baadajebage Xobugiwuge	Paiwoe

Particularly in the case of the Tugarege moiety, however, such a listing is so oversimplified as to be misleading. This is due to the

41

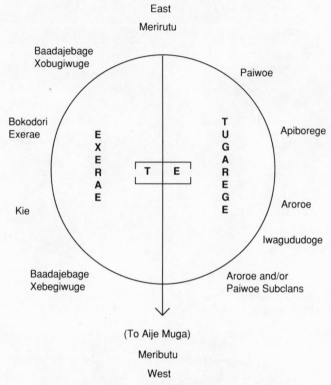

Fig. 3.3. Idealized scheme of a Bororo village

location at the western village end of either a subclan of the Aroroe or subclans of both Paiwoe and Aroroe (see figure 3.3).

Almost every investigator reports a different set of specific name groups. The different techniques of data collection, variations among the different villages researched, personal variations in ideas of correct location of social groups among Bororo individuals, and the Bororo tendency towards bestowing multiple names upon an individual all contribute to the various models to be found in the literature. Padre Angelo Venturelli, coauthor of the *Enciclopédia Bororo*, claims that the village scheme presented in volume 3 (the latest volume) most accurately represents the ideal Bororo village (personal communication, 1980; see *EB*III:0.9, and cf. the earlier models in *EB*I:436 and II:0.7–0.8). Considering the variety of models and disagreements among individual informants queried in the field, however, it seems likely that an absolute, "ideal" Bororo village model localizing exactly every minor social group exists primarily in the minds of investigators.[4]

In spite of certain discrepancies, there remains considerable

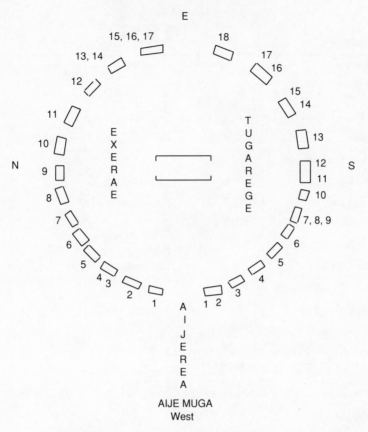

Fig. 3.4. Bororo village plan, Paiwoe version.
Source: Paiwoe culture chief (see table 3.1).

concordance among the Bororo concerning the principal village characteristics: circular shape; two moieties divided along an east-west axis, Exerae in the north and Tugarege in the south; four clans in each moiety, whose general disposition conforms to the layout described above in figure 3.3; a central men's house; and an *aije rea* and *aije muga* extending from the west of the village. The greatest discord arises in naming and locating the name groups which comprise the subclans.

Two Bororo cultural chiefs offered different detailed versions of the village plan. One chief was of the Paiwoe clan, the other was of the Bokodori Exerae, and both were critical of versions other than their own (including some published plans that were shown to them). The Paiwoe informant's village description is listed first (table 3.1), with an accompanying illustration (figure 3.4), and then the Bokodori Exerae informant's data are given (table 3.2), also with

Table 3.1
Bororo Village Plan, Version A

Exerae Moiety

Name Group	Subclan	Clan
1. Arua		
2. Bakorokudu	?	
3. Jakorawari	-----------	Baadajebage Xebegiwuge
4. Oxa Kudureu — same house		
5. Ki Bakororo - - - - - - - - - - - - - - -	Xebegiwuge	----- Kie
6. Torobaru - - - - - - - - - - - - - -	Xobugiwuge	
7. Inokuri	----------- Xebegiwuge	
8. (O)kogue Ekureu		
9. Barogo Bororo - - - - - - - - - - - -	Baiadodawuge	_ _ _ Bokodori Exerae
10. (O)kogue Erigiga		
11. Bokodori Baru - - - - - - - - - -	Xobugiwuge	
12. Kaigu		
13. Mamuyawuge Exeba		
14. Akaruyo Bokodori same house?	?	
15. Botonapa	-----------	Baadajebage Xobugiwuge
16. Buturagiri same house?		
17. Jerigi Otojiwu		

(continued)

a diagram (figure 3.5). In both cases the data are presented sequentially as they were recorded (although some points remained unclear even after several discussions of the information with my informants).

In the village plans presented in figures 3.4 and 3.5, a coincidence of nineteen name groups appears in both, with their corresponding clan and subclan identifications. Other name groups, though given different appellations, may actually be the same: the Bororo receive many proper names that are name group property and an individual may be known by any of these. In overall configuration the village versions are quite similar. In both, the Aroroe Xebegiwuge subclan is located near the *aije rea* in the west (with the remainder of the clan further to the south on the circumference, the two divisions being separated by the Iwagududoge clan). The

Table 3.1 (*continued*)

Tugarege Moiety

Name Group	Subclan	Clan
1. Manokurireu ⎤ – – – – – – – – – – – – –	Xebegiwuge – – – – –	Aroroe
⎟ same house?		
2. Toribugu ⎦ – – – – – – – – – – – –	Xoreu – – – – – – – –	Paiwoe
3. Aije Gugure – – – – – – – – – – – – –	Xebegiwuge – – – –	Aroroe
4. Tadugo		
5. Aroya Kurireu	Xoreu	
6. (O)kogue Enogwa Tabowu		
7. Jakomea Ekureu ⎤		– – Iwagududoge
8. Iwodudu Pradu ⎟ same house?	Kujagureu	
9. Jakomea Atugodojeba ⎦		
10. Butoregadu		
11. Baitogogo ⎤ same house – – – – – – –	Xobugiwuge – – – –	Aroroe
12. Birimodo ⎦		
13. Boroge		
14. Kurugugwa ⎤ same house? – – – – – – – – – – – – – –		Apiborege
15. Apuye Exeba ⎦		
16. Jokuruga ⎤ same house – – – – – – –	Xoreu	– – Paiwoe
17. Baiporo ⎦		
18. Aturuwa Paru – – – – – – – – – – – – –	Kujagureu	

Source: Paiwoe informant (see fig. 3.4).

overall number of name groups identified in each case is also similar. The alternative terms of Xoreu ("black"), and Kujagureu ("red") for Xebegiwu and Xobugiwu, respectively, for subclan nomenclature, appear only in the Tugarege moiety, if they appear at all; and the use of the term Baiadodawuge, "middle," to designate a clan section between the "upper" and "lower" subclans is infrequent.

Specifics such as the number of name groups and the use of the *baiadodawuge* subclan are those most likely to be affected by demographic shifts. The Bororo population has been drastically reduced in numbers, with a concomitant reduction in village size, over the past hundred years. Both informants who supplied the village models given above stressed the greater number of houses and size of villages in earlier days, claiming to have seen villages with at

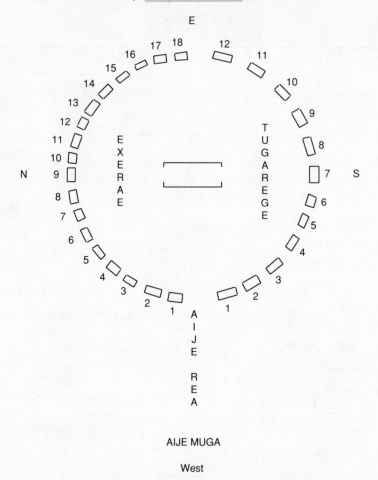

Fig. 3.5. Bororo village plan, Bokodori Exerae version.
Source: bokodori Exerae culture chief (see table 3.2).

least two concentric rings of houses, and said that larger villages would have more rings. In the plan of contemporary Garças village (described below), a number of gaps appear not only in name groups but in subclans as well, and extending even to the clan level, due to shortages in population. Such drastic reduction in numbers is likely to substantially affect native concepts and construction of ideal and real village plans. However, the relatively close correspondence of village plans described by members of different clans and from different regions of birth supports the significance of village organization in structuring Bororo society and in contributing to the noteworthy degree of Bororo sociocultural homogeneity.

Table 3.2
Bororo Village Plan, Version B

Tugarege Moiety

Name Group	Subclan	Clan
1. Manokurireu	Xebegiwuge	Aroroe
2. Tadugo	Xebegiwuge, Xoreu	Iwagududoge
3. Aroya Kurireu		
4. (O)kogue Bowu	Xobugiwuge, Kujagureu	
5. Butoregadu		
6. Kaboreu	Xebegiwuge	Aroroe
7. Birimodo	Xobugiwuge	
8. Akaruyo Boroge	Xebegiwuge	Apiborege
9. Apuye	Baiadodawu	
10. Kurugugwa	Xobugiwuge	
11. Xoreu (?)	Xebegiwuge	Paiwoe
12. Meriri Baru	Xobugiwuge	

Exerae Moiety

Name Group	Subclan	Clan
1. Bakorodudu	Xebegiwuge	Baadajebage Xebegiwuge
2. Arua		
3. Oxa Kudureu	Xobugiwuge	
4. Atugoreu		
5. Kie Bakororo	Xebegiwuge	Kie
6. Baadajeba Kudoro		
7. Baadajeba Merede	Xobugiwuge	
8. Torobaru		
9. Kugurireu or ?	Xobugiwuge	
Exerae Tevie	Xebegiwuge	
10. Aromerere	Xebegiwuge	Bokodori Exerae
11. Barogo Bororo		
12. Bara Meri	Baiadodawu	
13. Poru Yepa		
14. Bokodori Baru	Xobugiwuge	
15. Imoryo/Kaigu		
16. Akaruyo Bokodori	Xebegiwuge	Bakoro Exerae (Baadajebage Xobugiwuge)
17. Turugudu Pijiwu	Baiadodawu	
18. Jerigi Otojiwu	Xobugiwuge	

Source: Bokodori Exerae informant (see fig. 3.5).

The static dimensions of Bororo village and social structure are interwoven by dynamic processes defined within the life course (see chapter four) and within the set of "alliance" or *iorubodare* relations. *Iorubodare* is a reciprocal term used between a boy and his initiation sponsor but also extended to encompass the members of name groups of the opposite moiety with which the initiand's name group is bound in traditional, symmetrical exchange such as marriage partners, food, and a variety of services including ritual representations that are always undertaken by members of one moiety for members of the other. That a man's attention is most frequently and necessarily fixed upon the opposite moiety is illustrated by the village descriptions supplied by the two cultural chiefs: the Paiwoe informant (of the Tugarege moiety) began his description of the name groups with the Exerae moiety, whereas the Exerae informant began his plan in Tugarege space. Concern with the opposite moiety is reiterated for Bororo men as their process of social maturation includes exogamic marriage and uxorilocal postmarital residence, resulting in their actually inhabiting the side of the village opposite to that of their birth for the majority of their lives.

It is probably axiomatic that a man's ordering of village space will begin with the opposite moiety, as it is to this side of the village to which he looks (both figuratively and literally) for many of the social relationships that structure his life (e.g., father, initiation sponsor, wife), and the nature of these relationships provides him with the tangible substance of earned prestige. As he matures and exhibits his cultural knowledge and skills, he will be increasingly called upon to perform the *aroe* representations of his *iorubodare* and will also become the living representative of his deceased *iorubodare* (see Fabian 1985 and chapter 4). All of these relations are accompanied by an exchange of goods (e.g., food, clan-owned artifacts) as well as services, and the paths traversed by men between the moieties—especially during periods of peak ceremonial importance such as the funeral—crisscross and inextricably bind together the various subdivisions of the two moieties in a maze of Bororo-perceived *utawara* or "roads" (cf. Crocker 1979:290).

Neither of the informants who gave the detailed village descriptions presented above numbered the clans, subclans, or name groups but rather recited them in sequence.[5] One informant specifically stated, in response to my questioning, that the number of clans or social groups in general is not important, which can be taken to mean that the social groups are conceived of as a nonnumeric sequence that forms the village circle. Of apparent importance to the Bororo is not the number of name groups from any point A to point B of the village, but rather who these groups are and in what order they are arranged. The paradigmatic sequencing (with minor variations) of Bororo social groups composing the village bears certain resemblances to tables, lists, formulas, and recipes that Goody (1977) describes as features of literate traditions; similar nonnumeric sequencing is a major organizing principle of Bororo epistemology evident in all forms of narrative.

Another important concept and organizing principle revealed in the organization of Bororo social space is "layering." Name groups, subclans, clans, and moieties all overlap within the same village space, while *iorubodare* relations, naming sponsors (the *iedaga* and *imarugo*), friendships, *roça* or cooperative "garden" groups, possible age classes (see chapter 4), and relationships fixed by the *aroe maiwu* ("new soul") institution of the funeral are constitutive of relations that crisscross the village in a complex network of intersecting lines (see *EBI*:450 for a diagram representing marriage unions that illustrate such a scheme). Social layering and the intersection of different social relations within the village are also characteristic of neighboring Gê-speaking peoples; for the Bororo and Gê peoples, the use of nonnumeric sequencing and layering (or set overlapping/intersection) extends beyond the structuring of society to other facets of culture.[6]

Organization of the *Baimanagejewu,* the Men's House

As the center of ceremonial and male secular activity, as well as physically centered in the village, the *baimanagejewu,* or men's house, is the focus of village attention. It is the largest single structure, with dimensions depending upon village size. The *baito,* as it is commonly referred to, is faced by all clan houses on the village circumference, and functions as dormitory and workshop, as well as religious precinct. With its longer sides facing east and west, and doors opening to north and south, the structure cuts across the major village axis and opens into Exerae and Tugarege space. (A secondary set of doors opening onto the once screened dance plazas to east and west, as described in *EBI*:445–47 and illustrated on p. 436, no longer exist, presumably because these plazas are no longer screened to shield the participants from unqualified

49

observers.) The north door is entered by men of the Tugarege moiety and the south by Exerae men, a practice that reverses the men's natal positions on the village circumference but reflects their postmarital residence. The reversal is maintained in the men's house, where Tugarege men sit in the north and Exerae men in the south. Women are allowed to enter the *baito* only upon ritually significant occasions (with the exception of the "men's house associates" described by Crocker [1969a]) and are restricted to the eastern wall, Exerae women to the north and Tugarege women to the south.

In construction the men's house resembles most family dwellings in that it is rectangular, with three large pillars[7] supporting a long central ceiling beam that spans the entire length of the structure. From this central beam, wooden poles or rafters run down and lay atop the wall beams. Lengths of bamboo are attached perpendicular to the rafters and serve as a base for palm thatching. Walls are formed by a similar construction: three major pillars support beams along both long sides, and smaller vertical studs spaced between the larger pillars help support either horizontal bamboo poles on which buriti leaves are thatched or horizontal lengths of babaçu leaves attached directly to the vertical supports. The two shorter sides each have a doorway that may be closed by a plaited palm-mat door. Materials used to construct the men's house and all village houses are specifically chosen for their suitable characteristics for the intended use. Although some steel nails had been employed in fastening parts of the men's house and some family houses in Garças village, palm-derived braided rope was more extensively used.

An informant of the Bokodori Exerae clan gave a detailed model of the arrangement of men in the men's house based upon their name group. He and several others stressed that chiefs must sit near the central pillar, although the different categories of "chief" (e.g., hereditary or "cultural," the latter being men credited with profound traditional knowledge) complicate the issue. The detailed description is presented in figure 3.6 and shows men arranged by name group within their respective moieties, while also divided from east to west. The names correspond to those given on an earlier occasion by the same informant for the name groups in village organization (the numbers in figure 3.6 correspond to those of figure 3.5) except that one or two names are missing from each moiety.

In this plan the original Bororo chiefs Birimodo and Akaruyo

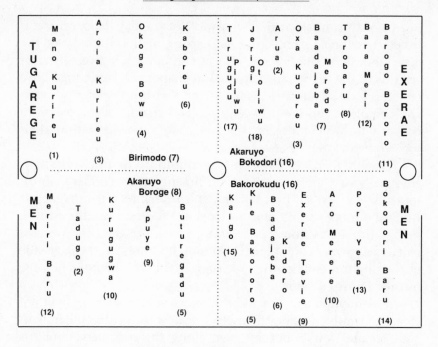

West

Fig. 3.6. Men's house organization. Note: see table 3.2 and figure 3.5.

Boroge are at the center, as are the subsequent chiefs Akaruyo Bokodori and Bakorokudu.[8] While Birimodo and Boroge are located just to the north of the central pillar in the men's house, they pertain to name groups in adjacent positions on the southernmost arc of the village circle. Although there is not an exact structural congruence between the positioning of men in the *baito* and in houses on the village circumference, to some extent those located nearest Birimodo and Boroge in the men's house are also nearest them on the village circle, and those farthest away are also so positioned in both cases: Manokurireu (1) and Meriri Baru (12) at opposite ends of their village half-circle occupy positions nearest the door. Meriri Baru was labeled by my informant as guardian of the Tugarege door (a position he did not assign on the Exerae side). That Meriri Baru is guardian of the door corresponds with his placement on the village circle, adjacent to the path leading out/in at the village's eastern edge, the "door" to the village. Furthermore, this spatial function is also linked to a temporal one: Meriri Baru is the last of five callers who "guard" the early morning (presunrise) hours by crying out at appointed times. Meriri Baru gives his cry

51

just prior to sunrise, at the "doorway" of the day. His position is fixed, therefore, in both time and space, at the doorway of the men's house, of the village, and of the day. (The five callers or "guards of the night" are discussed in chapter 5.) This congruence between location on the village arc and within the men's house, and the direct linkage between time and space, suggest a Bororo concern to structurally incorporate such concepts within their social organization.

That the men's house is quartered into north and south moieties with east and west halves intimates the secondary north-south axis described by Lévi-Strauss for Kejara village. In fact, it would be proper in the Bororo language to designate the eastern half of the men's house as *xobugiwu* or "upper" and the western half as *xebegiwu*, "lower." Such a division may preserve a villagewide organizing principle of the type suggested by Lévi-Strauss (a topic further discussed below).

In contemporary Garças, the most senior men or cultural chiefs generally position themselves nearest the central pillar, with younger and less important men along the periphery. There is loose correspondence in moiety location with Tugarege men in the north and Exerae in the south, although no strict rule is followed in occupying specific space, or even necessarily for entering the appropriate door. When women enter the *baito* for participation in activities and performances they arrange themselves along the east wall reflecting their moiety locations upon the village circle.

Garças Village, 1983

Garças village was originally named for its location on the bank of the Garças River, a tributary of the Araguaia River, the latter serving as the border between the Brazilian states of Mato Grosso and Goiás, and an informal eastern boundary of the territory traditionally occupied by the Bororo. At the time of my field study, however, the village had been moved to a new location several kilometers from the Garças River. Although in terms of ideal conditions for village location as described above, the new Garças location is characterized by some seemingly major contradictions, in fact its location does enhance its access to principal resources, the shift being in the nature of the desired resources. Built upon a level rise that overlooks thick cerrado, the village sits upon a sandy plain that had once been cleared for dry rice farming. The area has subsequently become barren, with a covering of only sparse grasses and short shrubs. This plain extends broadly to the north, where the village's current fields of dry-land rice are located. The plain slopes down gently in the east, and breaks off abruptly to the south. Although commanding an impressive view to the south, east, and partially to the west (a characteristic that elicited exclamations of delight from Bororo visiting from other villages), the openness of the setting creates several difficulties. Exposure to strong winds periodically results in clouds of dust and blowing sand covering the village; the poor soil quality makes the keeping of house gardens a continuous, low-yield challenge; no trees are near enough for shade, shelter, or visual interest; and the village is dependent upon small springs for its drinking and bathing water. These water sources, moreover, either dry up completely or become mere trickles during the dry season. Since the villagers no longer trek, seasonal water shortage poses a serious problem.

At the base of the escarpment to the south one stream flows constantly, and it is from this stream that the present Garças village receives its Bororo name, Tori Kujagu Paru Kejewu Boe E-muga (Village of the Bororo at the Stream of Red Stones), referring to the stream's characteristic red stones (*tori*, stone, and *kujagu*, red). (Since even among the Bororo the most common name for the village is by the name "Garças," I maintain this usage.) This stream is, unfortunately, about one kilometer distant and at the bottom of a steep decline; it is therefore seldom used as water supply for the village. The waterway also presents another difficulty, since it flows from west to east, or in the reverse direction of the ideal and cosmologically significant east-to-west flow—a relationship complained about by at least one village elder.

With the negative factors of an open and barren plain, difficult access to water, cosmological contradiction, and the distant location of fertile farming land on the banks of the Garças River, one wonders why the village was moved from its former location on the river where faunal and floral species are more abundant and in general conditions are more favorable for a life-style within traditional ideals.

Most of the villagers complain continually about the new location and rumors of a move are common. When asked why the village is located in its current position, many Garças Bororo replied that the current setting is "beautiful." One woman suggested that the Garças River, being large and fast, posed a threat to young children, and so they moved further from its dangerous banks. Since few of the men in Garças hunt with regularity and fishing is the preferred protein source, the availability of game is not a major consideration, while there are waterways accessible for fishing within a day's journey. But these conditions could also have been met at other, more advantageous locations, as some of the villagers themselves commented. Clearly, the advantages of the current location of Garças village must be measured by both traditional and contemporary scales of concern.

There are two major considerations for the present village location, and both involve access to resources: rice fields and the Meruri mission. Dry-land rice, which is planted, fertilized, and harvested with the aid of materials and equipment supplied (for a cost) by the mission and the Brazilian government, serves not only as the village's primary dietary staple but also as its principal cash crop. Eaten at every major meal, rice supplies the majority of the daily caloric intake. Bagged and trucked into the nearest town, the rice is sold and its proceeds (seldom very large) are used towards paying off debts and purchasing commodities such as cloth or clothing, blankets, tobacco, and liquor. As the dry, sandy soil of the cerrado is better than the wetter, richer soil of the river banks for this type of farming, easy access to these important fields is necessary, and a prime consideration for the village's current location.

Although the villagers fish, hunt, and gather the natural resources at their disposal, they are coming to rely more and more upon the materials obtained in trade from the mission. These include coffee, tea, sugar, tobacco, manioc, and wheat flour, and even rice when their own stores are depleted. Also available are thread, fishing line, bullets, soap, and other articles that the contemporary village life-style renders essential. In trade for these items most of the villagers manufacture tourist pieces such as bows and arrows, small headdresses, rattles, dusters, and so forth that the mission staff sells to the tourist trade. The Bororo state clearly that these articles are not true artifacts of their culture, possessing no Bororo names, and are made exclusively for trade. Nevertheless, the time, energy, and material required in their manufacture result in reduced attention and supplies for more traditional practices.

The mission also supplies the necessary and beneficial medical aid and facilities that have led to improved village health and more successful births. It is the base from which a visiting dentist (commissioned by the Brazilian government) attends to problem teeth, and it in other ways acts as liaison and mediator between Garças village and the "outside" Brazilian world. Although forty kilometers distant from the mission, Garças village is nevertheless in its current location to facilitate access to the supplies and services controlled by the mission. The village's previous location on the Garças River was further away, and, more significantly, the road linking mission and village was broken by two deep and treacherous streambeds that are impassible to vehicles for most of the rainy season. Although travel on the unpaved roads (which are essentially only wide paths) remains difficult especially during the rains, the present Garças village location is between the mission and the troublesome streambeds. The village has been shifted from a location stressing traditional values and life patterns to one recognizing more immediately practical concerns within the contemporary scene.

In general configuration Garças village conforms to the traditional layout of a Bororo village. More than a dozen structures form the circumference of a circle that measures approximately 80 meters in diameter, and all of these face inward to the cleared plaza and central men's house. The *aije rea* extends from the western end of the village (*ba paru*) about forty meters to the *aije muga*, which is about one-quarter the size of the main village plaza. There are also associated with the village several outlying structures at several hundred meters distance to the east and south. One of these housed the current (1982–83) village "chief": not a cultural chief or hereditary Baadajeba chief, but rather the government (FUNAI)-recognized representative who acts as liaison between the village and the Indian agency. Although bilingually conversant in Bororo and Portuguese and somewhat literate, this man's knowledge of *boe ero*, Bororo tradition, is limited, and his participation in ceremony and other cultural affairs is as marginal as his location. Another house, built of concrete and known as "the white house," is slightly further from the village and is occupied by an entrepreneurially oriented Bororo and his family, who also participate only infrequently in main village affairs. The families most removed spatially from the village were also generally those most removed from its cultural tradition.

Other features of the village include a dirt road that leads in from the north and out by the east linking the village to the state highway, the Salesian mission, and the Garças River. At the side of this road approximately 100 meters north from the village is a schoolhouse where mission-sponsored classes for Garças children are sporadically held. House gardens of different sizes with meager variety and yields are maintained by only some families. These are commonly surrounded by barbed wire to deter the village cattle from entering. Paths lead off to several small springs mostly located south of the village, each frequented by specific house groups.

The disposition of houses in Garças village is given in figure 3.7 and their occupants listed below (the sequence as given begins in the west at the *aije rea* and continues clockwise arbitrarily; it is not meant to represent native organizational principles):

1: Two families, the older and principal couple a Kie woman, her Aroroe husband, and an "adopted" Paiwoe boy, the second a Bokodori Exerae woman, her Kie husband, and their two children, one boy and one girl.

2: A Kie woman and her Paiwoe husband, their daughter and her Apiborege husband, and their children, two boys and two girls; an Iwagududoge man who was courting the eldest girl was also an occupant for one and a half months, but was otherwise a resident of house 14.

3: The house built for my wife and me, which after our departure was reported to be inhabited by members of house 2.

4: A Bokodori Exerae woman who later died and her husband of the Apiborege clan who, upon his wife's death, moved to the Meruri mission. This house was then occupied by house group 16.

5: Another Bokodori Exerae woman, her Paiwoe husband, their daughter, and her daughter and son.

6: Recently vacated before our arrival, it was later inhabited by the couple from house 8, a Paiwoe woman and her Kie husband.

7: Just after our arrival a family of eight (the woman a Baadajeba Xobugiwu) moved to Meruri when the husband left Garças to reside with a woman in another village. Then an elderly Paiwoe woman, a Kie woman with her two sons, two daughters, and one granddaughter, and another Kie woman moved in. The Kie group eventually moved out also and later became part of house group 16 (the unattached Kie woman later died). The elderly Paiwoe woman continued to reside in the house alone.

8: Originally a Paiwoe woman and her Kie husband, who later moved to house 6; a Baadajeba Xobugiwu woman, her Baadajeba Xebegiwu husband, and their two daughters moved in, with another couple, a Paiwoe woman and Kie man.

9: An Apiborege woman, her Baadajeba Xebegiwu husband, their two sons, two grandsons, and a granddaughter (their daughter, the mother of the grandchildren, lived in Meruri).

10: An unoccupied frame.

56

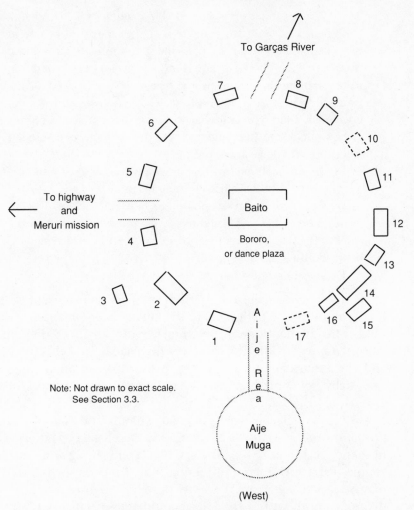

Fig. 3.7. Garças village, 1982–83

11: A Paiwoe woman, her Kie husband, and an elderly woman of the Aroroe clan.

12: Originally housed an Iwagududoge woman, her Baadajeba Xebegiwu husband, an infant daughter, and an adult daughter with her Kie husband and their child. The older couple, along with the wife's elderly mother (Iwagududoge), eventually moved to another village.

13: A woman of the Bokodori Exerae clan and her Iwagududoge husband. Occasionally the husband's brother from Meruri also stayed with them.

14: The largest single household, with an elderly Iwagududoge woman, her daughter, and this daughter's Kie husband, their two sons, and two daughters, the Kie husband of one of these daughters, and their child. One son eventually moved into the (then) chief's house distant from the village circle. In addition to this family, there were two other elderly women, one of the Iwagududoge and the other a Baadajeba Xebegiwu, an Iwagududoge man, and a young Baadajeba boy. Later, a Baadajeba Xebegiwu woman and her Apiborege (or possibly Paiwoe) husband from another village also moved in.

15: An uninhabited structure originally used as a schoolhouse, now housing the village rice-cleaning machine.

16: The first village schoolhouse, housing the Kie woman from house 7, her two daughters, a granddaughter born to the elder of the two, and the Kie woman's new Bokodori Exerae husband and their infant son.

17: An unoccupied frame.

In addition, a Baadajeba Xobugiwu man frequently slept in the men's house, while peripheral to the village were two other households, already mentioned. The "chief's house" included the "chief" who pertained to the Paiwoe clan, his Baadajeba Xebegiwu wife and their two daughters, the Kie husband of one daughter and their baby boy, and later, the Iwagududoge husband (from house 14) of the other daughter. The second house, the "white house," consisted of a Baadajeba Xobugiwu woman and her Apiborege husband, and initially their daughter, her Baadajeba Xebegiwu husband, and their two daughters; this family along with another couple (Paiwoe woman and Kie man) later moved to house 8. As may be appreciated from the above description, movement of family groups both within the village and between villages is a common trait (at least in a contemporary village) and makes census taking a tedious, unending task.

In all, the highest total population was 92, although frequent movement (of both a permanent and transitory nature), births, and deaths constantly altered the count. For couples in the village, the use of the term "married" and concomitant terminology is for practicality's sake: without ceremony to mark the unions, and with the relative ease of bonding and break-ups, "marriage" relationships can be ambiguous among the Bororo.

Four of the bonds are what traditionally would be labeled "incestuous" because they involve spouses of the same moiety. Residence patterns also vary from traditional ideals. Although female Exerae generally inhabit the northern portion of the village and Tugarege women the southern, there was considerable variance from the norm. Accepting that the village lacked a Baadajebage Xebegiwuge house in the west, houses 1 through 5 are relatively properly placed. Households 6, 7, and 11 with Paiwoe females are all out of place, although 11 is located in the appropriate moiety. House 8 is ambiguous with a Baadajeba Xobugiwu woman, a Paiwoe woman, and their families, a situation that to some degree affects the placement of the east-west village axis. Households 9 and 14 are correct as is 12, although its spot would more properly be Aroroe space, a clan of which there was no representative household in the village. Household 13 is completely mislocated since the woman, of the Bokodori Exerae clan, should be with houses 4 and 5.

Villagers are quite aware of incestuous unions and out-of-place households. The former are willingly accepted for the births they contribute to village population as there is considerable concern among the Bororo that they are dying out, prompted generally by the history of their demise since contact with non-Indians and specifically by their dramatic population decline since the 1930s. Two villages that hosted ethnographers in the 1960s are now defunct, while several women in Garças village remain childless (either never having given birth or having lost all of their off-spring). In partial response to this trend, contemporary Bororo are encouraged by the current rise in birthrate, even when the child-producing unions are against traditional patterns. Incestuous unions are also seen as practical, considering the shortage of marriageable partners.

A similar attitude of practical functionalism is applied to the location of clan houses. Although Garças village was originally formed by Bororo intent upon maintaining as much of an indigenous life-style as possible, and cultural traditionalists in the village lament the lack of order in clan placement, the small number of village occupants and lack of female representatives from certain clans (Aroroe and Baadajebage Xebegiwuge) as well as numerous subclans naturally result in breaches in the traditional pattern. Furthermore, village political factionalism influences village house placement and residency to some extent, as do emotional concerns between groups. To what extent these factors may have affected village organization in more distant times is unknown, but a fully traditional village presumably would have enough crosscutting affiliations and responsibilities to substantially reduce intravillage tensions, thus also contributing to the maintenance of ideal village organization.

Village Space and Beyond

Bororo social space can be considered in terms of both concentric and diametric models as discussed by Lévi-Strauss (1963a), an approach constructively applied by other researchers in central Brazil, such as Seeger for the Gê-speaking Suya (1981). Concentrically, the village center is most strongly related to society and culture, while increasing distance from this center places one further within the natural realm. Both sacred and secular activities characterize the use of the *baito* and central plaza, and this entire sphere is dominated by men. By comparison, along the circle of female-dominated houses, domestic and secular concerns are emphasized. Beyond this are house gardens and the broadening sphere of nature. However, the continuum from society to nature extending outwards from the village center is interlaced with oppositional elements such as objects from nature (fruits of the hunt, for example) that arrive in the village, and village elements, such as garden plots, that dot the more fertile and occasionally distant forested areas. Occupants of both the cultural and natural domains also commonly pass through and inhabit both: women on foraging trips and men on hunting and fishing forays going out from the village, for example, and certain species of wildlife such as rats, snakes, and insects entering it.

Since men are more far ranging in their travels, they relate the central-most part of social space with the farthest reaches of natural space, linking the center to outside, a link strengthened by the relationship of the *aroe* (ancestral, totemic, and natural spirit beings) with the Bororo. As depicted in the Toribugu myth, *aroe* live outside the village in what would concentrically be classified as "natural" or "wild" space. It is precisely from the *aroe*, however, that the essence of Bororo society and culture—names, social relations, ceremonies, decorations, ritual paraphernalia—is derived and defined. While *aroe* live outside the village, they enter the innermost village precincts (the men's house and plaza) during the most significant period of ritual performances, the funeral. Although part of both society and nature, they are also inherently outside both. Consistent with this analogy, representations of the *aroe* are performed by men.

Two *aroe* were once Bororo chiefs: Bakororo, who was once Birimodo (also called Baitogogo), now rules the village of the dead in the west; and Itubore, once Akaruyo Boroge, now rules the eastern village of the dead. These two beings and the east and west villages

60

Table 3.3
Characteristics Associated with Bakororo, Itubore, and the Hereditary Chiefs

Birimodo/Bakororo/Bakorokudu	Boroge/Itubore/Akaruyo Bokodori
Red and black horizontal body painting	Horizontal red and black stripes outlined with white down
Musical instrument: *ika*	Musical instrument: *pana*
One large and one small rattle	One large and one small rattle
Special *pariko* (headdress)	Special *pariko* (headdress)
Songs initiating hunting and fishing trips	Songs for the taking of game
Roia Kurireu ("Great Song")	Some songs of the funeral cycle
Perforates lips, ears, and nose; places penis sheath on initiand	Organizes war parties, communal hunting and fishing, and war parties
West	East
Plaza, inside the village activities	Outside the village activities

of the dead are a major link between the concentric and diametric organization of Bororo space. Their villages, at the extreme "outside" with respect to the Bororo village, are nevertheless connected to the village center, where remains of deceased Bororo are temporarily buried and prepared by ceremony for their final burial, and to where the *aroe* (including Bakororo and Itubore) arrive in order to accompany the new spirit to its final abode.

The diametric division of north and south, established by the east-west axis stretching between the villages of the dead and characterized by the Exerae and Tugarege moieties, is crosscut by an east-west dichotomy polarized within the locations and characteristics of Bakororo and Itubore and the sets of hereditary powers possessed by the Baadajebage chiefs Bakorokudu and Akaruyo Bokodori. Bororo mythology (cf. *EB*II: myths #7 and #8) tells of Birimodo who cedes his powers to Bakorokudu before becoming Bakororo and chief of the western village of the dead, and of Boroge who likewise cedes his powers to Akaruyo Bokodori before becoming Itubore, chief of the eastern village of the dead.

Z. Levak (1971:155–57) reports certain key elements in the chiefly sets of power. Bakorokudu is responsible for perforating lips, ears, and nose and for the placement of the penis sheath in *rites de passage* and is generally related to peace and cultural acts. Levak describes the power of Akaruyo Bokodori as that of ordering communal hunting, fishing, and other activities that occur outside the village, including the waging of war. Table 3.3 summarizes the characteristics associated with Bakororo, Itubore, and the hereditary chiefs. Diametric organization is again combined with the

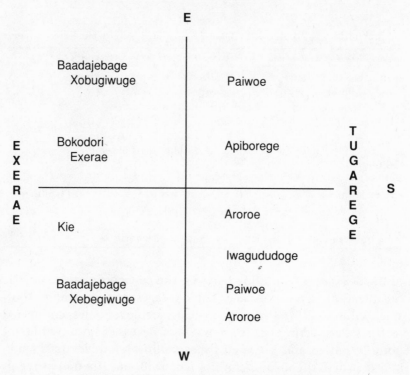

Fig. 3.8. Quadripartition in a Bororo village

concentric, since features related to inside-the-village functions are connected with the west, and cultural features extending outside the village are connected with the east.[9]

The two sets of dyadic models that can be applied to Bororo village organization effectively quadripartition social space. As principal axis, the east-west line running through the village between the villages of the dead and paralleling the flow of celestial bodies and terrestrial water divides the northern, Exerae moiety from the Tugarege in the south. As mentioned earlier in this chapter, Lévi-Strauss describes a secondary north-south axis in Kejara village.[10] Such an axis is implied by the juxtaposition of Bakororo and Itubore as chiefs of the villages of the dead located at the extremes of west and east, respectively, and their powers as reflected in the hereditary responsibilities of Bakorokudu and Akaruyo Bokodori. Structurally, these latter two personages occupy western and eastern extremes in the Baadajebage Xebegiwuge and Baadajebage Xobugiwuge clans, respectively, as well as in the Exerae moiety. A north-south axis is even more graphically suggested by the positions of the two original Bororo chiefs Birimodo and Boroge, who

62

are structurally located at the southernmost portion of the village residential arc. The north-south axis would then be defined between them, since by their subsequent positions as Bakororo and Itubore they are equated with west and east, respectively. Further evidence of the dual axes has already been presented in the description of the men's house organization, where the northern and southern halves of the *baito* are subdivided into eastern and western portions.

A feature of Bororo village organization worth noting appears when a quadripartition is applied, a scheme graphically represented in figure 3.8. In this figure the four clans of the Exerae are separated from the four clans of the Tugarege by the primary east-west division. The north-south line further divides the four Exerae clans into two parts of two clans each. In Tugarege space, however, two clans in one quarter are opposed to four social groups in the other. The southwest quarter is often simplified in published texts to contain only the Aroroe and Iwagududoge clans (as represented in figure 3.2). Most schemes of the village drawn from informants' reports, however, consistently present a more complex situation, in which Aroroe and Paiwoe subclans (or name groups) occupy non-contiguous sections of the village arc with the other social groups of these clans. The resulting reduplication within one quarter of the quadripartition is a feature reminiscent of studies on Andean social organization (cf. the work of Zuidema, and Rivière 1983).[11]

Although concentric and diametric models of spatial organization are useful in describing Bororo concepts of space, they are only approximations of native spatial perceptions. Furthermore, since the different models are inherently related, neither should be applied without reference to the other. Bororo conceptualizations of their cultural space are characteristically complex, multilayered, and intimately related to their perceptions of time. It is the element of time applied to the spatial structure of Bororo social and village organization that yields the dynamic social processes that are statically depicted in the village plan.

Four

The Life Course

The passage of time in a Bororo's life is indicated by physical growth and noteworthy stages of development rather than by the counting of years. These stages are marked for both men and women, although marking is more pronounced and elaborate for men, whose movement in social time is accompanied by changes in the occupancy of social space. Thus, the elements of Bororo social organization that are graphically represented by the layout of the localized social groups that comprise village space are animated by male movement accompanying the transition of marked stages of the life course. Efforts are also made to synchronize the marking of social time cycles with time cycles perceived in the natural environment.

Birth

Traditionally a Bororo woman leaves the village to deliver her child in the nearby forest with the aid of at least one female kinswoman (Crocker asserts that normatively the midwife should be the husband's father's mother or sister who, due to customary marriage practices, would be a member of the wife's clan; 1985:53; Sylvia Caiuby Novães asserts that the midwife would not be a member of the wife's clan, but rather the husband's sister or husband's mother [personal communication, 1990]). The newborn is placed on softened bark cloth, and the group returns to the village where clan (consanguineal) relatives express their joy, but no major ceremonies are held.[1] Both parents observe dietary and activity restrictions that gradually diminish until their child's birth is socially marked by the name-giving ceremony.

Name Giving

Infants are considered to be still forming, or "soft," for several months after birth and are therefore not suitable to receive a name

Painted and down-covered woman prior to the ceremony incorporating her back into society after debility from a serious wound. The special headpiece and down covering are equivalent to a baby's at name-giving, appropriate as both are being socialized into human society.

and its concomitant social identity. Once the infant has "hardened" it is given a name chosen from the set belonging to its mother's clan, thus becoming socially "born" and recognized. Both the midwife—the child's *imarugo*—and the mother's brother—the child's *iedaga*—preside over the naming, marking a lifelong relationship between themselves and the child somewhat analogous to Christian godparentage. The child's *imarugo*, who at its birth held the power of life and death over it (deformed babies or those whose parents have had dreams of ill omen prior to the birth are traditionally not allowed to live, the responsibility of action in such cases falling upon the midwife) now introduces the child to its new social life. It is this relationship, between a child and its name-giving godmother, that is emphasized in the Toribugu myth, for although the relationship is determined genealogically, it is the role of the *imarugo* with respect to the child she sponsors that is significant.[2]

There are, however, some differences in the literature on the specifics of the name-giving ceremony. The *Enciclopédia Bororo*, for example, states that the ceremony takes place only days, not months, after birth, and that the principal adult male involved is the maternal grandfather of the child, who is of the opposite moiety, in contrast to the mother's brother who is of the child's own moiety and clan. In all accounts, however, a boy's naming ceremony differs from a girl's in that during the former a boy's *iedaga* uses a special tool to pierce the baby's lower lip, making a hole from which ornaments will be suspended. This ceremony is called *ipare enogwa porododu*, "the piercing of the lower lip of the youths" (*EB*I:624–26).

The only naming ceremony that took place during the period of my field study was that in which my wife and I were the principal participants. We were never asked if we desired such a distinction; that we would be given Bororo names was simply announced to us one day by a village elder, about six months after our arrival in the village, and so analogous to the typical period of "hardening" of the newborn. The ceremony began two days later at sundown, when we were led to the western village plaza where most of the men were gathered and were seated upon a mat facing the crimson and blue western horizon. Our names were told to us, and we were instructed to write them down so as not to forget them. Then we were sung over briefly from behind. We were led twice, counter clockwise, around the western plaza, a young woman of my adopting clan—the Bokodori Exerae—leading me, and a girl of the Tugarege moiety leading my wife. Our marriage was thus appropriately exogamous. (A woman from a clan other than my wife's, the Aroroe, actually led my wife as there are no young Aroroe women living in Garças village.) Before it was completely dark, and when we were once again standing near the *baito* facing west, my wife's sponsor/*iedaga*, a village elder and the only adult male representative of the Aroroe clan in the village, faced her from several paces away. An old *pariko*, headdress, of macaw tail feathers adorned his head, and he played the *ika* or transverse resonating "flute." He turned in a circle, leapt up and down while flapping his arms in silhouette against the fading western glow (appearing very much like an oversized bird), and then advanced towards my wife in a low, shuffling step, *ika* held before him. He stopped halfway to her and repeated his birdlike movements, then resumed his quick approach. When he reached my wife he stopped abruptly and blew forcefully over her three times[3] and then stepped aside.

Presumably because my *iedaga* is old and half-blind, he led out another village elder of the Exerae moiety who performed essentially the same rites for me as had been done for my wife. We then sat down and were again sung over briefly before being told that we could go. It was not long after, however, the night by this time fully dark, when singing began outside the *baimanagejewu*, roughly in the same place as earlier in the western plaza. We took up sitting positions as directed behind the main male singer facing west and were flanked by much of the rest of the village, the women following the male singer's lead with a droning chant. It had been our responsibility to provide refreshments for the performers, and as the June night became colder and the hot drinks, food, and tobacco we were providing thinned out, so did the attendant villagers. The singing, however, continued without interruption through the night, the main singer alternating between men of the two moieties. At full dawn the singing ceased and everyone left the plaza.

After sunrise we were led to our adopting clan houses (although my wife went to the house of her *iedaga*'s wife, as the Aroroe clan is not represented in Garças by a household) where our hair was cut in Bororo fashion and our faces painted with urucu, a red pigment, and further decorated with appropriate clan designs. (Babies are in addition given special headpieces and their bodies covered with down.) Led again to the western plaza, we stood facing west, with two *pariko* diadems and two *ika* flutes placed on *baku*, or ceremonial trays, in front of us. My wife's *iedaga*, with his hands on her shoulders, announced her Bororo name and the names of her American parents, then blew over her from behind. My *iedaga* did likewise with me, except that his hands were under my arms, as if simulating the way in which an infant would be held up in the air at this stage of the ritual. These procedures ended the ceremony, after which we were congratulated by a line of villagers, each one shaking our hands.

Due to the specific circumstances of this ceremony (the fact that it was held for adults, and particularly adults without actual Bororo parentage), the ethnographic particulars can only serve as a partial illustration of traditional practice. Nevertheless, it did reveal to us the significance of this rite within Bororo culture: from that time on we were expected to learn to "act" properly, use the appropriate terms of address for our fellow villagers, and participate as best we could in village activities. It also highlighted the relationships formed between ourselves and the kin network established by our adoption, particularly with our *iedaga*. Although the newly named are still only down-covered and awkward fledglings (Bororo culture is replete with this avian metaphor), they are not only brought to life in social time but are already completely oriented in social space, since most of their relationships will to greater or lesser degrees be based upon their name(s), that is, upon the clan into which they are born.

Ear Piercing

The earlobes of young boys and girls are generally pierced prior to puberty. Although itself a festive occasion, there is an attempt to perform it conjointly with either a name-giving or male initiation (Colbacchini and Albisetti 1942:175–76). Called *ipare evia porododu* ("piercing the earlobes of young boys and girls," *EBI*:626–27), the ceremony is poorly described in the literature and was not observed during the field stay.

Certain relationships are established by the ceremony, the man who actually does the ear piercing addressed as *iedaga* by either a boy or a girl, while he would refer to a boy as *iwagedu* (literally "my grandson," but also serves for "my godson") and to a girl as *irago* ("my granddaughter/my goddaughter"). These are also the appropriate terms used by the name-giver for the children he names. It is not clear if this is the same *iedaga* that functions in the naming ceremony and pierces the lower lip of a boy. Although the term of

A Bororo elder with traditional face and body paint and adornments.
Note the earrings and mother-of-pearl labrette emphasizing the ear and
lower lip perforations associated with marked stages of the life course.

address *iedaga* is again in this case glossed by the *Enciclopédia Bororo*
as "my maternal grandfather," Z. Levak glosses it as father's father
or mother's father as well as mother's brother (1971:11–12), and as
already pointed out, the same term is applied to the male name-
giver, reported by Crocker to be the mother's brother, or at least of
the mother's clan (a classificatory mother's brother), as in our
naming ceremony. As in all ritually marked relationships the par-
ties exchange food and goods; in this case the *iedaga* manufactures
and supplies ear ornaments as well as fruits of the hunt, from
which he is given his appropriate cooked portion.

Puberty

Perhaps the greatest disparity between the sexes in marking the life
course is observable in their respective puberty celebrations. For
young women today, the arrival of their first menses is essentially
unmarked ceremonially. Traditionally they were painted with
urucu and given the female belt (*kogu*) and loincloth (*ruguri* or
okwamie; *EBI*:88–90), although these items of apparel were sometimes given to the girl prior to puberty. Contemporary Bororo

females begin wearing a skirt or dress while still quite young, so that puberty is even less marked than in earlier times.

For boys, however, elaborate preparations and rituals were traditionally performed to usher the male child into the adult world. There are two major phases concerning male initiation: the *ipare eregodu*, "running of the youth," and the *ipare eno o badodu*, "(imposition of) the penis sheaths on the youths" (*EBI*:627–42).

The *ipare eregodu* is a "bush camp" period of training during which boys at the appropriate stages of development (physical stature and relative maturity are the primary criteria for selection) are taken from the village and led through various rigors to develop them into warriors and hunters, with additional instruction in the traditions of the Bororo (*boe erore*, "the things/way of the Bororo"). During this period, which may last a year (Colbacchini and Albisetti 1942:239; *EBI*:642 reports that the boys were allowed to return to the village only after their unkempt hair had grown to cover their whole face), the boys were led, challenged and trained by elders of their opposite moiety, called collectively *erubadarege* or singly *iorubodare* (the term used herein; it is generally translated as *padrinho* in Portuguese, or "godfather"). *Iorubodare* is the term of address used by a male for another male who has either married into his clan or is likely to do so according to traditional prescribed marriage rules. Since marriage itself only serves as one level of exchange between two groups already joined by other traditional exchanges of goods and services, the *iorubodare* relationship is one that goes far beyond "in-law" status: it is a fundamental block upon which the structure of Bororo society rests. The significance of the relationships is dramatically demonstrated in the role of the adult men in preparing boys from the opposite moiety to become proper, knowledgeable Bororo adults in their own right: to hunt, fight, embody the *aroe* spirits in ceremony, and procreate. Just as these activities ensure the survival of traditional Bororo culture, the relationship by which they are maintained and transmitted ensures the effective functioning of Bororo social organization.

While enduring the rigors of forest life away from the village and the security of their relatives, the youths are further stressed by the threat of encounters with the *aije-doge* (sing. *aije*), powerful, aquatic *aroe* spirits. Uninitiated boys and all females risk death if they see the *aije*, whose distinctive sound is replicated by the bullroarer. With their *iorubodare* leading them onward and chased from behind by the menace of the *aije* whose eery and awesome whirring can be heard for several kilometers, the youths literally "run" or "flee" for much of their training. This atmosphere of threat and hardship helped develop skills the boys had been developing on their own through play, increased their knowledge of their environment and culture, and enhanced their strength and survival ability.

When the training of the youths is considered complete, they are led back to the village. Dirty and with unkempt and overgrown hair from the long period of privation and lack of grooming, they are on the threshold of forever leaving the world of the child and entering that of the adult. To accentuate their wildness and their changing nature, they are further rendered unrecognizable to the village before their entry by the use of leaf coverings. Standing in the village plaza, they are carefully scrutinized by their mothers who must correctly identify their offspring and lead each back to his maternal home. There, ritual wailing that both greets a long-absent relative and sends off the departed is performed in honor of the youth. It is a particularly fitting rite for these boys who, although returning from an extended period away from the village, are now preparing to leave their child's existence and their mother's house for the traditional comradery and unity of the bachelors' group, which sleeps and centers its activities in the *baimanagejewu* or men's house. Once received in their maternal homes the boys are cleaned, their hair properly cut in traditional fashion, and their facial and body hair plucked out in preparation for receival of the penis sheath.

The most detailed account of the *ipare eno o badodu*, the imposition of the penis sheath, appears in the *Enciclopédia Bororo* I (629–41) and is based primarily upon an account given by the principal informant Tiago Marques Aipobureu in 1953 that compares favorably with an earlier version [c. 1913?] given by the same informant (Colbacchini 1925:165–67; Colbacchini and Albisetti 1942:173–75). Briefly recounted, the youths are not allowed to sleep during the night of their return to the village and at dawn are painted with urucu and led to the village plaza. There the ceremony is presided over by two Baadajebage, or hereditary "chiefs," a *bari* shaman (one of two types of shaman present in Bororo culture), and the *iorubodare*. The penis sheaths are made from babaçu previously collected by the boys' maternal relatives (a reference to which begins one version of the Toribugu myth); one sheath is provisionally fitted on a boy by a Baadajeba, then fixed in place by his *iorubodare*. The *ba* or sheath is the outward sign of the youth's adult status, without which he must never appear in public. The *iorubodare* also gives his young charge a name, different from that bestowed in infancy and one that the youth repeats when he kills a jaguar. (The name bestowed at this time may actually have been one shared by initiates in a pseudo age-class system, a topic returned to below.) Before the youths leave the plaza, a chant is sung to Bakororo and Itubore (*aroe* who were the original Bororo chiefs and who now preside over the western and eastern villages of the dead, respectively), and the *bari* reveals something of each youth's future.

These rites are planned to coincide with the final days of the funeral,[4] the most significant of Bororo ceremonies (discussed below). It is precisely at this time that the *aije* make their appearance in the plaza, coming up from the *aije muga* directly to the west of the village. Once the initiates have received their penis sheaths they are attacked by the *aije-doge*—represented by young men of the Exerae moiety covered with white clay (*noa*) and with fearsome black markings on their faces—and it is the *iorubodare* who intervene and support the initiates. Just as the village member who has died is undergoing a transition in state of being from that of *boe*, "Bororo" or true "human," to that of *aroe*, "soul," male youths undergoing initiation that culminates during the funeral have also "died," leaving the child's world for that of the adult.

Once barred from witnessing the *aije* and other powerful *aroe*, the initiate now has the responsibility of representing these awesome beings in ceremony. The *aije-doge*, embodiments of a cosmic, male, and somewhat ungovernable power, make their only appearance at this stage of the funeral and initiation proceedings, to symbolize the forces that dominate Bororo culture and society and the human effort to control their effects.[5]

Although trained and prepared for their roles as new adults and ushered into the set of privileged male knowledge, initiates must undergo one more trial before the completion of their ordeal. At night (precisely which night is not clear; most likely it is the night following the day when penis sheaths are imposed and the *aije* appear) a bonfire is made over which the youths must leap (or into which they are thrown by their *iorubodare*), and from which firebrands are hurled at the Pleiades. Here the *iorubodare* execute control, impeding the youths' mothers who attempt to shelter their sons with mats (Colbacchini and Albisetti 1942:240; *EBI*:629). By the end of this rite, the youths are considered appropriately "cooked," transformed now into young adult males who particularly embody *boe ero*: Bororo culture.

Three details of male initiation merit further discussion: the degree of "openness" or "closedness" of the initiates, the timing of the initiation ceremonies, and the names that the youths receive upon initiation.

Bororo youths are "closed" by means of the penis sheath, a state compared with the relative "openness" of women and children. However, this physical closing may actually acknowledge the new state of "openness" of the initiates to deeper cultural truths and to the realm of the spirits and the sacred. S. Hugh-Jones reports that Barasana males of the Colombian upper Vaupés River region are "opened up" during their initiation, and that because of this they must stringently adhere to food and other taboos. If not, their anuses will become so large that they will literally drain away (1979:200). By becoming adults, Bororo males also have to observe culinary and other taboos, mythically risking the same fate as that of Barasana initiates for failure to do so: Toribugu, although ambiguously defined with respect to age, commits an act that breaks traditional taboos and as a result begins to drain away through his enlarged anus. This reiterates the significance of the Toribugu myth in its relation to male initiation, maturation, and the marking of social time. The characteristic of being "open" or "closed," while expressed by food-related metaphors, affects the new Bororo adult male not only physically but morally and spiritually as well.

The timing of initiation with the funeral services is appropriate, as both involve a transition in state of being for society's members, and both are also extremely significant for cultural and societal renewal (see below, and Fabian 1985). However, one Bororo elder at Garças specifically related the initiation not only with another cycle of social time, but with a "natural" time cycle as well, that of the heliacal rise of the Pleiades (a star cluster or asterism in the constellation of Taurus). He said that there used to be a festival called Akiri-doge Ewure Kowudu ("burning the feet of the Akiri-doge, Pleiades," *EBI*:45) that occurred when the Pleiades first appear on the horizon at dawn, when a bonfire would be lit from which torches were thrown at the Pleiades in order to burn their feet, thus slowing their progress and prolonging the dry season (the heliacal rise of the Pleiades occurs in June, when the dry season is sufficiently advanced to permit trekking and its related lifestyle for the Bororo).[6] He added that it was during this ceremony that the *iorubodare* would give the *ba* or penis sheath to youths passing into adulthood. Therefore a three-way correlation of male initiation can be seen within Bororo ceremonialism and time cycles: the readiness of a group of boys to enter adulthood, the closing of their initiation at the same time as the closing of a funeral, and the further congruence of this occasion with a seasonal and astronomical cycle.

The name that is given to the initiate by his *iorubodare* upon the imposition of the penis sheath may locate the youth in a system of age classes. Z. Levak initially made this suggestion (1971:173) based upon informants' statements and a set of five names, one of which would be given to all of the boys initiated at the same time and which would thereafter supersede any other kinship-derived term when used to address each other. The *Enciclopédia Bororo* defines eight names (the number of Bororo clans), including Levak's five, but makes no such claim as to their function. Rather, the terms are defined as those given only to members of specific clans. The eight are said to be legendary animals.[7] (The corresponding lower-case letter for each can be located in figure 4.1.) The asterisks indicate the five names given by Levak.

a: *Kuruie Eimejera** (gloss unknown), a name given to members of the Baadajebage Xebegiwuge Xebegiwuge during the ceremony of the imposition of the penis sheath

b: *Inojie** (no gloss), name given to members of the Aroroe Xebegiwuge during the imposition of the penis sheath

c: *Marogorege* (no gloss), name given to members of Iwagudu-doge Xebugiwuge at the imposition of the penis sheath

d: *Rikaguruie* (no gloss), name given to Iwagudu-doge Xobugiwuge at the imposition of the penis sheath

e: *Kunonae** (no gloss), name given to Aroroe Xobugiwuge with the imposition of the penis sheath

f: *Baxereuge** (legendary animals similar to herons), name given to Apiborege Xebegiwuge with the imposition of the penis sheath

g: *Kuaru (Kowaru)-doge* (no gloss), name given to Apiborege Xobugiwuge with the imposition of the penis sheath

h: *Adoro-doge** (no gloss), name given to Paiwoe Xobugiwuge with the imposition of the penis sheath (*EBI*:629)

Although the *Enciclopédia Bororo* states that these names are given to members of specific clans at initiation, Z. Levak's data claims that they were used as terms of address between co-initiates regardless of kinship ties. If the names were given only to members of specific subclans, a more equal distribution among the clans of both moieties would be expected. Instead, with only one exception the

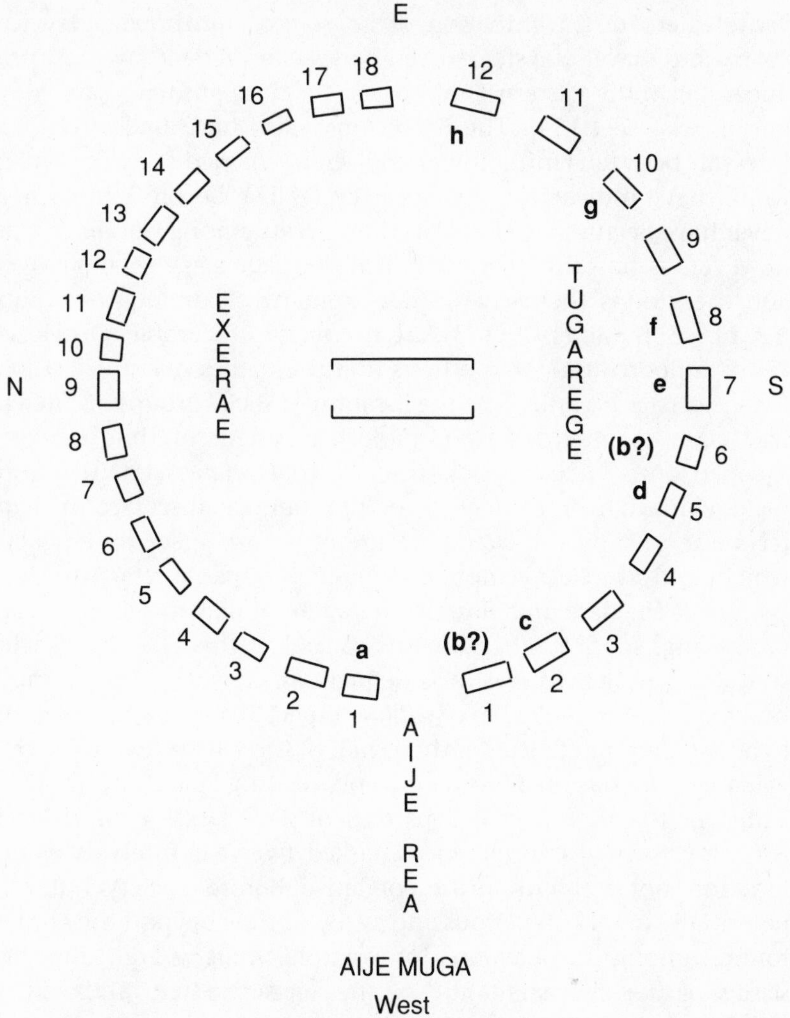

Fig. 4.1. Bororo pseudo age classes. Note: see table 3.2.

names appear spatially related only to the Tugarege moiety. A reasonable hypothesis for the data is that the eight names correspond to age classes found primarily along the Tugarege arc of the village.

Based upon comparative material, it is plausible that the eight names functioned as denominations for age classes within Bororo culture. The Eastern Timbira, as described by Nimuendajú (1946:90–92), have an age-class system based upon an estimated forty years of active, adult male life. In this system, four age classes are localized on the village plaza and are animated by an approximate ten-year cycle of initiation. Closer to the Bororo, the Shavante celebrate the initiation of boys into adulthood every five years, and have a system of eight specific age-sets, which produces—as in the Eastern Timbira case—a cycle of forty years (Maybury-Lewis 1974:154). The Bororo may also have had a five-year interval between initiations, and eight named classes, which would have indicated a forty-year cycle. The Bororo system may never have been as developed as the systems among the Gê groups, however, as no other evidence on Bororo age classes has survived and the groups themselves, aside from two individuals encountered by Z. Levak (1971:173), are no longer observable. Other evidence supporting the hypothesis that the names may have served for age classes organized by the location of social groups on the village circle is provided by (1) another system of time marking mapped onto village social structure that relates certain Bororo males with nighttime directly preceding sunrise (discussed in chapter 5), and (2) by the overall nature of Bororo space-time beliefs, which tends to relate temporal sequences to spatial referents.

While the data on a functional system of Bororo age classes are tantalizing, supportive arguments cannot at this time be conclusive. The problem is not inconsequential, however. Determining how the system might have worked, especially as the groups seem to be localized along the southern half of the village, could provide valuable material on Bororo concepts relating space and time. In addition, the presence of a pattern of age classes comprising a recurring forty-year cycle with marked five-year intervals would function not only to further organize Bororo society but also potentially to reckon periods and cycles of time beyond the annual round. Among the Shavante, for example, villagers are "fully conscious of the cyclical nature of the age-set system and will, if pressed, explain that time passes in a series of such cycles, expressing its passage by a series of circles drawn on the ground. The cycles themselves are divided into periods corresponding to the passage of age-sets through the bachelors' hut. . . . Each of these periods, they say, is of five years' duration, and they count up to five and tick the years off on their fingers to drive the point home" (Maybury-Lewis 1974:154). Such a concept of cyclical time, and its reckoning or counting, is similar to the time systems of the Maya and other Mesoamerican peoples and further begs the question of the nature of native Brazilian concepts of time and the extent and degree of precision and systematic knowledge in these native cultures, topics to be further discussed in later chapters.

Unfortunately, contemporary village life can give little assistance for resolving the interesting questions posed by Bororo initiation. Penis sheaths are no longer worn (in favor of gym shorts and trousers), youths no longer live in the men's house but rather with their maternal relatives until marriage, and there is little collective training of youths for manhood.

Marriage and Parenthood

Marriage, like birth, receives virtually no ritual elaboration, placing these two occurrences out of the realm of the sacred, wherein spirits are invoked through song and ceremony, and into the realm of the secular. While the newborn is not considered a member of society until he/she receives a name, marriage "is looked upon as a continuation of an alliance arrangement which was established in mythical time by other cultural exchanges, e.g., those of ceremonies and goods" (Z. Levak 1971:76). This alliance arrangement is signaled by the reciprocal use of the *iorubodare* address and relationship. While at one time such intermoiety ties were traced between specific name groups, recent population decline and reduced village size has resulted in a broadening of the *iorubodare* categories, as well as reduced stigma upon incestuous unions, and recognition of affines (potential and actual) today encompasses in essence the entire moiety opposite to one's own. Since the *iorubodare* alliance is particularly significant for exchanging performances of clan-specific ceremonies (which must be enacted by members of the opposite moiety), the generalization of alliance ties allows Bororo culture to remain viable in villages where many name groups, subclans, and even entire clans are no longer represented.

Traditionally, postpubescent young women are eligible for marriage, although in fact the alliance may have been arranged earlier. Young men, on the other hand, the core of the village's fighters and labor force as a group of relatively unattached bachelors residing in the *baimanagejewu*, both desired and were encouraged to remain unmarried for as long as possible to maintain their freedom and virility. A class of women referred to in the literature as "men's house associates" was comprised of young women involved sexually with their *iorubodare* counterparts as a group in the men's house via affairs typically carried on in the *baito* or during treks (Crocker 1969a; Von den Steinen 1940:chapter 17). To be a member of this class was apparently without stigma or distinction for the young women, nor did potential pregnancy and birth (although traditional herbal mixtures are reputed to have been capable of preventing pregnancy) present any social or moral dilemma: children produced by such unions were considered legitimate members of the woman's clan and thereby guaranteed an appropriate relationship with both consanguineal and affinal relatives. In Garças village I observed no such association of women, but neither is there a single definable group of young bachelors.

A "marriage" is recognized when a man's possessions are moved to his "wife's" house, although the two are probably involved sexually for some time previous to this move. As the cultural ideal is for young men to remain bachelors for as long as feasible but encourage motherhood for young women, the ages of spouses is often disparate.

Just as no real ceremony marks the beginning of a marriage, none marks its end. Divorce is, and apparently was in the past, comparatively simple and commonplace among the Bororo. Beliefs in the material and spiritual composition of the child (see, e.g., Crocker 1985) and the ready set of consanguines (clan relatives of the mother) and affines (those already established in the *iorubodare* alliance) that accompanied each person through his or her clan membership at birth and traced through the mother are factors in easing both forming and breaking of marital unions. In the contemporary village, cultural decline and deleterious external influences only serve to place further stress upon the union of spouses, in spite of concerted missionary efforts to stabilize Bororo marriages.

Once a child is born to a couple their union is considered more "stable," while they themselves are now regarded as mature members of society. The father, upon the birth of his first son, will traditionally have his nasal septum pierced in a ceremony called *ipare ekeno porododu* (*EB*I:624); few details are known of this rite, which is rarely practiced today. It is performed conjointly when the infant is named and its lower lip is pierced. Status in Bororo culture is not linked—especially for men—specifically to one's increasing family or parenthood but is linked for both men and women to the demonstration of appropriate comportment, and especially to one's command of ceremonial knowledge and participation.

Death

In spite of the number of stages recognized by the Bororo in the human developmental cycle, no ceremony celebrates life and

Bororo culture as much as their ceremony for death. When a village member dies, the entire village population is mobilized for the performance of a complex set of services and ceremonies, which may also involve the participation of members from distant villages. A funeral is the most demanding Bororo ceremony in terms of time, energy, and materials and requires prodigious traditional knowledge to ensure observance of its prescribed format. It thus renews and reiterates Bororo culture and society, reestablishing vital relationships among the participants and with nature and the spirit realm.

The importance of the Bororo funeral and partial descriptions of its elaborate structure have been reported in the literature (e.g., *EBI*: Itaga entry, 647–68; Colbacchini and Albisetti 1942:153–66; M. Levak 1979–80; Kozak 1963; Crocker 1983), although it has yet to receive the comprehensive treatment it merits. While residing in Garças I observed and participated in one complete and one partial funeral (Fabian 1985).

Despite variations in the descriptions of the Bororo funeral, it is possible to distinguish the following principal and common features: initial songs and the preparation of the corpse for preliminary interment; primary, temporary burial in the western village plaza; a set of ceremonies that can be villagewide or clan-specific in scope; special social observances, including communal hunts and fishing, strict exchange patterns, and daily mourning, while the corpse decomposes; a three-day series of continual rituals immediately preceding the exhumation of bones; the exhumation, cleaning, and decoration of the bones; and final burial (in marsh, grottos, or today in an actual cemetery).

The funeral has a key role in Bororo sociocultural reproduction. The village plaza is cleaned with special attention given to the scraping and cleaning of the *aije rea* and *aije muga*. Extensive repairs are effected on the *baimanagejewu*, which as the precinct of the sacred houses some of the most significant funerary proceedings. Cultural artifacts such as headdresses and musical instruments are either repaired or replaced, so that the village is made to look "new."

In a like manner, traditional patterns and relations are reestablished. The impressive variety of performances and ceremonies call upon the most profound details of cultural tradition. In the preparation of costumes and the application of decorations, in dance movements, ritual chants, and songs, cultural values are expressed while the extensive knowledge which underlies these activities is

Clan-specific funerary ceremony. *Foreground:* temporary burial
with discarded materials from previous ceremonies.
Background: the western side of the *baimanagejewu,* or men's
house, with its new wall of layered babaçu palm fronds.

refreshed and passed on. The bonds of society are strengthened in
shared grief as friend and foe alike participate. Particularly emphasized are *iorubodare* ties since clans do not perform their own ceremonies but rather decorate and adorn their *iorubodare* to perform
the ceremonies for them: the primary responsibility towards the
deceased and his or her family lies with the members of the opposite moiety.

All of the features that comprise Bororo funerary practices have
in some way to do with Bororo beliefs of the *aroe. Aroe* can be
defined as "soul," but as a class the *aroe* are natural, totemic, and
ancestral spirit beings, "the representatives of immutable categorical form," juxtaposed in Bororo beliefs with *bope* spirits, entities
that embody "the principle of organic transformation" (Crocker
1985:36). The two spirit categories both complement and oppose
each other, are approached through two distinct shamanic complexes, and exemplify the profundities of the Bororo dualistic
world view.[8]

The *aroe* define Bororo village organization and social relations.
Specific sets of *aroe* actually appear (represented by appropriately
costumed adult males) during certain funeral ceremonies, which
constitute the only time that these entities are physically present

in the village. During a funeral, therefore, Bororo villagers come into direct contact not only with the organizing principles of their culture and society but with the actual beings who embody these principles.

The *aroe maiwu* ("new soul") is a man chosen from the moiety opposite that of the deceased to represent the deceased (whether male or female) throughout the funerary period. If possible, he should be an *iorubodare* of the deceased. Through his position as *aroe maiwu* he becomes related to the deceased's family via ritual nuclear family ties, becoming their "son" in a lifelong relationship manifested through the observance of particular behavior between the new family members, by the use of appropriate terms of address, through the receiving of new proper names, and by the exchange of food and services.[9]

Qualifications for the *aroe maiwu* include that he should be an outstanding member of the opposite moiety who has exhibited hunting skill and a respectable level of cultural knowledge. One of his most weighty responsibilities is to kill a jaguar or other member of the class of animals for which the jaguar serves as prime representative: the *marege mori-xe*, defined by Crocker (1985:281) as "animals of revenge" and as "carnivores of warm-blooded animals." The *aroe maiwu* must present to the deceased's parents (his own new ritual parents) one of the predators of this set of animals, as partial retribution (*mori*) for the death of their loved one. The animals after which Toribugu is ordered by his father all belong to this set (listed by Crocker, 1985:282), and the incidents described in the myth can be read as the incipience of the observance of supplying "revenge animals," an example of the myth's theme of cultural development.

Two other institutions of the funeral are significant to Bororo social reproduction and social time: the investiture of Baadajebage chiefs, and the appearance of the *aije* along with the final stages of the initiation of male youths, both of which are related to the myth of Toribugu.

Toribugu's father is a member of the Baadajebage Xebegiwuge clan, one of the two clans (the other being the Baadajebage Xobugiwuge) whose members may inherit the rights and responsibilities of the two original Bororo chiefs. These two chiefs ceded their powers to Bakorokudu (Baadajebage Xebegiwuge) and Akaruyo Bokodori (Baadajebage Xobugiwuge), respectively. As described in chapter 3, these powers include the right to lead certain songs and call for performances, abilities which Toribugu's father demonstrates in the myth.[10] It is another indication of the funeral's overall importance to Bororo culture that the investiture of new Baadajebage chiefs occurs during one of the prescribed performances, that of the Parabara, one of the most complex performances and the only one during which a sociopolitical status is bestowed.

Among the set of villagewide performances, that is, performances that require the participation of a host of actors from a number of clans and that must be performed during the funerary period, the Parabara ceremony is conspicuous on several counts. Whereas most performances begin in the late afternoon (the period known as *meri rekodu*: see chapter 5), the Parabara ceremony begins in midmorning. During its course several important and distinctive *aroe* make their appearance, which varies from the customary appearance of only one type of *aroe* during a specific ceremony. "Parabara" is the name of the major group of *aroe* who perform in this ceremony, and the name also extends to the bamboo "clappers" (lengths of split bamboo) that they wield. Their leader, *parabara-doge eimejera* ("chief of the Parabara"), is the Baadajeba who will be newly invested as chief. Although no reference is made to this investiture in the *Enciclopédia Bororo*, Colbacchini and Albisetti (1942:141) report upon it, and their description concurs with the ceremony witnessed in Garças village.

In the Garças Parabara, a young Baadajeba boy was guided by a cultural chief through an involved series of actions, including a special chant. Informants related that the boy was actually the chief of the *parabara* but was too young to perform alone in that capacity. Although the boy's clan membership as Baadajebage was inherited matrilineally, his access to the powers of a Baadajeba chief required his official investiture. As there were only two active Baadajebage men in Garças, it may have been considered preferable to invest a young boy into this position, to allow him time to be properly instructed for his forthcoming roles.

As described earlier in this chapter, the final stages of boys' initiation into adulthood are performed towards the end of the funerary period. Specifically, this occurs during the three-day series of continual rituals that immediately precedes the exhumation of the bones that still lie buried in the western plaza. By integrating male initiation with the funeral ceremonies, the Bororo use the occasion of individual death to ensure continued life for their culture and society. This integration brings together the services of the shaman of the *bope* spirits (called *bari*), who functions during the initiation,

Men returning to the village after hunting and foraging expedition
during the funerary period.

with those of the *aroe etawarare*, the shaman of the *aroe* who presides over the funeral proceedings.

At Garças village in 1983, the funerary observances for one
deceased villager had already proceeded through several stages
when another death occurred. For the second person, the appropriate ceremonies were performed until the two funerals were
"synchronized," at which point subsequent rituals involved both
of the deceased and their *aroe maiwu* . However, the village elders
decided to terminate the funeral of the first deceased when the
corpse had sufficiently decomposed (the corpse is periodically
checked to determine its state of decomposition), while the second
funeral continued for several more months. One consideration
that influenced this decision was the fact that the second corpse
would take an inordinately long period to decompose as it had
been buried in a coffin, rather than in the traditional palm matting
(resulting from the deceased's having died of an infectious disease
at a distant hospital). The decision resulted, however, in what may
have been a foreshortening of some of the services due the first
deceased, as some villagers complained that the amount of materials, time, and energy required to properly perform the rites for the
one and then repeat them soon after for the other would overtax
the limited resources of the community.

These details bring into question the nature of funeral proceedings in more indigenous eras, when village size was considerably

Final rites in the village for the deceased. In the specially made and decorated basket are the painted bones of the deceased which were buried in a private ceremony the next day in the mission cemetery. View is due west.

larger (and therefore offered greater human resources) and when materials were probably more plentiful and accessible. It also suggests the need for some rethinking about the length of the funeral, since overlapping funerary periods, and traditional patterns of village residency based upon seasonal activities, would affect the observance of funerals.

When Lévi-Strauss visited Kejara village in 1936 during the rainy season months of January and February, he was able to witness parts of an ongoing funeral, which many of his photographs depict. In these photographs the number of participants and spectators is much greater than the village population at Garças, where the same men are required not only to make the elaborate ritual preparations necessary for the various ceremonies but to perform them as well, participate in the frequent collective fishing and hunting expeditions at this time, and maintain the tasks necessary for everyday living. Naturally, Garças village men complained of the trying degree of *serviço* (labor or work) with which they were beset. They were also hampered by insufficient materials for the manufacture of certain articles required by the funeral services. The source of manpower evident at Kejara village would have lessened an individual's burden, allowing for the fuller performance of traditionally prescribed functions.

Transporting a slain giant armadillo to the village. Coming as it did during the funerary period, this prize was considered a gift of the *aroe* spirits. In the immediate background is a "sweet" manioc garden; the barbed wire is strung to keep out village cattle, barely visible in the far background as white specks.

It may also be significant, however, that Lévi-Strauss observed and photographed these proceedings during the rainy season, as did Von den Steinen who reports a funeral in March and April towards the end of the rains, for as was evident in the Toribugu myth and as will be described further in the next chapter, there was considerable seasonal differentiation in residency and activity patterns during indigenous times. While large villages housed a relatively stable population during the rainy season months, the dry season afforded the opportunity for groups to embark upon distant trekking expeditions. These would create a substantial decline in the village's population, while the individual groups on trek would remain relatively out of contact with each other and with the main village.[11] This reduction in the number of village occupants and the often considerable distance between trekking groups make the dry season a poor time during which to conduct funeral services and lead to the hypothesis that rainy season months were the primary period for such observances.

The overall length of a funeral is variously reported as between one month (Kozak 1963:46) and six to ten months (Crocker 1983:170). The complete funeral observed in Garças village lasted fifty-two days from death until final burial, with the corpse temporarily buried in the western plaza for forty-eight days. It is possible that in precontact times the entire rainy season may have been a single, extended funerary period, juxtaposed with dry season activities that emphasized long trips and small groups and served for the collection of some of the materials necessary for proper funerary attire. This situation would correspond to Crocker's report of a six- to ten-month funeral, a period I suggest was contemporaneous with the rainy season. Further support for this hypothesis is the synchronization of Bororo male initiation with both the end of the funeral and with the Akiri-doge ceremony, a rite that occurs specifically at the heliacal rise of the Pleiades star group, an annual occurrence observed in June that serves to initiate the trekking season, most avidly conducted during the months of June to September. (In contemporary times this seasonal dichotomy is neither likely nor necessary, since the village population is relatively stable throughout the year.)

It is possible that the rainy season, and the concomitant main village residence and ceremonial activity, may at one time not have been a "funerary" period per se, but rather that period of the year when society was visited by the *aroe* spirits. With the physical presence of these ancestral beings in the village, not only were the traditional societal patterns and relationships reinforced and renewed but the investiture of Baadajebage chiefs, the initiation of boys into manhood, and the burial of the deceased could all be properly attended to. This emphasis on the presence of the spirits in general, as opposed to the specific practice of funerary proceedings, would help account for otherwise contradictory data such as the length(s) of the funerary period, the coincidence of male initiation with the funeral (even though both sets of ceremonies were not likely to occur every year, especially considering a possible five-year initiation cycle as has been suggested above), and the performance of certain ritual activities such as a *mano* race (analogous to Gê log races) or even the naming of the newborn, which technically are not supposed to be performed while a funeral is in progress. While it can be accepted that the funeral was always of great importance to the Bororo, its significance in contemporary times may reflect one level of indigenous response to intense outside pressures and dramatic population decline.

Five

Cycles of Time in Nature

While the village orients the Bororo in space through its paradigmatic, major east-west axis and localized social groups, it also contributes to orienting them in time. For males, aging and social growth are accompanied by changes in spatial positioning in the village. And, as the village's major east-west axis parallels the prevailing celestial movement, an immediate relationship is established with the sun, moon, and stars, celestial bodies that are all used in time reckoning. Additionally, the village itself is traditionally characterized by a seasonal pattern of residence, as evidenced in the Toribugu myth.

Day Time

The Bororo word *meriji*, which analogously expresses our concept of "day," has at its base *meri*, "sun." The period, therefore, that can be distinguished for day time as opposed to night time encompasses the period when the sun is above the horizon, from *merirutu* ("sunrise" and also "east") to *meributu* ("sunset" and "west"). The common way for Bororo to mark the passage of time during the day is by noting the position of the sun. Certain positions have been established into named periods of the day (presented in tables 5.1 and 5.2) as related by informants in Garças village. Table 5.3 presents data arranged from the *Enciclopédia Bororo* (I:294–95) for comparative purposes.

Even though certain periods of the day are designated by name, the most ingenious scheme of which locates the sun with respect to points on the face and head (table 5.2), by far the most common means of marking and telling time is simply by pointing with the arm and hand, fingers together and extended, to the sun's position, and saying *meri woe* ("the sun here"). This technique is used in reference to day time that has passed or is yet to come. It is never performed in a sloppy or careless fashion: the angle of hand/arm and

Table 5.1
Bororo Day Time, Version A

Bororo	Portuguese	English
Merirutu	O nascer do sol	Sunrise
Boe akudo	O cedo do dia	Cool/clean time, early morning
Meri jeturi barae etaia keje; Barae etaia	O meio dia	Sun over the center of the non-Indians, noon
Meri rore goroxije; Meri jo godu	A tarde	Early afternoon
Meri rekodu godu; Meri rekodu	A tarde	Sun flees/runs, late afternoon
Meributu	O por do sol	Sun descends, sunset

Table 5.2
Bororo Day Time, Version B

Bororo	Portuguese	English
Merirutu tabo	O nascer do sol	Sunrise
Meri dieta pagogwa kejede tabo	O sol está no nivel da boca	The sun is at the level of the mouth, just past sunrise
Meri paidiaka kejede tabo	O sol está no nivel dos olhos	The sun is at eye level, early morning
Meri dieta pagudo kejede tabo	O sol está no nivel do testa	The sun is at the level of the forehead, mid- to late morning
Meri dieta pagaia kejede tabo	O sol está encima da cabeça	The sun is overhead, noon.
Meri terawuji pagawora diokido tabo	O sol está em nosso cangote	The sun is at the back of the head, early afternoon
Meri diati pagabara kejede tabo	O sol está no rumo de nosso cangote	The sun is at the base of the head, midafternoon
Meri diati pagidoru kejede tabo	O sol ja está na pescoço	The sun is at the level of the neck, mid- to late afternoon
Meri rekodu tabo	Ja correu o sol	The sun runs/has fled, late afternoon; equated with sunset
Meributu tabo	O por do sol	Sunset

direction must all be exactly precise. (I was consistently corrected when using this technique; although the gesture is done quickly, the Bororo accurately "aim" their hand as if shooting a projectile.)

Today in Garças village one man possesses a functional wristwatch, and although he wears it constantly and is occasionally consulted by others, the man himself can only laboriously read the time from it. Since no one else owns a timepiece, its usefulness is

Table 5.3
Bororo Day Time, Version C

Bororo	Portuguese	English
Meri rutu	Subida do sol, nascer do sol	Sunrise
Meri kajeje	O sol parece subir ao céu, do nascer do sol até as 10 horas	The sun is climbing, from sunrise to 10 A.M.
Meri togi	O sol bate na frente, manhã adiantada	The sun hits one's front/face, late morning
Meri baru o-iadadu	O sol ocupa o centro do ceu, meio-dia e horas vizinhas	Sun in the center of the sky, noon and the hours around it
Barae et-aeiadada	O sol bate sobre a calvicie dos civilizados, meio-dia e horas vizinhas	The sun beats over the baldness of the non-Indians, noon and the hours around it
Meri baru ku kajeje	O sol está sobre o ventre do ceu, de tarde	The sun is over the belly of the sky, afternoon
Meri jogodu	Sol que está para cair, das 15 horas até pouco antes do ocaso	The sun is inclining/falling, from 3 P.M. to just before sunset
Meri rekodu	Fuga do sol, por do sol	Flight of the sun, sunset
Meri butu	Queda do sol, ocaso	Fall of the sun, sunset

Source: EBI:294–95.

dubious. Usually it is used in a comparative manner with native reckoning, although all villagers have some familiarity with Western time designations.

A typical day's activities begin prior to sunrise, usually by the first beginnings of dawn. However, events such as late-night or all-night ceremonies, early outings and expeditions, the relative heat or cold and wet and dryness of the night and day, as well as other factors, influence the type and time of all activities. Generally the dawn-to-sunrise period is characterized by preparations for the day's activities and visits to neighboring houses. Women will stoke the family fire and begin preparation of food and drink; men will often make a fire in the plaza and stand by it, talking. Traditionally an invigorating bath in a nearby stream initiated a man's day, but only a couple of hardy individuals were observed in such a practice today.

Usually by sunrise (merirutu) or shortly thereafter, any industrious projects have begun: men have left the village to fish, hunt, or attend to gardening and other service projects, while women have gone off gathering or gardening or are taking advantage of the early morning's (boe akudo) dampness to work on palm plaiting.

By early afternoon (meri jo godu) most projects give way to rest, especially on very hot days. The later afternoon, specifically desig-

89

Table 5.4
Bororo Night Time, Version A

Bororo	Portuguese	English
Boe eka modo godu	Escurecendo	Getting dark, twilight
Boexo paru	Boca da noite	Night beginning, nightfall
Boexo oya	Meia noite	Midnight
Boexo oto	Já apontou a noite	The night has reached its peak, late night
Ba aregodu	Madrugada, dia clareando	Predawn to dawn
Barogwa kododu	Amanhece	Dawn increase, full dawn, daylight

nated as *meri rekodu* ("the sun flees") and encompassing a period from approximately two hours prior to and up to sunset (or when the sun is past its halfway point between noon and the horizon), is the most common time for ceremonies. This is particularly so for most of the villagewide performances of the funerary period, although some ceremonies continue into and through the night, while others begin only after sunset or in the morning. Usually by sunset the village begins to settle into a more nocturnal pattern.

Meals are traditionally taken throughout the day without regard for any schedule other than one's own hunger and the availability of food. While in the village men typically gravitate to and remain in the *baimanagejewu*, fashioning articles and weapons, talking, lounging, or sleeping. Today the manufacture of tourist articles occupies much of the villagers' time. Women characteristically remain in or near their house or that of a friend or relative while in the village, attending to domestic chores or making tourist articles. When both sexes leave for collective work projects, it is the woman's responsibility to have cooked food ready for the men (although usually at least one man has been designated to supply the protein portion of the food). These outings (for example, to clear a large garden patch) are usually only one-day trips in which the group returns to the village by nightfall. However, a simple shelter is often erected at a work site so that one or more persons can remain, particularly if the group is to return on another day or if the distance to the village is substantial.

Night Time

"Night" is known as *boe xo* or *boe xodu*, the *xo* of which derives from *xoreu*, "black." *Boe* is a more problematic word, glossed by the

Table 5.5
Bororo Night Time, Version B

Bororo	Portuguese	English
Boexo godogu	*A noite está escurecendo*	It is getting dark, early nightfall
Boexo okwa torugodure	*Está escurecendo mais*	At the margin of night, nightfall
Boexo motudure	*A noite já está pesada*	The night is heavy, full darkness
Boexo oyare	*Meia noite*	Midnight
Boexo aregodure toyado	*A noite chegou a metade*	Midnight
Boexo kodure toyakure biagatijye	*Passou um pouco da meia noite*	Shortly after midnight
Boexo kodure toyakure rakarugade	*Passou muito da meia noite*	Well past midnight
Boexo pure dugodure	*A noite ja está no lado do fim*	Approaching the end of night
(A) *Boegigadowodu biagare tujye*	*Está clareando um pouquinho*	Just beginning to get light
(B) *Boegigadowodu oto aregidyre*	*Está surgindo o clarão do dia*	Getting lighter
(C) *Ba aregodure*	*Madrugada*	Lighter, but predawn
(D) *Boegigadowodure mawure*	*Ja está quase claro*	Early dawn
(E) *Boerore jytaukujye*	*Agora está claro*	Full dawn

Table 5.6
Bororo Night Time, Version C

Bororo	Portuguese	English
Boe xo paru	*Inicio da noite, boca da noite*	Nightfall
Boe xo godu	*Boca da noite*	Nightfall
Boe xo okwa	*Margem da noite, boca da noite*	Nightfall
Boe xo oia	*Centro da noite, meia noite*	Midnight
Barogwa	*Aurora*	Dawn
Barogwadodu	*Aurora feita*	Full dawn to sunrise

Source: EBI:294–295.

Salesians as "thing, Bororo, astronomical time, atmospheric condition" (*EBI*:280). Night is appropriately, therefore, "the time or thing of blackness" and is that period when the sun is not present in the sky.

Bororo schemes of night time are given in tables 5.4–5.6. To tell time during the night poses no more difficulty than day time readings and is accomplished in the same fashion: rather than pointing to or otherwise referring to the sun's position, on nights when the moon is visible its position is the common reference, although alternatively major stars or constellations are also used. Among the latter are most notably the Pleiades and the Southern Cross (chapter 7 is specifically devoted to astronomical observation). A Bororo village does not lie in quiet slumber throughout the night. To the contrary, certain songs and ceremonies must occur specifically during the night, and on occasion hunters or fishermen will return late or leave the village "early," during the heart of the night. Even during nights that are otherwise unmarked by performance or expedition, most households stir intermittently throughout the nocturnal hours.

Commonly at nightfall (*boexo paru*) the men of the village will congregate in the western plaza near the men's house, sprawling on mats, sitting or squatting on makeshift seats, or occasionally standing. At the same time the women and children sit in front of their own or their neighbors' houses. Everyone talks, passes on news and stories, discusses important issues, and generally relaxes. Announcements are made at this time to inform the village of major items of information, including plans for the following day. In Garças village announcements are made by an elder of the Kie clan, standing among the men in the western plaza and shouting out to the surrounding houses. Once these are finished, other cultural chiefs or knowledgeable elders can and usually do speak, delivering anything from harangue to humorous anecdote or occasionally a poignant traditional myth. All public night addresses are performed in a loud singsong and frequently make use of special phraseology and vocabulary of the native tongue. (Typically at Garças there was much reference to *barae* or "non-Indians" during these addresses, indicating the extent of outside relationships and the pressure they created within the village.) The duration of this session varies, but the night is generally fairly young by the time the plaza is clear of people, who have retired behind the closed doors of their houses. Such sessions were less frequent during the funerary period, when night time ritual observances were often required. Night time also serves for counting short periods of "days"—that is, Bororo traditionally reckon several days' elapse by the number of nights or "sleeps" there were within this period (*EBI*:295). They share this trait with neighboring groups, such as the Shavante (Maybury-Lewis 1974:155) and the Tapirapé (Wagley 1983:32).

As a result of both their observations of the positions of celestial bodies and a keen awareness of the subtle changes in the quality of light, atmospheric condition, and other environmental indicators, the Bororo are acutely attuned to the approach of dawn (*ba aregodu*), and most households are active well before full dawn (*barogwa*) brightens the sky just prior to sunrise. The Bororo have a codified set of presunrise observations and announcements encompassing the predawn and dawn period. These presunrise times are called *uwadodureawuge*, for which I have no satisfactory gloss. They are included in table 5.5 and marked by capital letters *A–E*. Each of these times is announced by a different man, of a specific social group. These men are called *eiamedu*, glossed by my informants as *tomadores de atenção* in Portuguese, or "those who pay/call attention." Their function and that of the calls they make is to act *como um guarda da noite*, "like a guard of the night." The following list gives the name of each man and what he says, as provided by two Bororo elders, one of the Bokodori Exerae clan, the other of the Iwagudu-doge.

A. *Manokurireu Tugarege Aroroedu Xebegiwu.* (Call unknown.) He yells to inform everyone that day is approaching.

B. *Tadugo Iwagududogedu Xebegiwu.* "*Gugugu.*" After making this sound he tells everyone to wake up, to go and urinate and defecate.

C. *Akaruyo Boroge Apiboregedu Xebegiwu.* "*Wawawa.*" He yells for all to awaken, to light fires, to straighten and harden their arrows (over the fires).

D. *Kurugugwa Apiboregedu Xobugiwu.* "*Buri buri buri.*" He yells for all to get up and get something to eat.

E. *Meriri Baru Paiwoedu Xobugiwu.* "*Kukuku.*" He yells for all to awaken, to cover themselves with urucu for hunting, and to kill all danger.

The first word given in each case is the name of the man (synonymous in each case with his respective name group), followed by his clan and subclan affiliation. All of the names are easily located on the village diagram, figure 3.5, and for ease of reference have been provided in figure 5.1. The repetitive sounds uttered by each caller mimic some natural species, about which my data are unfortunately incomplete. Each announcement is made in the same loud singsong that characterizes evening public addresses. The informants who provided this data also stated that the stars are used to tell the hours of the night and gave as an example a myth similar to the segment of the Toribugu myth wherein the rising of specific

93

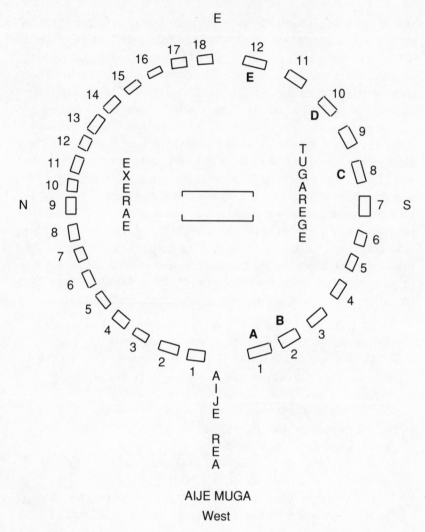

Fig. 5.1. Bororo "Guards of the Night." Note: see table 3.2.

stars is called out in Bororo whistling language. They said that the
Bororo know how to tell night time because Birimodo (Aroroe
Xobugiwu, one of the original Bororo chiefs) taught them. Such a
system of night guards would have been an aid in alerting the village to the danger of enemy attack, for which the preferred time is
just before dawn. The technique of predawn attack has been
described in Bororo mythology as practiced both by and against
them; the implementation of the "night guards" may have contributed to the powerful presence and stability of the Bororo in
their vast home territory in indigenous times.

The scheme of presunrise hour callers is particularly significant to this study as it exemplifies an indigenous, codified system of detailed observations and time marking, while graphically relating time and space. Although our knowledge of the system is incomplete (it is not commonly practiced in contemporary Garças village), it is evident that specific astronomical and other environmental observations were systematically made in order to properly time the announcements. Among the astronomical observations significant for timing these calls is a series of "morning star" observations. At least three Bororo terms refer to different morning stars: Barogwa Jeiba, Barogwa Tabowu, Barogwa Kudodu, one of which— Barogwa Kudodu—is synonymous for a planet/star and for time that immediately precedes sunrise. As these observations functioned sequentially, they help orient the time announcers with respect to approaching sunrise. (A more detailed treatment of the morning star observations is made in chapter 7.)

Time and space are intricately linked in this scheme, as the temporal sequence of calls corresponds to the directional, spatial sequence of the callers (see figure 5.1). The sequence begins just south of due west on the village circle and continues counterclockwise to just south of due east, all callers being of the Tugarege moiety. Particularly illustrative of the space-time congruence is the fifth and final caller, Meriri Baru, who as an "upper" Paiwoe is positionally adjacent to the village east-west axis. His is the easternmost position of the night guards, and as both spatial and temporal "gatekeeper," is replicated by his position in the *baimanagejewu* (see figure 3.6) where he is positioned next to, and said to guard, the Tugarege (northern) door. Appropriately, his name, Meriri Baru, can be glossed as "bright sky" (*meriri*, "metal, bright," from *meri*, "sun"; and *baru*, "sky"), a descriptive reference to the sky just before sunrise.[1] The function and structure of the set of night time announcers is also important in relation to the positions and hypothesized function of the pseudo age classes described in the previous chapter. That is, the night guards sequence might serve as a model for the sequence of the set of names connected to male initiation and proposed as age classes.

There is no myth of which I am aware that specifically describes the scheme of hour callers, but a version of the Bororo flood myth depicts the sole survivor as whistling at dawn in order to announce the day to his fellows (all of whom have perished in the flood) in an attempt to call them back, a technique reminiscent of the guards of the night calling for the villagers to awaken. Per-

Table 5.7

Bororo Lunar Month Terminology, Version A

Bororo	English
Ari rutu	Moonrise (applied to first appearance of the waxing crescent)
Ari maiwu	New moon (literal)
Ari rixadure	The moon is growing, waxing moon
Ari tuyokukuridu	The moon's eye is large, full moon
Ari jyoku biagare	The moon's eye is getting smaller, waning moon

haps coincidentally, the hero of this myth, Jerigi Otojiwu, is structurally located just north of east in the Baadajebage Xobugiwuge clan of the Exerae moiety, a position analogous to that of Meriri Baru, whose call immediately precedes the sunrise. The calling out of stars throughout the night by Toribugu must also be related to such a practice, as the hour callers' announcements were based upon astronomical observations. Some vestige of the complete system remains in Garças village, where presunrise calls arouse the village when major, villagewide undertakings have been planned for the day and an early start is crucial. Contemporary villagers also note the passage of postmidnight time by successive rooster crowings; several cocks in the village begin their crowing very early each morning, gradually picking up in frequency and intensity as the dawn approaches. Plans to begin a task, for example, "after the third cock-crow" are common and may hearken back to the indigenous system of the night guards.

Lunar Cycles

The Bororo term for both moon and lunar month is *ari*. It appears that the lunar month referred to is a synodical one that concerns the moon's phases or position relative to the sun. Both phase and position are significant in lunar terminology, two schemes of which were obtained from Garças informants (tables 5.7 and 5.8). One of the most interesting characteristics of Bororo lunar month terminology, evident in table 5.8, is the tendency prior to and including full moon to refer to the physical appearance of the moon (its size and shape), while after full moon to emphasize its position as observed at dawn or sunrise. The *Enciclopédia Bororo* states that the Bororo are unable to say how many days or weeks have passed since an event has taken place (I:295), an attitude similar to that expressed by Baldus in his paper on native Brazilian

Table 5.8
Bororo Lunar Month Terminology, Version B

Bororo	English
Ari rutu	Moonrise, new moon
Ari maiwu	New moon
Ari renonu bokodori nogire	The moon is similar to the claw of the giant armadillo, early waxing moon
Ari yoku kuri godure	The moon's eye is growing, first quarter
Ari tuyoka kuridu	The moon's eye is large, full moon
Arire barogwadu	The moon dawns, when the moon is visible after sunrise, waning moon
Ari yoku biaga godure	The moon's eye is getting smaller, waning moon
Arire barogwadu etuya parikadeje	The moon dawns behind the trees, just past full moon
Arire barogwadu etuya otoji	The moon dawns over the trees, past full moon
Arire barogwadu baru oya puredogodu	The moon dawns near the center of the sky, before third quarter
Arire barogwadu baru kajeji	The moon draws near the center of the sky, just short of third quarter
Arire barogwadu baru oya keje	The moon dawns in the center of the sky, third quarter
Arire barogwadu barae etaya keje	The moon dawns over the baldness of the non-Indians, third quarter
*Arire tuya wuji barae etaya jyok*i	The moon descends from the crown of the non-Indians, past third quarter
Arire barogwadu barae etabaru keje	The moon dawns behind the head of the non-Indians, the small waning crescent
Ari butu	Moonset, the last visible crescent
Ari akedure	The moon ends, no visible moon

time concepts (Baldus 1940). However, such attitudes do not account for the Bororo method of referring to a period of time more than one or two days in the past simply by noting the appropriate lunar phase or position, which all other Bororo would recognize and understand.[2]

Another interesting feature of Bororo lunar terminology is the reference to moon "rise" as being in the west. This describes the first reappearance of the waxing crescent moon as a sliver hanging abruptly above the western horizon after sunset.[3] While recognizing that the moon, like all other regular astronomical features, proceeds during any specific day or night in an east-to-west direction, by saying that the moon rises in the west they are also indicating their observation that the moon proceeds steadily from west to east as observed at each sunset during its waxing phase. In other words, whereas the new crescent appears above the western horizon at sunset and shortly thereafter follows the sun in setting, by first quarter, when the moon appears half-full, it will appear more or less at the meridian (its highest point of the night) at sunset, and at full moon will be seen ideally just coming over the eastern horizon as the sun sets in the west, therefore having apparently "traveled" from west to east in half a month's time.

Besides its obvious use in marking time within a monthly period, the moon is also used to indicate the passage of night time, as well as periods beyond a single lunation. For the former, the procedure with the moon is exactly analogous to that used for the sun or any other astronomical body: its position is marked through verbal description or precise pointing. For periods beyond a single lunation, tally counting can be used if necessary to sum up elapsed months. Such a system could have been used for month counting in ways suggested by the work of Marshack (1972). In addition, one male informant of the Bokodori Exerae clan claimed that the Bororo recognize a system of ten months and provided their names:

> *Ari boe tojiwu*
> *Ari boe tojiwu rekoda jiwu*
> *Ari pobedu eregoda jiwu ari*
> *Ari pobema awu metuya bokwaredu eregoda jiwu ari*
> *Ari pobe poibiji de eregoda jiwu ari*
> *Ari pagere awu bodu eregoda jiwu ari*
> *No ari jiyo ewaje pagera aubowu todu eregoda jiwu ari*
> *No ari pobe pagera awu bowu tadadii eregoda jiwu ari*
> *No ari pobema awu metuya bokwaredu eregoda jiwu ari*
> *No ari pobe poibiji pagera auboda tadadii eregoda jiwu ari*

As this data remains largely uncorroborated and the names have yet to be satisfactorily translated, it must be treated with some reserve.[4] However, it is interesting that the informant, an elder with considerable cultural knowledge, described ten moons or months, not twelve. (Since a synodical month comprises 29.53 days, twelve such months come close to the period of a solar or "tropical" year of 365.24 days: $12 \times 29.53 = 354.36$; ten synodical months equal 295.3 days.) Other indigenous calendars also include only ten months, such as the Trobriand system described by Leach (1950), as well as the pre-Julian Roman calendar, in which the months September to December were (as their names imply) the seventh through tenth months, with December the last named month. The Bororo naming of a recognized set of ten months may indicate a more detailed and codified calendar than is today evident in their culture. Observations of the moon along the horizon may also have been significant for calendric purposes (a topic returned to in the next chapter). In contemporary Bororo villages any necessary reference to specific months is made with respect to the Brazilian (Gregorian) calendar.

Lunar observations are also significant for a number of associations only marginally calendric in function. For example, two older informants expressed the belief that there is a direct relationship between lunar phases and human health and fitness, and that this relationship had been traditionally marked by an observance of certain rules of conduct, such as fasting at both new and full moon. Other comments relevant to lunar associations include: a child cuts its first tooth when "the moon is in the zenith," referring to third-quarter moon when it is at its highest point at sunrise (cf. table 5.8, *arire barogwadu baru oya keje*); this belief is paralleled by the notion that teeth grow when the moon is "descending," a general reference to the waning moon. Fish eggs are also said to be growing during waning moon, while palm shoots are said to open at full moon.

My wife was instructed by one of her basket-making mentors that the best time to get the important shoots of the babaçu and buriti palm is just before full moon, that is, when the shoots would reach their fullest length prior to opening. After opening, a shoot is no longer suitable for most weaving purposes. However, as some weaving does require different lengths and qualities of shoots, it is logical to assume that different times of the month would be selected for collection of these materials. Such a palm/lunar calendar would be particularly significant to women and might also suggest a relation to the cycle of "moons" of women, i.e., the menstrual cycle (see Blatt-Fabian 1985). According to Sylvia Caiuby Novães, the Bororo associate both menstruation and the gestation period with the moon and moon phases, suggesting an effective female lunar calendar (personal communication, 1990).

The growing of domesticated plants is also affected by lunar phases, but there is little agreement between different informants' opinions on this relationship. One opinion has it that all crops (manioc, rice, potatoes, and corn were specifically mentioned) should be planted during full moon, although the period of waxing moon could also serve; planting during the waning moon would be useless, as nothing would grow. However, another opinion held that manioc, unlike other plants, could be planted during any month of the year, when the moon is in the middle of the sky at daybreak (i.e., the waning, third-quarter moon).

The moon is also significant for certain prognostications: the newly appearing crescent is observed for its angle, although again differing interpretations accompany such observations. A vertical crescent means cold and rain for some, while others consider it a good omen. A horizontal crescent with points up means sun and heat or alternatively can predict death. The new moon of months at the commencement of the rainy season (those in September, October and possibly November) are particularly related to bad weather.

The potential for bad luck and threatening situations with animals is said to increase during the periods of new crescent moon and also during the last days of waning moon. There is an obvious correlation between these periods and the darkest nights (those with least amount of moonlight), and such beliefs may derive from this relationship. The dark, nocturnal forest is certainly considered dangerous.

For the Bororo then, the moon serves for the marking of night time and for longer periods such as a synodical month and is also correlated in some fashion with the period of a solar (tropical) year. Traditional beliefs also relate lunar phases with seasonal data, crop planting, and the growth and development of humans and animals. There is, therefore, a great deal of significance in lunar observations for the Bororo (and probably for other native peoples as well), a topic deserving additional, concerted study.

Seasons

Beyond month-long time periods the Bororo recognize an alternation of two seasons: *butaokau* or *butaobutu*, the rainy season, and *jorukau* or *jorubutu*, the dry season. As most Bororo activities are paced so as to adequately exploit environmental resources, and as the availability of these resources is intimately connected with seasonal and meteorological phenomena, traditional activities differ substantially between the two seasons.

Butaokau, Time of Rains

According to the Salesians (*EBI*:295–96; Colbacchini and Albisetti 1942:98) *butau* is a word that relates to the Butau-doge, long-haired and bearded spirits who are said to cause the rain, *bubutu*. Garças villagers referred to the period of rains as *butaokau* or *butaobutu* interchangeably.

Strengthening winds and increasingly oppressive heat and humidity are characteristics of the month of September, along with thickening, dark clouds and a sense of intensifying atmospheric pressure. While rain may fall once or twice in September, it generally becomes regular in October, announced by a period of severe electrical displays and gradually building up in frequency and intensity, providing relief to September's discomfort. From November through January rain falls heavily each day; by February the rains subside, but intermittent and occasionally heavy showers continue into April.

With the onset of the rains, the baked, brown cerrado begins to green again, and dried-up water courses rise from a trickle to eventually overflow their banks. Many areas of the central Brazilian highlands have high water tables, and the abundant rains pouring from the sky are met by gushing springs and marshes: the dried savannah becomes boglike, and sandy paths turn muddy and treacherous. Streams and rivers turn brown with eroded sand and soil, and water, which had become so scarce and precious during the dry months, is now everywhere available.

In general the rainy season is characterized by home-based activities as the muddied paths and swollen waterways greatly inhibit travel (especially since the Bororo did not traditionally use the canoe). Some fishing and hunting are necessarily always practiced—in the former case hook and line is the most successful strategy to use in the high, opaque waters—but the dry season remains the preferred period for these pursuits. Certain wild, edible plant foods come into season during the rains, such as the *eko* (piki) fruit and the fruit of the cashew (*jatugo*). Unfortunately, although there is much talk of the abundance of wild foods in times past, very few wild plant species are a significant part of the contemporary daily diet in Garças, contributing greatly to the villagers' overall nutritional poverty. (The *Enciclopédia Bororo* I:320–29 gives a detailed description of Bororo foods and food preparation, although very few data are given on seasonal variation.) The availability of wild plant species also varies between forest and cerrado varieties, making access to all major ecological zones a priority for sufficient quantity and quality of foodstuffs.

The contemporary Garças villagers depend more upon domesticated plant food than upon wild foods. Planting is undertaken just before the onset of the rains on ground cleared by slash-and-burn methods during the dry season. Both house gardens and larger plantation-style gardens are maintained, the latter usually located several kilometers from the village on the fertile banks of the Garças River. Crops include corn (*kuiada*), "sweet" manioc (*jiu*), potatoes (*tadari*), cane (*taborewu*), banana (*bako*), squash (*powari*) and tobacco (*mea*), as well as some fruit such as melons, papaya, mango, pineapple, and citrus fruits. There is also an effort to raise sweet potatoes and beans.[5]

Dry-land rice (*iro* or *aro*) is now planted as a partially mechanized cash crop by the Garças Bororo, with the assistance of the Meruri mission and FUNAI, and its planting is timed during the rainy season so as to be ready for harvesting when the rains end. This can be difficult, as the growth period varies by specific rice variety. As a dietary staple, white rice (cleaned and semipolished by a battery-run machine) supplies the people of Garças with calories of questionable nutritional content, nor is it completely successful as a cash crop because of its risks and low returns. Current dependency on it for food and income and attention to its cycle are major factors in the shift of interest, energy, and village location away from sites of traditional food sources and food-related practices. It is also probable that certain nutrition-related health problems, such as poor teeth, general lassitude, skin lesions, and other conditions, are related to the ingestion of large quantities of such simple carbohydrates uncomplemented by higher quality foods.

While a number of cultivated species other than rice are planted, quantities remain small primarily as a result of inconsistencies in the amounts and types planted, soil infertility, and indifferent garden care. Three *roça* or "garden" groups of families work plots collectively, but this organization centers more specifically on rice cultivation. Two or three nonrice plantations were maintained, planted principally with relatively low nutrition sweet manioc, and almost no corn was available the entire year of our stay in the village.[6]

Harvesting of all crops except rice is done piecemeal as the varieties ripen. Corn takes about four months to mature and its harvest is celebrated with a green corn ceremony, *kuiada paru*. Such a ceremony was not performed in Garças during our stay, but the FUNAI official in residence at the Bororo village of Corrego Grande reported its performance there (personal communication, January 1983). An elderly informant at Garças related that this ceremony should entail two groups, one headed by Bakororo, the other by

Itubore, who sing in response to each other throughout the night. The corn itself is gathered and put in the men's house, where it is rendered safe to eat by the *bari*.

In general the rainy season has more ceremonial complexity than the dry, due at least in part to traditional residence patterns: the Bororo stay in and around the main village during the rains but roam and trek much more widely in the dry months. The entire rainy season may traditionally have served as a time of direct communion with the *aroe* spirits, a practice that eventually developed into a somewhat extended funerary period (see the discussion in the previous chapter). It is also possible that there may have been some alternation in years with a funerary period and years without, allowing for the observance of nonfunerary rituals and performances. That the funeral was seasonal is substantiated by the synchronization of its performance with male initiation, and the latter with the heliacal rise of the Pleiades in June that ends both rituals and begins the trekking season. Such a period would also account for Crocker's observation that a Bororo funeral lasts for six to ten months (and so corresponds to the rainy season), whereas other reports are of one- to two-month periods. Perhaps individual funerals were completed within this shorter period, but as observed in Garças, there is a tendency to combine performances for overlapping deaths. Because the funeral is the epoch when the *aroe* physically enter the village, the seasonal duration of this appearance would be comparable to the period of Katchina visitation in the U.S. Southwest, which among the Hopi begins near the December solstice and extends slightly beyond the June solstice (e.g., Parsons 1933).

The Bororo therefore correlated natural, ecological time cycles with cycles of the spirits and with the life course. A similar "layering" or synchronizing of different types of temporal cycles is described by Wagley for the central Brazilian Tapirapé. "As the rainy season ended, the real season of masked dancing and of visits of a variety of *anchunga* [spirits] began. It must be remembered that the beginning of the dry season was marked by the harvest ceremonies . . . , the dancing and singing at Kawió when there was an exchange of personal property, and the coming of age ceremony for young men" (1983:216). Such synchronization was probably a widespread phenomenon among native Brazilian and South American peoples, significantly contributing to indigenous patterns of interrelation with all aspects of their environment.

Another event that appears to be limited to the rainy season is a race run while carrying large cylinders or wheels made from a marsh plant called *mano* (*caeté* or *piripiri* in Portuguese) available only during the rains according to my informants. Moiety-based teams construct the wheels in a clearing located several kilometers from the village and then race back—reminiscent of Gê log racing—with two individuals struggling to carry each of the heavy and awkward wheels. These races are run for enjoyment and exercise and are unlikely to occur during the somber and ritually active funerary period (the Salesians report that such races occurred only outside of the funerary cycle; *EBI*:152–54). While this may challenge the rainy season/funerary period hypothesis, it does not necessarily negate it, as it is likely that during some years no funerals or initiations occurred, and in such years they could have held the *mano* race.[7] Two performances during the funerary period are similar to the *mano* races: one that involves dancing while carrying miniature *mano* cylinders behind one's neck and the *marido* ceremony (performed twice within a funeral cycle), which involves a pair of large and heavy wheels constructed of buriti (*marido*) frond stems. These are carried atop a dancer's head. All three performances (the *mano* races and the funerary *mano* and *marido* ceremonies) involve a pair of wheels or cylinders used simultaneously by two groups. Since indigenous cycles and patterns have been greatly influenced by the changing contemporary situation, concrete data relevant especially to the timing of such performances are difficult to achieve.

Much of each day during the rainy season in Garças village is occupied with the manufacture of tourist articles that are sold or bartered to the missionaries for desired and needed items or to pay off debts. While no funeral was going on during the rainy season in which we arrived, neither were any *mano* races held. Soccer was played between moieties on occasion, while ceremonial activity was limited to songs performed for hunting and fishing success: a nocturnal ritual with two versions, one all-night and the other (more common) of about an hour's duration, neither of which is seasonally limited.

Jorukau, Time of Fire

Joru is "fire" and refers at least in part to the scalding sun that beats mercilessly from a cloudless sky. The sky does not remain clear throughout the dry season, however, as large tracts of the cerrado are burnt off in sweeping range fires (nowadays set by the local Brazilian population as well as by indigenous peoples), the more

Transfer of the marido wheel of buriti palm during
villagewide funerary ceremony.

relevant seasonal reference. These fires billow forth smoke that
combines with wind-borne dirt and sand to gradually obscure
much of the sky, not only blocking out stars at night but limiting
even the dulled disc of the sun from view for a couple of hours
after sunrise and before sunset. Traditionally the cerrado and
forests were burnt as a hunting strategy, to clear land for later
planting, or simply to "clean" the land, as some informants
expressed it. These days local landowners have agribusiness and
pasturage lands that are also burnt off. The fires can be hazardous
as changes in wind direction may threaten an entire village; stories
of burned villages were recalled by older informants.

Intermittent rain showers occur in April, and occasionally into
early May, eventually ceasing altogether. The dryness of the
months of May through September is relieved only rarely by contrary southerly or southwesterly winds that bring some rain but are
also accompanied by biting cold that may last with the rain for
three or four days. Such weather produces little lasting effect on
the parched land and dried-up waterways and is generally a miser-
able period when most villagers huddle near their fires. June and
July are noted for their cool to cold, clear nights and sunburning
days, although by late July the smoke, dust, and heat haze is
already advancing across the sky. Frequent breezes make day time
temperatures more bearable than the sultry heat of the early rainy
season but contribute to the dryness; dust storms can be a problem. In September clouds begin to blow in from the east, and a seasonally early shower forecasts the coming deluge.

Hunting and particularly fishing are the preferred dry season
activities to this day. The latter includes the use of nets, weirs, bow

and arrow, fish poisons, and deep-water line fishing, which can produce enormous quantities of fish for minimal energy expenditure. Early dry season fishing can be quite poor, however, as the height of availability extends from July through October. In Garças village we saw only a small portion of the variety of wild foods available exclusively during the dry season (such as the fruit of the jatobá [*bokwado*] and a considerable variety of wild tubers) used by the villagers.

Access to different areas and ecological zones within Bororo territory is greatly enhanced during the dry season, giving rise to the traditional *maguru,* "trek." Groups of varied size and composition struck off from the village for long-range forays, sleeping in makeshift camps said to reduplicate in their outlay the structure of the Bororo village. Unfortunately, trek details such as provenience, range, duration, and group composition are no longer available to study as contemporary Bororo remain relatively confined.

Garden sites are chosen and preferably cleared during the early dry season to allow the cut material to dry for burning before the arrival of the rains. This scheduling leaves the entire middle period of the dry season free for nonagricultural activities both in and away from the village.

Ceremonial activity traditionally lessens during *jorukau,* but one ceremony during this period is of extreme importance: the Akiri-doge Ewure Kowudu, the "burning of the feet of the Pleiades." Performed when the Pleiades star group makes its first appearance above the eastern horizon before sunrise (an event that occurs in June), the ceremony includes both jumping over a fire (for the young male initiates) and hurling firebrands at the Pleiades. The intent is to burn the feet of the Akiri-doge (the Pleiades) and thereby slow the advance of the dry season that is favored by all. Although not practiced today, the Akiri-doge ceremony remains vestigially present in the celebration of the day of São João. In Garças village on the night of 23 June 1983 bonfires were lit on the plaza in front of the houses, in stated reference to the Catholic saint but with little or no overt ceremonial behavior. However, two months prior to this, my principal informant explicitly connected the *"fogo de São João "* (the "fire of Saint John") with the Akiri-doge Ewure Kowudu ceremony, claiming the former to be reminiscent of the latter and performed like a seasonal indicator at the same time (details of the Pleiades and other stars as time indicators are treated in chapter 7).

While some Bororo are knowledgeable about the Western calendar, my principal informant scoffed at marking the specific day and time of the beginning of a particular season: in his opinion natural indicators were more appropriate to this function, while the "beginning" of any season could not be so minutely pin-pointed. As there is more to defining the rainy season than simply when the rains begin or end, the knowledge of environmental indicators used traditionally to mark time are vitally important in appreciating the indigenous system. Unfortunately, investigation of this topic is hampered by two factors: the current demise of tra-ditional practices in contemporary villages, and the lack of detailed studies of the seasonal availability of resources.

Blooming flowers are among the single most significant indica-tors or markers of time for the Bororo. Informants gave examples of the blooming of certain flowers and their indications: the *kuoga*, a yellow flower of the cerrado, signified the onset of cold weather. A red flower called *ema oko* marked the rains. The *mana i* flower marked the time when parakeets had young (in June), while the blooming of the *mana guru oko* (Portuguese *arika*) announced the coming of fish up the rivers (in July). The relation of flowers and the origin of fish is also the theme of two Bororo myths (Colbac-chini and Albisetti 1942:211; *EB*II:#21; Wilbert and Simoneau 1983:#75 and #76). While important, such indicators are not taken alone as time markers but are combined with other observations, as failure to do so can result in misleading information. (For exam-ple in 1983, fish were found to be coming up the river in quantity even before the *mana guru oko* bloomed.) Environmental indicators for marking time include the horizon observation of sun and moon and the appearance and positions of various star groups, especially the Pleiades (topics treated in more detail in the next two chapters). The practice of relying on multiple observations for precision in time marking, a crucial feature of native Brazilian time concepts, results in increased effectiveness in resource exploita-tion, especially since many of these resources are interdependent or related.

Awareness of the extent to which traditional Bororo activities are and were affected by seasonality is a prerequisite for apprecia-tion of the cultural time-space system, an awareness increasingly more difficult to realize. The relationship is evident, however, in one of the few truly traditional pursuits still maintained by the Bororo: their native palm working. As my wife describes in her work (Blatt-Fabian 1985) the entire process of palm working is tem-porally related, from the collection of appropriate materials, to their preparation, and to the manufacture of basketry and other products, and includes seasonal availability, lunar cycles, and sensitivity to atmospheric moisture levels.

Time periods longer than one season are noted and marked by the observation of astronomical bodies such as solar horizon position and heliacal rising, occurrences that transpire annually. Beyond this, tally counting of annual phenomena is possible, while time passage is casually noted and referred to with particular reference to the change in height of village children: in answer to a question about when a certain incident occurred in the past, a Bororo will point to a child and say, "When he was only this tall," showing the height level with an outstretched hand. In more traditional times, the Bororo age-class system may have functioned for organizing periods of five years in a forty-year cycle.

Six

The Meri-doge: Sun and Moon as Celestial Bodies and Mythical Heroes

Meri (the sun) and *ari* (the moon) are of primary importance within Bororo space-time. Their movement and positions and the latter's phases are always part of Bororo awareness, on a daily/nightly basis and throughout the course of a month and year. As celestial bodies they are models and guides for village planning, directions of social movement, and seasonal activities; as anthropomorphized heroes they are also models and guides for social interaction and personal character. In general they have a profound effect upon the natural, social, and cosmological environments of the Bororo.

Colbacchini and Albisetti (1942:97) describe the Bororo notion of the celestial sun as a shining gold disc that is carried by the spirits of dead *bari* shamans (*baire*, pl.: shamans who communicate with the *bope* spirits and so are juxtaposed to the *aroe etawarare*, shaman of the *aroe*; for detailed information on Bororo shamanism, see Crocker 1985). These spirits start off lightly with their load at sunrise but by midmorning are toiling up the arduous ascent of the sky; finally about midafternoon descent facilitates their work. After reaching the horizon they arrive at an impassable body of water that they skirt by going north, arriving in the east for the next sunrise. Movement of the celestial moon is similarly described, with its phases said to be controlled by the degree of openness of the spirits' eyes.

In Garças village, one informant related that at sunset *meri* sets on the shoulders of Bakororo, the culture hero and chief presiding over the western village of the dead, and rises on the shoulders of Itubore, who presides over the eastern village of the dead. Each of these entities is associated with a specific type of musical instrument (*ika* [transverse flute] for Bakororo and *pana* [a multilobed horn] for Itubore), which they play to announce the arrival of *meri* at their respective villages. This informant said that after sunset *meri* passes through another world and then returns to ours. Another informant believed that *meri* was so powerful that he could return from west to east by willing to do so, being first at one place and then simply reappearing at the other.

The contemporary beliefs of the Bororo of Garças concerning the nature of the celestial sun and moon are somewhat unclear, expressing an uncertainty that stems mainly from statements they have heard from outside the village that markedly conflict with their traditional cosmology. For example, one of the first questions I was asked by the men of Garças was if it were true that someone had actually walked upon the moon, an inconceivability within native tenets. When I had hesitantly replied in the affirmative, one of the men resolved this inconsistency with native belief by using it to contrast the relative strengths of the sun and moon. The moon, he said, was weak, but the sun strong, and although neither are very far away, the sun would never allow himself to be reached like the moon but rather would appear to always move beyond reach of any who tried to approach. This quandary and its attempted solution are exemplary of the current dilemma of the Bororo, who daily experience the stark confrontation between the underpinnings of their native beliefs and opposing views from the modern world culture that encompasses them.

There is a consistent tendency to anthropomorphize the celestial sun and moon. Meri and Ari, collectively known as Meri-doge, are important mythical entities and cultural heroes for the Bororo and occupy a prominent place in Bororo folklore. The Salesians have suggested that the mythological Meri-doge are not to be confused with the celestial sun and moon, which the Salesians contend were only given the names of *meri* and *ari* from the folk heroes in admiration and recognition of their power (*EBI*:773). Wilbert repeats this depiction in his introduction to *Folk Literature of the Bororo Indians* (Wilbert and Simoneau 1983:6), suggesting only a "tenuous" identification of the brothers (Meri as older brother, Ari as younger) in Bororo mythology with the celestial sun and moon. Such an attitude results from a primary concern with an empiricism that is intrinsically impossible to dispute: that as humanlike culture heroes and powerful mythical entities, Sun and Moon are obviously not the same as bright celestial orbs. Such opinions, however, disregard the inherent metaphorical identity in Bororo thought that relates the celestial and mythical beings. Bororo Sun and Moon mythology demonstrates an "understanding and experiencing [of] one kind of thing in terms of another," which is the essence of metaphor as defined by Lakoff and Johnson (1980:5). By looking at the characterizations explicit in the myths, Bororo identifications between the celestial and mythical entities can be readily understood.

Acceptance of an essential metaphorical relationship conceived of by the Bororo between the celestial and mythological sun and moon is also supported by beliefs held among the neighboring Gê peoples, for whom solar and lunar observations are also very important. In these cultures the celestial bodies are clearly anthropomorphized and related to mythical beings and culture heroes. Among the Sherente, for example, Nimuendajú reports, "Waptokwa and Wairie are the anthropomorphized sun and moon. The celestial bodies are called *bdu*, 'sun,' and *wa*, 'moon,' . . . yet when I asked where and who Waptokwa is, the Sherente simply pointed at the disk of the sun" (1942:84; I have simplified some of Nimuendajú's orthography).

The Bororo First Encounter the Meri-doge

One myth (Colbacchini and Albisetti 1942:196–97; Wilbert and Simoneau 1983:#44) tells of Rikubugu, a Bororo of the Paiwoe clan, who while hunting encounters a path of glowing red footprints. He follows these until he is forced to stop by the increasing heat and while resting hears two voices, one stronger than the other. He gets closer and sees that the speakers are the brothers Meri and Ari; he becomes so frightened with this discovery that he flees back to his village. There he recounts his adventure to his father, Bakorokudu (of the Baadajebage Xebegiwuge clan), and the two of them argue about whose clan Meri and Ari will belong to (Bororo clans may claim a newly discovered item for their own by right of first discovery; recall that clan membership is matrilineal). Some days later father and son go together to follow the same path and upon finding the brilliant red footprints again discuss the clan membership of Meri and Ari. Bakorokudu decides that the Meri-doge and also the path of the sun called *meri etawara* are to be of his clan, while the *bororo*, or plaza, of Meri and Ari would be of his son's clan. The two then try to walk further along the path but are forced to turn back because of the increasing heat.

In another version of this myth (*EBII*:#46; Wilbert and Simoneau 1983:#45) it is not a member of the Paiwoe clan but rather Tadugo of the Iwagududoge (although both are Tugarege clans) who first encounters Meri and Ari, when he is with his father, again Bakorokudu. In this version Meri wears a shining red headdress and Ari a yellow one. Father and son argue as to whose clan the Meri-doge will join, and again Bakorokudu wins them for his clan, but their representation in ceremony, always effected by members of the opposite moiety, is reserved for, respectively, Tadugo (and the Iwagududoge clan) as Meri, with the Aroroe Xebegiwuge subclan as Ari. The red and yellow headdresses of the Meri-doge carry implicit meaning for which another Bororo myth gives us the interpretation. In it, men jumping through a fire turn into beautifully plummaged birds; one who jumped directly through the hottest part of the fire emerged as a macaw with red feathers, while another, jumping only over the fire's periphery, was transformed into a macaw with yellow feathers, "as there was not enough heat to turn the feathers red" (*EB*II:#26; Wilbert and Simoneau 1983:#68). Thus in the myth about Meri and Ari, the red-feathered (macaw) headdress of Meri marks him as hotter (that is, stronger) than his brother Ari, whose yellow-feathered (macaw) headdress is cooler (weaker), characteristics consistent with those described in the first myth version recounted above, where Meri's greater strength was evidenced by his more powerful voice.

Another myth of the first encounter between the Bororo and the Meri-doge (*EB*II:#47; Wilbert and Simoneau 1983:#46) again includes a Paiwoe member, Kaidagare, who while visiting what he believes to be a Bororo village is treated with a medicinal/magical herb. This treatment enables him, like the other villagers, to see Meri and Ari when they appear on the branch of a jatobá tree, singing and dancing, each wearing his characteristic red and yellow headdresses. After discovering that the villagers are not true Bororo, Kaidagare returns home and tells his tale, whereupon his father (again Bakorokudu) claims the Meri-doge but allows Kaidagare to represent them. In yet a fourth version of this myth, collected from an informant in Garças village, it is a member of the Baadajebage clan who first comes upon Meri and Ari: he sees their tracks and a light shining in the distance along the *meritawara*, road of Meri. After he returns to the village, Meri and Ari themselves arrive and stay for a time in a Baadajebage Xebegiwuge house. They later leave, only to return with a member of the Paiwoe clan, who cares for them. However, the Baadajebage pull the Meri-doge to their clan house, and there they stay as members of the Baadajebage Xebegiwuge clan.

Several features of these myths deserve emphasis: (a) the path of Meri and Ari; (b) their color association; (c) the heat experienced in their proximity; (d) the relationship of Meri as older (and stronger) brother to Ari; (e) the relationship between Meri and Ari and a path, *meri etawara*, and the village plaza, *bororo*, and (f) the ultimate clan affiliation of Meri and Ari as Baadajebage Xebegiwuge of Bakorokudu's name group. Features (a) through (d) connect the qualities of the celestial sun and moon with the mythical entities, while (e) and (f) depict an intrinsic relationship between the Meri-doge, the Bororo village, and social ordering. The village plaza, *bororo*, is divided by an east-west axis, a division predicated on the perceived daily east-to-west movement—presumably the path called *meri etawara*, literally the "path of the sun"—of the celestial bodies, primarily of the sun. This east-west axis also separates the village moieties, Exerae in the north and Tugarege in the south. Apinayé villages are also characterized by an east-west dividing line, also predicated on the sun and moon and also related to social structure. "Then Sun said, 'Let us lay out a village for our children.' [Sun and Moon] looked for a high site and laid out a circle, which Sun divided by an E-W line, saying, 'I put my children on the N side!' 'And I put mine on the S side!' answered Moon. Thus the two moieties arose" (Nimuendajú 1967:164).

The clan to which Meri and Ari pertain is situated adjacent to the east-west axis, path, or both, at the "base" of the village in the west. Bakorokudu, who claims the Meri-doge for his clan, is one of the hereditary chiefs of the Bororo. As "constructors of the village," the Baadajebage, with clans both in the east and the west, are responsible for properly aligning the village and ordering the placement of its localized social groups. The myth implies that such planning relies directly upon solar observation, an implication substantiated by the traditional layout of contemporary Garças village and statements and practices made by its residents in relating the principal axis of the village to the course of the sun.

The Adventures of Meri and Ari

Published myths about the Meri-doge are numerous. In these myths, Meri is consistently credited with an impressive transformative power. At times he uses this power in a positive fashion, such as to improve the beaks of certain birds, or to give humans their teeth and nails (see *EB*II:#53; Colbacchini and Albisetti 1942: 249; Wilbert and Simoneau 1983:#81 and #82). At other times, however, a mischievous, covetous side of his character encourages the pernicious exercising of his abilities. For example, Meri trades his own worthless axe for the good axe a group of Bororo are using to collect honey; when they complain, he transforms them into woodpeckers (*enare*) who must from that time forward rely upon their beaks for nourishment (*EB*II:#49; Colbacchini and Albisetti 1942: 250; Wilbert and Simoneau 1983:#85 and #86). In a different episode, Meri, desiring the fine bow employed by a Bororo for fishing, trades the man a weak, poorly made substitute, then punishes the man's complaints by turning him into a kingfisher (*kadogare; EB*II:#48; Colbacchini and Albisetti 1942: 251; Wilbert and Simoneau 1983:#83 and #84). And on yet another occasion Meri, envious of a man's red macaw-feathered chest ornament, forces the man to trade for an inferior article. Dissatisfied, the man scuffles with Meri over the finer ornament, which falls upon the Bororo's head; Meri transforms him into the red-crested finch, *aogwa* (*EB*II:#50; Colbacchini and Albisetti 1942: 251; Wilbert and Simoneau 1983:#87 and #88).

Meri's mischievous intelligence and cruel cleverness also win him control over the night. Originally the ibis *O* (*socó* in Portuguese) controlled the darkness. Meri kills the bird's two fledglings and then bargains with the ibis, offering to bring the young back to life in exchange for the power over darkness. The bird agrees and the deal is made, with the stipulation that Meri must bring night to an end when the ibis cries "oó, oó, oó," in order that Meri not abuse the power (*EB*II:#59; Colbacchini and Albisetti 1942: 250; Wilbert and Simoneau 1983:#12 and #13).

The myths of Meri describe his capriciousness, his transformative power, his relationship with the color red, and his control over the night, as well as over death. When his brother Ari appears with him in myths, the latter's comparative weakness, lack of intelligence, and ineptitude are evident. Ari is tricked, for example, into giving his jaguar skin and his women to Meri, who finds them more beautiful than his own (*EB*II:#51, 52; Wilbert and Simoneau 1983:#14 and #15). Several myths dramatize the one-sided relationship of the brothers, as well as their relationship with the Bororo.

The Deaths of Ari and His Resuscitation

Several instances of Ari's death and his eventual resuscitation by his brother Meri appear in Bororo mythology. Although both the *Enciclopédia Bororo* II and Colbacchini and Albisetti give these in sequence (i.e., "first," "second," "third") it is not readily apparent if this order is significant to the Bororo.

In the first myth, the Bororo themselves attempt to kill the Meri-doge with fire in revenge for tricks played upon them by the brothers. Caught by the encircling flames, Meri tells the weaker Ari to climb up the *kuogo i*, a short tree of weak wood, while Meri himself scales the *tara i*, a large, strong tree. The fire reaches the tree in which Ari has sought refuge and consumes both tree and occupant, while Meri remains safe in his perch. The remains of Ari are then eaten by a foxlike animal (*okwa*) which Meri later succeeds in killing, after which he collects the few remnants of his brother from the animal's entrails. Arranging the remains with pieces of wood in roughly human form and covering the whole with leaves and a medicinal mixture, Meri re-forms his brother and jars him back to life with excited shouts warning of impending danger (from venomous snakes, felines, whites, enemy Indians; *EB*II:#54; Colbacchini and Albisetti 1942:233–35; Wilbert and Simoneau 1983:#1 and #2). Essentially the same procedure is used by Meri to revive his brother after his other misadventures: attacking jaguars scale and devour Ari as he attempts to flee from them up a tree with thick bark (*bie i*), and Ari is killed accidentally by Meri as they compete in an archery bout (*EB*II:#55 and #57; Colbacchini and Albisetti 1942:236–37; Wilbert and Simoneau 1983:#4–#7).[1] In a fourth version of Ari's death collected during my fieldwork, Ari is killed in a fight with the mythical Adugo (Jaguar), who throws him into a lagoon where piranha devour him (some of Ari's viscera float to the surface and become aquatic plants, *anabo*, as did Kiareware's in the Toribugu myth). Ari's resurrection in this fourth version is effected by his brother in the same fashion as in the other versions.

The theme of Ari's repeated deaths does more than emphasize the contrast in strength and other abilities between Meri and him. The multiple deaths of the mythical moon correspond to the repeated monthly "deaths" or disappearances of the celestial moon, which, as occurs in the myths, is revived by the sun: in the sky by the sun's light, and in the mythic context by Sun's magical ministrations. In both contexts the two entities are contiguous. Alternatively, the number of Ari's deaths as compared to the isolated incidence of his brother's demise (see below) may be a way of illustrating their other deaths, eclipses: *ari bi* and *meri bi*, "moon death" and "sun death," respectively. In fact, lunar eclipses are observed with greater frequency than are solar eclipses in any given geographic area.

115

The Death of Meri

Meri also dies, killed accidentally in a competition with his brother. Published versions recount an archery contest; Garças informants describe a contest wherein Meri and Ari throw a large, heavy *mano*—a wheel made of a swamp plant and used in races similar to Gê log races—that strikes Meri in the chest, killing him. Unable to revive his brother, Ari wanders sad and lonely until he finds a village in which he takes up residence, only to be badly mistreated by its residents. Each time a flock of birds passes through the village Ari inquires as to his brother's whereabouts, and finally Meri does arrive with a flock of macaws, having apparently revived himself. Reunited with his younger brother, Meri transforms himself into a *dourado* fish (*okoge*) in order to feed his starving brother.[2] The two eventually move across the river away from the village in which Ari was so poorly treated. Meri is determined to avenge his brother, and to do so sends heavy winds and rain that destroy the village houses and extinguish all fires (similar to events in the Toribugu myth). To get fire, the villagers are forced to swim the river to Meri and Ari's house, which remains undamaged by the storm. Meri cleverly ties firebrands into the men's hair in order that they may swim more easily across to their village, but he purposely makes knots in the brands on the heads of Ari's tormentors. These latter suffer burned heads, becoming bald-headed birds (primarily vultures and herons).

In this myth, descriptions of Meri's self-regenerative power and his control of the elements are undoubtedly references to the celestial sun's perceived cycle and its relationship to the seasons, especially illustrated by a series of flocks of birds that pass through the village, strongly indicative of (seasonal) time passage.

The Meri-doge Ascend to the Sky

The use and misuse of their powers by the brothers Meri and Ari eventually lead the Bororo to force the Meri-doge up into the sky: they become literally "too hot" or "too bright"—as the myths themselves describe—to handle.

In published Salesian versions of this myth (*EB*II:#61; Colbacchini and Albisetti 1942:237–78; Wilbert and Simoneau 1983:#16 and #17), the Meri-doge ask for water from members of the Iwagududoge clan and, once offered it, break the large clay jar in which it is contained. Angered by yet another instance of the brothers' pranks, the Iwagududoge clan members apprehend them (or Meri alone in one version) and, after seating the brothers in their midst, begin to fan them. To Meri's remonstrations the Iwagududoge respond, "You produce a lot of heat," and fan even more vigorously until Meri and Ari are lifted up by the wind into the sky.

One version collected in Garças village from a Paiwoe informant relates how a Paiwoe woman collecting honey is killed by a storm sent by the Meri-doge. Seeking retribution, her brother and another Bororo go to the house of the Meri-doge in order to take the beautiful adornments there as payment. Meri and Ari return to find the two Bororo accoutered in their own ornaments, dancing in the plaza. Meri asks them to spin slower as they dance, but instead the Bororo spin faster, and the metal ornaments of the Meri-doge spin so fast and get so bright that Meri and Ari disappear.

Having been so presumptuous as to forcibly remove the powerful Meri-doge from their midst, the Bororo are punished by the celestial/mythical entities, forbidden to consume a large category of favored foods until these foods have been blessed by a *bari* shaman. Failure to do so will result in illness and death (lists of these taboo foods appear in *EBII*:#61, pp. 1139–53; *EBI*:240–43; and Crocker 1985:140–42). This belief is an example of the multiple and complex notions regarding elements of Bororo cosmology, such as the sun and moon as both culture heroes and celestial bodies, the spirit world (particularly the *bope*), and Bororo shamans, specifically the *bari*, who is related to the *bope*. (Discussion of these complexities is continued in this book's concluding chapters, but for additional details see especially Crocker 1985.)

A Garças informant related that once they were forced to leave, the Meri-doge would no longer give the direct counsel they had once supplied to the Bororo, such as the appropriate times and places for carrying on particular cultural activities, especially those related to basic subsistence. Such counsel could subsequently be heard only from the mouth of the *bari*, who would divine it from his *bope* familiars, and from omens they would see in the world around them.

The Characterization of Meri and Ari

The Bororo myths related in this chapter demonstrate that, rather than few or no grounds existing for considering the mythical Meri-doge as the celestial sun and moon, in fact Bororo characterization and depiction of these entities illustrates an understanding and experiencing of the sun and moon in terms of the mythical heroes and vice versa. The grounds on which this metaphorical identity rests are often explicit and multidimensional.

Inherent in the differentiation between sun and moon as observed in the sky is the characteristic that although the two appear roughly equal in size, the sun burns hotter and brighter and has a more regular cycle than the moon. In Bororo mythology, Meri (Sun) is the stronger, elder brother of Ari (Moon). Color symbolism is regularly used to distinguish the quality of brightness and heat that are intrinsic to Meri, qualities in which both the mythical and celestial suns surpass the mythical and celestial moons. Ari's repeated deaths and resurrections effected by Meri illustrate the moon's monthly cycle—and possibly eclipses—and resuscitation by the sun. Whether or not the Bororo explain lunar phases in terms of reflected sunlight, they relate the reappearance of the new moon as a sliver of crescent in the western sky at sunset to the sun's effect, based on their proximity. Empirically the moon is at its strongest when furthest from the sun (at full moon), but Ari is still so weak that he cannot live adequately separated from his brother, as the myth of Meri's death portrays (after its full phase the moon again draws closer to the sun, while also diminishing in size).

In the mythical depiction of Meri the Bororo relate their observation of the sun's capriciousness: while it gives life and rejuvenation through heat and light, it may just as easily burn and parch with its relentless power. Meri as culture hero is described as "bad" and "mean" by informants in a manner analogous to the use of these terms in slang or black English, with a hint of respect and even admiration in the expressions: although "bad," Meri is not evil. His character is a model that Bororo men attempt to emulate: strength, cunning, and boldness are all desired male traits, while most men exercise their mischievous side with some frequency. Even Meri's relationship with his younger brother serves as a behavior pattern for this important sibling relationship among the Bororo. As elder brother, Meri cares for Ari by avenging his ill-treatment by the villagers, by offering himself as food in the form of a fish, and by actually bringing Ari back to life. But Meri has also taken his brother's jaguar skin and women for his own and apparently knowingly suggests the inadequate trees that Ari climbs in a futile effort to escape flames and attacking jaguars. Meri and Ari's relationship highlights the ambivalence of the brother relationship among the Bororo in which ideally the elder brother is respected and emulated by the younger, while the two nevertheless must compete as adults for many of the same resources (e.g., positions of prestige, women, etc.).

Sun and Moon as mythic heroes also have social positions that relate to their celestial counterparts and to village structure. Meri and Ari pertain to Bakorokudu's name group within the Baadajebage Xebegiwuge clan, located at the base of the village in the west, just north of the principal axis. Bakorokudu chose them for his clan, for as he put it, the village plaza is connected with the Meri-doge and their path. Empirically, the sun, moon, and other celestial bodies are observed to rise in the east and set in the west, and the Bororo have chosen this significant directionality and course of movement as the major foundation for orienting their village and its central men's house. This pattern also serves as the underpinning of all Bororo social and cosmological structure. As "constructors of the village" the Baadajebage are active agents in the planning and layout of this structure. They are situated as two clans, one to the extreme east and one to the extreme west in Exerae space, the northern half of the village. By locating Meri and Ari just to the north of the east-west axis, the Bororo may be expressing a characteristic of the sun and moon as perceived through consistent observation: in the southern hemisphere the sun and moon appear for a greater portion of the year in the sky north of the zenith (and an imaginary line connecting it to east and west). They are therefore more frequently over or within Exerae space, to which the celestial and mythical sun and moon pertain. It is also important to note the relationship of the "path of the sun" or *meri etawara* to the Paiwoe clan: in many village plans (if not in actual practice) there are Paiwoe segments located at both eastern and western ends, flanking the east-west axis similarly to the positions of the Baadajebage clans of the Exerae moiety.

The celestial sun and moon not only apparently move from east to west, however, but course between northern and southern extremes as well (on a yearly basis for the former, and on a monthly basis for the latter).[3] This north-south-north movement may be an alternate "path of the sun" and resembles the movement of men in the village: males born in the southern or Tugarege moiety traditionally move their residence northward to the men's house at puberty and then continue northward after marriage for cohabitation with women of the Exerae moiety. Exerae males have a similar but opposite movement to the south. North-south movement, or movement between moieties, is furthermore the principal direction of intravillage exchange of goods or services, as the basis for most exchange patterns are the intermoiety *iorubodare* relationships.

Bororo sun and moon myths explicitly substantiate the metaphoric relationship between the mythic heroes and celestial bodies by recounting how Meri gains control of the night and how the Meri-doge are forced into the sky. The latter incident is the incipience of an extremely significant cultural pattern, the recognition and special treatment of a large class of taboo foods. This complex of behavior is related to the cult of the *bope*, spirits described by Crocker as involved in the "processes of physical change" (1985:13). However, Meri and Ari are themselves *aroe*, a class of spirits related to the "immutability of physical reality in its 'givenness' as the regularity of night and day, seasons, natural species" (ibid.). Although an *aroe* and therefore an antithesis to the *bope*, Meri is credited by some Bororo as being "father of the *bope*" (cf. Crocker 1985:132). While much of Meri's mythical conduct may be described as "anomalous, immoral and disordered" (traits characteristic of the *bope*), he nevertheless "creates natural order, originating species and assigning them a perpetual ecological, symbolic, and categorical status in the universe. It appears that the *bope*, although the animating principle of organic transformation and serial change, are themselves subject to the prescription that things must be themselves, reflect the attributes and roles implicit in their names [i.e., traits characteristic of the *aroe*]. . . . The Bororo, by identifying Meri and defining the terms of their relationship with him, establish the principles whereby the reciprocal transactions between society and the *bope* must be governed" (Crocker 1985:139).

The Meri-doge are crucial therefore to the integration and comprehension of both *aroe* and *bope* for the Bororo, and are in a similar way crucial in defining both time and space and in relating the two. Similar material concerning the sun and moon is also described by Nimuendajú for the Eastern and Western Timbira (Apinayé), and the Sherente (consult especially Nimuendajú 1942:84–85; 1946:231–33, 243–45; and 1967:132–39, 158–65). While the quality and amount of detail vary in each account, the Gê societies seem also to have held the sun and moon in high regard, to the extent of deifying the entities. Among the Apinayé, for example, features recounted in the sun and moon myths relate these entities directly with the creation of humans and the founding of the first human settlement and in general "form the basis of religion and social structure" (Nimuendajú 1967:133). The sun and moon myth cycle recorded for the Eastern and Western Timbira has elements similar to Bororo sun and moon mythology, namely a steppe fire that threatens Sun and Moon, the significance of the color red for Sun, involvement with woodpeckers, and the characterization of Sun as the stronger, more intelligent of the sun and moon pair, with a mischievous, even malicious nature. However, among these Gê groups, the mythical Sun and Moon are considered companions, not brothers as among the Bororo. Additional comparative research on the respective myths of native central Brazilians is pivotal for establishing the degree of relatedness of these cultures.

The Excursions of the Meri-doge

At least one myth explicitly describes the movement of the Meri-doge through space in a manner interpretable as a calendric reference. One version of this myth (from Colbacchini and Albisetti 1942:257; Wilbert and Simoneau 1983:#23) is paraphrased here.

> The Bororo say that the sun and his companions of the sky undertook a journey from west to east, marking the places they passed with mountains and so forming that chain of heights that goes in the direction of their journey, during which they also created some animals, such as *ki*, tapir, *jui*, wild pig, and others.
>
> Observing that people did not have a good line from which to make cord for fishing, they made the *rito* emerge from the earth, a small palm from whose leaves a very tough fiber could be taken by the Bororo for fishing and for making nets.
>
> At a certain moment they let out a strong and prolonged yell that startled the caymans that were on the bank of the river. Then the Meri-doge said, "The *aroe* caymans were startled to hear the shouts of the *aroe meri* at the passage of the river." They said the same when with their shouts they frightened the *aroe pai*, the howler monkey.

The myth presents a direction of movement from west to east, and therefore contrary to the observed daily motion of the sun. This may be a reference to nocturnal solar movement, when the celestial orb must travel from its setting point in the west to once again rise in the east. The myth may also be describing the apparent west-to-east movement of both the sun and moon with respect to the background of relatively fixed stars. The moon, for example, is explicitly said to "rise" in the west when it reappears each month as a waxing crescent; it is then observed and talked about coursing eastward, as on successive nights leading up to its full phase it is seen progressively further from the setting sun. The sun's apparent movement against the backdrop of stars is more problematic, as the presence in the sky of the sun and the stars is mutually exclusive. Specific stars can be perceived as appearing higher in the sky each night at sunset, making the sun appear to be moving eastward through their midst. It is also possible that the west-to-east motion may be an idiom for expressing the observed yearly peregrination of the sun and moon between northern and southern extremes: it is for this north-south movement that the hills created by the sun to mark his journey would be most effective for solar observations on the horizon.

In another version of this myth (*EB*II:#56; Wilbert and Simoneau 1983:#22) the Meri-doge's excursion is marked by encounters with a number of animals: *ai/adugo* (jaguar), . . . *awagodori/aipobureu* (ocelot), *aiguio/aigo* (puma), *kurugugwa* and fledgling (a large hawk or falcon), *aroe exeba* and fledgling (harpy eagle), *toroa* and fledgling (another large hawk or falcon), *baruguma/barugi* and fledgling (a smaller hawk or falcon), *baxe* (heron) . . . *kidoe* (parakeets), *pai* (howler monkey), and *aroe utaboio/uwai* (cayman) (ellipses mark breaks that seem to occur in the format of the narration as recorded in the *Enciclopédia Bororo* [II:1061–73]). In each encounter the named animal is apparently startled and is said to "flee over the road of Bakororo." This ambiguous reference is linked by the Salesians to a Bororo song. But Bakororo is also the name of the chief presiding over the village of the dead in the west and can also be applied to that direction. Therefore the implication is that the frightened animals flee westward, the daily direction of celestial motion and terrestrial water in the Bororo area.

Exactly what the sequence of animals might be referring to is not clear. Although no fish species are mentioned, the animals listed refer to the three environments of land (felines), air (hawks/falcons, other birds, and perhaps the howler monkey as arboreal), and water (cayman and heron), in that order. The animals do not seem to constitute a particular set as recognized by the Bororo, nor do they all conform to any single category of species (cf. Crocker 1985, tables 4.1, 6.1, 6.2, 6.3, 9.1, and 9.2). Furthermore, the significance of the animals' apparent fear of the Meridoge and of their subsequent flight over the road of Bakororo is obscure. The implied western movement of the species is a possible reference to either the daily/nightly movement from rising in the east to setting in the west, or again a reference to the apparent eastward movement of the sun and moon against the general westward progression of the stars.

That actual observations of the sun are being referred to is clearly suggested in the final part of the myth when the Meri-doge arrive at the summit of a hill (and frighten the howler monkeys), descend onto the adjacent plain, come to the Rio São Lourenço (and frighten the caymans), and finally "arrive at the place from where they had started." This last reference clearly implies an annual cycle, when after apparent north and south migrations along the horizon, the sun will rise and set in its location of a year earlier (assuming that observations are made from the same place). The use of geographic features to mark the apparent motion supports this hypothesis.

In addition, the eleven listed encounters, with up to two other possible encounters implied by breaks in the myth's sequence, suggest an annual period based upon observed lunations. That is, 12–13 synodical lunar months, or months based upon lunar phases and the moon's position relative to the sun, comprise a solar or tropical year (12 synodical months of 29.5 days each falls short of the tropical year by somewhat more than 11 days: $12 \times 29.5 = 354$). The occurrence of fledglings among some of the encounters—specifically with the hawk species—must be interpreted as a seasonal reference based upon the breeding cycle of these birds. I cannot say conclusively whether the other species relate specifically to calendric periods or not, but parakeets, for example, are considered garden pests in the Andes, especially destructive of maturing corn (R.T. Zuidema, personal communication 1986; on March, cf. Guaman Poma de Ayala 1936:1137–38) and may also have threatened Bororo corn plantations near harvest time (January–March).

The sequence of animals encountered by the Meri-doge on their excursion through space-time is indicative of the common Bororo practice of using a nonnumeric sequence as an organizing principle for both space and time. This trait is evident in many examples of native lore, as it is in certain features of village organization, e.g., the arrangement of the "guards of the night" and pseudo age classes along the Tugarege moiety, and by extension the complete arrangement of Bororo localized social groups.

It seems evident that this sequenced myth describes the movement of the sun and moon over the course of a year, linking their positions with geographical referents and seasonality. Both the sun and moon are observed on the horizon by the Bororo; a cultural chief of the Paiwoe clan once described the moon's position and movement as being contrary to that of the sun, claiming that when the sun is in the north, the moon is in the south, pointing to the horizon as he said so to illustrate his point. While the moon can be observed to move between northern and southern extremes within a month's time (as opposed to the sun, which traverses this expanse within one year), my informant was referring to the full moon, which is by definition located diametrically opposite to the position of the sun. Probably much more use of horizon observations of the sun and moon was made than has survived into contemporary times. What is clear from the myths of sun and moon is that the Bororo were making consistent solar and lunar observations and preserving the knowledge gleaned from these observations in an allegorical code.

Seven

The Stars as a Paradigm of Order

Unrecounted in other versions of the Toribugu myth as presented in chapter 2 is the sequence of star risings announced by the hero as he waits in the jatobá tree surrounded by belligerent *aroe*, although this myth segment does occur in other Bororo myths. Whether or not the sequence corresponds to an empirically observable succession of stellar risings, its use in indicating the passage of night time in the myth suggests similar schemes actually employed by the Bororo to mark nightly (and by extension, longer) periods of time passage.

Without streetlights or the towering forms of urban structures, and exposed to full view from the cleared center of the village plaza, the star-studded sky of the southern tropics demands and receives considerable attention. The nightly practice of Bororo men is to lie stretched upon mats near the central *baito*, where gazing skyward affords ample opportunity for consistent stellar observations. This practice was also noted by Lévi-Strauss during his 1936 sojourn in Kejara village (1975:240). Especially in June, when the rain clouds have dissipated and before the *fumaça* or smoky haze of the later dry season obscures the sky, nights are exceptionally clear, and the Bororo enjoy the celestial display of a myriad of shining, colored lights.

While interesting in themselves, the variously colored and grouped stars provide the Bororo and other observers with a way to mark the flow of time and a measure against which other environmental observations can be compared and coordinated. The stars in their fixed patterns progress sequentially across the sky and eventually repeat themselves in time and position over the course of a year. Although the observation of individual stars at specific times and in particular positions is significant, stellar observations also comprise an intricate scheme of relationships that include stars observed with respect to other stars, with respect to the horizon or other fixed points in the celestial sphere (such as the zenith), and with respect to the passage of time and contemporaneous nonstellar events. These synchronic and diachronic properties are utilized by the Bororo as part of a process of orientation and integration of themselves in space, time, and the cosmos as they perceive it.

The Origin of the Stars

Stars as a group are referred to in the Toribugu myth as Kiege Barege, a name also employed by several Garças informants. This expression is related to wildlife (*kiege* is literally "birds" and *barege* "animals/mammals") and is also the title of a song genre. More commonly, however, the stars are collectively known as (I)kuieje-doge (the initial "i" was usually not pronounced in Garças), which the *Enciclopédia Bororo* glosses as *ikuieje*: "the face of the possessors of the line" (*EBI*:611; *-doge* is a pluralizer), an odd-sounding expression that nevertheless refers explicitly to the Bororo myth concerning the origin of the stars, in which the eyes or faces of children who ascend to the sky by means of a long string or cord become the stars. Another term for the stars, Ipare, "youths," is a more literal reference to the children who become the stars as told in the stars origin myth. The Salesians have published two versions of the origin of stars myth (Colbacchini and Albisetti 1942:218–19; *EBII*:#22; see also Wilbert and Simoneau 1983:#18 and #19). A version that I collected in Garças village, and that compares favorably with the published versions, is given below.

Origin of the Stars (from a Paiwoe culture chief)

Corn was growing without being planted. The women went to look for corn, but returned with nothing. They left all the children and youths with nothing. [The men were off hunting and fishing.] There was no corn: the women would always return without anything.

There was a child that wanted to go, but the women did not want him to; they did not let him. And they returned a third time without corn. Finally a child went behind them; he had put some *uro* [a red clay or gravel] in his mouth. His mother hit him, and it appeared that blood came from his mouth: the other women said to let him go with the group. He went with the women.

They arrived at the place [where there was corn]: he saw a lot of corn. The women made many things from the corn, such as *kuiada amireu*, a corn bread or cake. The boy put the corn bread in his arrows [he took off the points and put it inside the hollow bamboo tube of the arrow shafts]. The women told him, "Don't tell any of this there in the village." They returned with nothing another time. [Everyone saw that he too had nothing, but he had!] They said, "There isn't any corn."

The next day the women said, "Let's go look for corn." But the little boy did not want to go anymore; his mother now wanted him to go. He ran from his mother's hands and stayed behind.

When the women were already far away, he called the rest of the children, getting them all together. He spoke. "This is what our mothers do; they're doing bad to us. There, they have a lot of corn, but when they arrive here they say they don't have any. They don't like us. You'll see when they arrive they'll say they don't have any corn again." He took off the points of his arrows, hit them, and the corn came out.

"You can eat it, you can eat."

Everyone ate a little. Then he said, "What are we going to do? Where can we go to get away from our mothers? If we hide in the forest the beasts will eat us, and our mothers can find us there also."

One youth [Akaruyo Boroge] said, "Let's go to the sky."

"How will we climb to the sky?"

"We'll go with this line [*akigo*, of thick cotton] to the sky."

"Okay, let's go."

They called all the birds to go up with the end of the line to the sky, but it did not work, the sky was too far.

Piodudo Porerewu [the smallest hummingbird] was called.

"Carry this end up to the sky."

"Okay." He went, the others waiting behind. And then he returned. He fell in the midst of the others; he did not say anything, only lay there panting. They fanned him, and then he spoke. He said, "I tied it at the foot of the *api i* [sucupira] tree."

"In this way it's good."

An old woman had stayed in the village who always took care of the children when the other women left. They cut her tongue, so that she could not speak to the other women.

So then the children got together to climb up the line. They climbed and they climbed, the elder brothers carrying the younger brothers on their shoulders. They climbed and came out of the forest; and then their mothers arrived.

The village was sad. "Where are the children?" "Son, daughter, come, I'm back." Nothing: the village was sad.

They asked the old woman, "Where's my son, where's my daughter?" She said nothing [it was for this that they had cut her tongue], but she indicated towards the sky with her eyes and the motion of her head. The women looked up into the sky and saw the group there.

"Come here, my child, come here and suck," they said, moving their breasts with their hands to attract the children.

Nothing: the children did not want to return.

The group of women began to climb up after the children. Looking back, the children saw the group of women come out above the forest. The last boy [an older boy] cut the line while all the women were on it. All of the women fell, some on top of trees, others on the ground. The line that fell became a vine. Those women who landed sitting upon the ground became tapir, capybara, paca, aguti, collared peccary, white-lipped peccary, that is, animals without a tail. Those others on the ground became mammals with tails: giant anteater, giant armadillo, anteater, porcupine. Those women who fell atop trees became monkeys [*juko* and *bakure*], the howler monkey, coati, and porcupine.[1]

He that cut the tongue of the old woman turned into a cayman.

The women became beasts. The children became something beautiful in the sky. Because of this there are stars in the sky. This is what the Bororo say.

That the origin of the stars myth is also the origin of wild (game) animals marks a perceived relationship between stars and game. It is in this regard that the expression *kiege barege* (literally, "birds mammals") is used for the stars; it is also a reference, like the other Bororo expressions for the stars as a set, to the stars origin myth. The nature of and the relation between stars and game implies a temporal coordination between the two, with stellar observations of pertinent stars or constellations paired with important animal cycles. Such a scheme has been described by Urton in Quechua astronomy (1981a, 1981b). The details of such a system among the Bororo, however, are still obscure, an unfortunate situation whose resolution is hampered by the decreasing reliance on game characteristic of the contemporary Bororo life-style and diet.

The origin of stars myth is concerned with social order and behavior. Traditionally, it was the women's responsibility in

Bororo culture to harvest corn and vegetal foods in general, and to prepare foods for consumption; the men supply the village protein, principally via fishing and hunting. By hoarding the corn for themselves and denying their social responsibilities, the women in the myth threaten the very foundation of society. As a result of their anti-social behavior they become animals, the very food sources hunted and supplied by men. In contrast, the children become something "beautiful" in the sky, stars, which in their orderly arrangement and metered movement serve as both measure and reminder of the significance and process of social order.

By their actions, the women can also be described as attempting to keep their children at the stage of infancy: they do not supply their children with solid food but rather offer them their breasts to suck. This theme is similar to that of the Toribugu myth and of the Gê bird-nester myth as interpreted by Turner (1985): once identified as a fledgling by metaphor and contiguity, Toribugu (the bird-nester) cannot descend to join his waiting relative. If he did so and returned to the family house, he would in effect be condemning himself to perpetual existence as a fledgling/child.[2] Toribugu does eventually come down, but only after a severe period of separation and trial, much of it suspended well above the ground level of his people. When he does return, he is transformed—graphically attested to by his appearance as different animals, particularly the *atubo* deer—or matured. The children in the stars origin myth cannot return to earth; if they did they would continue to be confined to infancy. They remain in the sky as things of beauty, and as reminders of the proper order of things: temporal, spatial, and social order, order they have established at least in part by effecting the origin of game animals. With abundant game for men to hunt, society will be balanced with men's and women's activities, assuring appropriate attention to its requisite order.

Furthermore, at least one version describes the corn as not yet cultivated, but growing wild. The women, by eating the corn outside the village and not bringing any back with them, are maintaining corn in a nonsocialized state. This is analogous to their desire to keep the children as children, for full socialization only occurs with maturation and participation in the adult roles concerned with production and reproduction. The myth, then, talks about both the maturation of the children and the maturation of the corn, relating their respective growth and life cycles and depicting the women's role in cultivating both. Corn takes about four months to ripen, if planted at the beginning of the rains (late September–November), and mature corn can be available from as early as January. In indigenous times the Bororo had access to agricultural produce until at least the beginning of the dry season, and the period of maturation of corn (and by extension other cultigens) is linked in general with the rainy season.

Significantly it is at the end of the rains, simultaneous with the commencement of dry season trekking, that boys are initiated into manhood. The Bororo not only attempt to synchronize different cycles of time but actually superimpose or layer cycles upon one another, seeing the maturation cycle of garden produce as analogous to the maturation and life course of their children. At least one central Brazilian neighbor of the Bororo makes explicit relations between seasonal time and the human life course. The Tapirapé specifically relate the changing seasons to the life-course stages of a culture hero, Petura, who "lives and re-lives his life cycle as the cycle of seasons. In the early rains of October to December, Petura is a small boy (konomi). During the heavy rains of January to March, he is an adolescent youth (churangí). He is a mature man (awachewete) as the rains diminish in April and May, and as the year draws to its close, Petura becomes a marikeura (old man). . . . This symbolizes the agricultural year" (Wagley 1983:178).

In the stars origin myth, the children escape to a plane beyond the nature-culture dichotomy: they become stellar entities in fixed patterns and cycles. It is to the sky and stars that the Bororo turn in order to integrate their social cycles with ecological cycles.

The Bororo recognize and name a large number of stars and constellations (see figure 7.1 following page 146),[3] although what had been the extent of their knowledge and use of celestial lore under the circumstances of a more traditional existence can only be hypothesized today. Data relevant to Bororo-perceived celestial phenomena are arranged in Appendix A (cross-referenced in Appendix B) and include the names and descriptions of stars and constellations, and other topics related to the sky, based on published literature as well as on my own fieldwork.[4] It should be emphasized that the list of Bororo stellar lore in Appendix A, although extensive, must be considered incomplete. Native stellar observations and time concepts are intimately related to their aboriginal life-style, and changes in the latter have particularly affected the former. The once rich and culturally integrated body of Bororo astronomical lore must be appreciated today through the glimpses we have of its surviving remnants.

Akiri-doge, the Pleiades

It is not surprising that the Pleiades, an asterism in the Western constellation Taurus (see figure 7.1), is one of the most important stellar entities observed by the Bororo with reference to marking time, as this distinction is characteristic of native cultures the world over. In South America, for example, the Pleiades cycle is related to that of maize among the Quechua Indians of Misminay (Urton 1981b:118–21) and among the Barasana of the Rio Pira-Paraná to the complex cycle of male initiation, the seasons, and the availability of certain fruit (S. Hugh-Jones 1979:65–66). The French monk Claude d'Abbeville makes one of the earliest references from the New World of the use of the Pleiades by the Tupinambá to predict the coming of rains (1963/1614:317 [chap. 51]). For the Tapirapé, another Tupian group, Wagley reports that the Pleiades were used to mark both rainy and dry seasons. "Their appearance on the horizon in late October or November announces the beginning of the rains, and their disappearance in April promises the coming of the dry season" (1983:50). Among the Eastern Timbira, Nimuendajú describes the Pleiades as the most important constellation, saying that "when they become visible above the western horizon after sunset, this is taken as a sign that the rainy season is approaching and that it is time to make clearings for planting" (1946:233).

The Bororo most commonly call the Pleiades Akiri-doge (two other appelations, Okire-doge and Ikuie, are rarely used today); *akiri* is "white down" but also refers to the *anjiko* (Portuguese) tree whose leaves or flowers are said to resemble down (-*doge* is a pluralizer). The Akiri-doge are used to mark time on both a nightly and seasonal scale. There is also a probable correlation between the *anjiko*'s annual cycle, e.g., when it blooms, and the annual cycle of the Pleiades, but this has not been confirmed. Nightly, the position of the Akiri-doge is used effectively to measure the passage of night time, especially from October through February (conditions permitting, as this is the rainy season) when this group is most prominent in the night sky. The group's presence or absence in the night sky, the time of its rising or setting at night, and its position in the sky at culturally significant times throughout the year are all observed for seasonal references.

The Bororo especially note the position of the Pleiades at dawn or dusk and coordinate certain of these observations with specific cultural and ecological events. These observations (including a

Table 7.1

An Akiri-doge (Pleiades) Calendar

Calendar Date	Sun Time	Pleiades/Akiri-doge	Cultural/Ecological Events
Mid-June	Dawn	First heliacal rise	Akiri-doge Ewure Kowudo ceremony; trekking; full dry season
Mid-August	Dawn	"Overhead"	Strong winds
September equinox	Dawn	60° in West	Burning fields
Early October	Dawn	45° in West	Planting; rains begin
Late November	Dusk	Rise	Full rainy season
Late April to early May	Dusk	Set	Rains ending
May through mid-June	(Night)	Not visible	Gardens can begin to be cleared

period of nonvisibility) encompass the solar year in a set, summarized in table 7.1, that can be related at any time by those knowledgeable; such knowledge is fundamental for and indicative of possible further codification of a calendar based on stellar observation. Watched consistently, the Pleiades serve as one reference to mark pertinent cultural and ecological events. For example, when the Pleiades are low in the west at dawn, around early October, crops should be planted as the rains are imminent. Similarly, their setting at dusk in late April to early May signals the end of the rainy season and the beginning of preparations for the boys' initiation ceremony. The system of noted Pleiades positions is not an absolute clock or calendar, however, but rather is combined with other environmental particulars to yield temporal information accurate enough to result in the strategic and adequate utilization of available resources and the integration of social and natural cycles.

Particularly significant is the relationship between the position of the Pleiades and the performance of the Akiri-doge Ewure Kowudu ceremony ("the burning of the feet of the Pleiades"), a ceremony that closes the initiation of Bororo boys into manhood, marks the incipience of the trekking season, and corresponds with the final rites of the funerary period. This ceremony occurs when the Pleiades first appear heliacally over the eastern horizon preceding sunrise in mid-June, after a disappearance from the night sky for over one month. By burning the feet of the Pleiades, the Bororo hope to slow their progress in the sky and, by extension, that of their favorite season. This "slowing down" is perhaps suggested to

132

the Bororo by solar movement, since at this same time of the year the sun is seen to "stand still" at the June solstice: *sol* (sun), and *stice* (from the Latin *stare*, "to stand"). The Akiri-doge Ewure Kowudu synchronizes astronomical, ecological, and social time, links the realms of nature, society, and the spirit world, and highlights the significance of astronomical observations in Bororo culture.

Other Stars of Importance

Stars, as a named set, pertain to the Apiborege clan. The major, perhaps only, exception to this is the star (actually a planet) called Orowaribo Kajijewu, "the star that is/rises over the great water"—Venus in its western appearance as evening star. According to some informants this name refers to the Paraguay River, which was once the western boundary of the Eastern Bororo culture area. Orowaribo Kajijewu pertains to the Baadajebage Xebegiwuge clan, but no explanation for this anomaly could be elicited (note, however, that Baadajebage Xebegiwuge is the westernmost clan of the Exerae moiety and is the clan of the hereditary chief Bakorokudu, and of Meri, Sun). Nor is it clear why the stars pertain to the Apiborege clan. One possible explanation concerns the role of Akaruyo Boroge, of the Apiborege clan, in the origin of the stars. As the apparent leader of the children—he was named in one version collected in Garças Village—it is his plan and organization that result in the children's escape to the sky, and therefore the origin of the stars. Akaruyo Boroge is also the name and name group of one of the original hereditary chiefs. Another relationship between the stars and the Apiborege clan is that empirically a large number of Bororo-named stars and constellations rise over Apiborege clan space as seen from the village plaza.

The stars are named in a myth or myths separate from their origin tale. In the most common versions a frightened boy who has angered his father hides in a tree in the forest; that night forest spirits call out the names of certain stars as they rise (Colbacchini and Albisetti 1942:253–54; *EBII*:#23; Wilbert and Simoneau 1983:#20 and #21). Several features of this myth are similar to the segment of the Toribugu myth in which the stars are named: in both cases a boy is in conflict with and separated from his father; in both cases the boy is hiding in a jatobá tree; and in both cases the boy is surrounded by (the same) belligerent spirits. Four different sequences of star names as they are either given in published myth versions

Table 7.2
Star Sequences as Given in the Naming of Stars Myth

Version A (Toribugu myth)	Version B (Fieldwork)
(O)Koge Joku	Tuwagowu
Bokodori Jari Paru Kajeje-wuge	Barogwa Jeiba
Tugiga Kiwu	(I)Kuieje Kujagurewu
Tuwagowu	Barogwa Tabowu
Jekurirewu	Jekurirewu
Barogwa Tabowu	Akiri-doge
Akiri-doge	
Barogwa Kododu	

Version C (*EBII:#12*)	Version D (Colbacchini and Albisetti)
Jekurireu	Bika Joku
Akiri-doge	Akiri Dogue
Bace Iwara Arege	Baxe Iwararegue
Pari Burea-doge	Kuddoro
Tuwagou	Upe
Kudoro	Pari Burea Dogue
Bika Joku	Geriguigui
Jerigigi	Gecurireu
Upe	
Bokodori Jari Paru Kado Jebage	

or supplied by Garças informants are listed in table 7.2. These sequences differ in the number, order, and identity of named stars/constellations, and the preliminary identification of the sequence elements reveals little correspondence to empirical observations of star sequences.[5]

Accurate identifications of stars and constellations are difficult to obtain. Many young Bororo today appear ignorant of the names of all but the most prominent stellar entities, while among older informants the amount of celestial knowledge varies. Additional problems arise in actually perceiving which stars pertain to the identifications proffered by informants, a situation that the beam of a high-powered flashlight and accessible sky charts can only partially alleviate. Nor were consistent nightly observations with all of the village elders feasible during my field stay in Garças village. On the other hand, gaps or contradictions in stellar information may serve as data in themselves. In the noteworthy work of Von del Chamberlain on the astronomy of the Skidi Pawnee (1982), similar gaps and contradictions, including multiple names for certain astronomical bodies, are apparent in the identifications of Skidi stars/constellations.

Bororo informants are unanimous in citing the dry season months, particularly June, as best suited for stellar observations. Throughout the nights of June the stars are bright and bountiful, including many of the best known Bororo constellations and a particularly impressive section of the Milky Way. Depending upon their own cycles, some planets are also generally visible (while undistinguished as a named set from the stars, planets do comprise distinct observations), and more than occasionally the momentary brilliance of a shooting star trails across the night sky. In the following paragraphs I describe the positions of some stars at sunset, midnight, and dawn in early, middle, and late June. Reference to figure 7.1 will be helpful in following the description, as would consulting either a celestial globe or adjustable star chart.

At sunset in early June, the pincers of Scorpius, one of the Bororo Upe or turtle constellations, are rising, with Corvus as Jerigigi, a type of tortoise, high in the east and the Southern Cross—Pari Burea, the "foot/track of the rhea"—with the Coalsack, the rhea's head, high in the south. In the west Rigel and accompanying stars—another Jerigigi—sits above the horizon (Orion's belt is known as Baxe Iwara Reuge, for which no clear gloss could be obtained). Other prominent stars are also observable. The head of Hydra is another Upe high in the west, while the cayman Uwai is identified as either Canopus and its neighboring constellations or stars of Virgo, Hydra, and Corvus. Near the Southern Cross are other features of the rhea: α and β Centauri as Pari Bopona, the rhea's thigh; Pari Itoru—the "rhea's neck"—is a black area of the Milky Way near the Coalsack; and a large patch of black Milky Way comprises the body of the celestial Pari or rhea (figures 7.1 and 7.2). Also near the Southern Cross much of the constellation of Centaurus is identified as a rifle and shotgun (Boeiga Kurirewu and Boeiga Biagarewu). The brightest star of the sky, Sirius—known as Tuwagowu—is visible in the west, and near it black parts of the Milky Way are known as Kaia and Kaibore, a mortar and pestle, respectively (an alternative mortar and pestle were identified in the Milky Way next to the tail of Scorpius). Far to the north the Big Dipper sits cup-down to the horizon; it is called Ke, a type of Bororo headdress, but is also labeled in the *Enciclopédia Bororo* I as Ba Paru Kadoda Jebage, which might refer to a role in orienting the village, as *ba paru* is the western portion or "base" of the village.

By midnight of early June Scorpius/Upe is at its highest point, followed by Sagittarius among whose stars the Bororo recognize a pair of small deer, Pobogo Imedu and Pobogo Aredu. The Pari con-

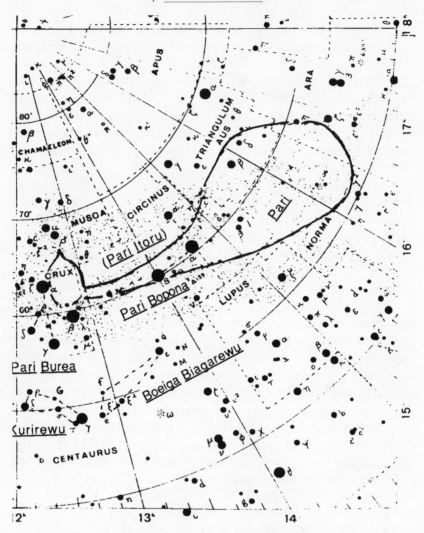

Fig. 7.2. The region of the Southern Cross

stellation and Corvus/Jerigigi are low in the west, while in the east is the small but distinct Delphinus, which Bororo see as the dark blue or hyacinthine macaw, Kudoro. Just preceding sunrise in early June, Scorpius/Upe is setting, the Pobogo pair in Sagittarius is high above it, with Kudoro also past the meridian, and high in the east is Cetus, the Western constellation I identify as the large-antlered Atubo deer of the Bororo. β Ceti, which I identify as Tugiga Kiwu (referring to the antler of Atubo and described as a reddish star rising over the house of Paiwoe, slightly south of east), is part of this constellation and is also given as part of the constellation Bokodori Jari Paru Kado Jebage.

Sunset in mid-June reveals the stars of Orion already set, and Tuwagowu (Sirius) low in the west. Corvus/Jerigigi is near the zenith and the head and foot of Pari (Rhea) are near the meridian to the south. Scorpius/Upe is already high in the east. By midnight Corvus/Jerigigi and the Southern Cross are near setting and Scorpius/Upe has passed the meridian. The Pobogo pair nears the meridian and high in the east Kudoro the macaw is plainly visible. At dawn Scorpius/Upe has set with the Pobogo in Sagittarius nearing the western horizon, Atubo (Cetus) is nearing the meridian, and briefly visible above the eastern horizon before being lost to the sun's glare appear the Pleiades, Akiri-doge (such an observation would traditionally signal the ceremony Akiri-doge Ewure Kowudu).

Sunset in late June is quickly followed by the set of Tuwagowu (Sirius), while Pari Burea (the Southern Cross) and Corvus/Jerigigi stand at the meridian (the latter very close to zenith). Scorpius/Upe is high in the east, and just rising are Pobogo the deer in Sagittarius. After half the night Corvus/Jerigigi has set, the Pobogo are at the meridian, and Delphinus as Kudoro the macaw is high in the east. Just before sunrise the Pobogo are low in the west, Atubo nears the meridian, and the Akiri-doge are high in the east, followed by Aldebaran known as (O)koge Joku, the eye of the *dourado* fish (which may be part of a larger constellation in which the Hyades form the head). Also just visible is Rigel and the Orion/ Jerigigi rising heliacally in the east after their disappearance from the night skies for most of June.

This description of constellations and their movement through time and space as observed from Garças village demonstrates several significant stellar characteristics: (1) the stars stand in fixed patterns relative to each other; (2) the stars move relative to the horizon or other fixed reference point (e.g., meridian, zenith); (3) the motion of the stars is regular and constant; and (4) following from the above, the stars can be—and are—used to accurately gauge the passage of time. To measure time by the stars it is not necessary to make computations or refer to a running count of hours, minutes, and seconds as in our time system. Rather, night time is gauged by the shifting of the stars in space. It can be readily established from the above description that a star or constellation rising at sunset (and positioned diametrically opposite the sun) will cross the meridian at or near midnight (when the sun is at its lower culmination or meridian crossing) and will be setting at sunrise. Such an awareness does not presuppose any knowledge of either the sun's nocturnal position or movement or the notion of a spherical earth. It is knowledge gained from consistent empirical observation.

Thorough knowledge of the stars and their relationships in constellations can result in extremely astute temporal knowledge. Because of their fixed patterns, star positions can be known through the observation of even one stellar entity when viewed at a marked period of time, optimally sunset, since this will cue the observer into all of the remaining length of night time. This is precisely when Bororo men lie stretched upon their mats on the village plaza, looking up at and discussing the stars.

Furthermore, although such knowledge is useful to indicate the advancing "hours" of the night, the relationships of star positions can serve to reckon longer periods of time on a monthly, seasonal, and yearly scale. For example, the sky at sunset in mid-June is essentially the same sky visible at midnight in mid-March and near sunrise of mid-December. Thus, while lunar and other environmental observations are made with reference to monthly and seasonal time, they are all made against a backdrop of regular stellar patterns and movement.

Such detailed and consistent observations of the sky result in the awareness of a period of a "year," even though the Bororo have no precisely corresponding term for such a period. The awaited return of the Pleiades in the dawn sky of June is a yearly occurrence, while other stellar heliacal rises are also almost certainly watched for. The heliacal rise is not observed as an isolated event; rather, it is well placed in the context of both the observed yearly cycle of the particular stellar entity (as evidenced in the case of the Pleiades, whose position is noted with respect to time throughout the year) and the observed recurrent cycle of that star with respect to the myriad other stars amidst which it stands in a relatively fixed relationship.

Bororo conceptualizations of an annual period, however, apparently differ from Western conceptualizations, possibly because of differences in perception and description of celestial mechanics and their underlying cognitive patterns. The Bororo propensity for dual organization, observable in the moiety structure of their village and social system and in their cosmological/ religious beliefs such as those concerning the *aroe* and *bope* dichotomy, is extended to the temporal dimension. Rather than labeling a single period equivalent to our twenty-four-hour day, the Bororo perceive two distinct periods, "day" or *meriji* when the sun is observable in the sky, and *boexo*, night, when it is not, and the world, consequently, is in darkness. Similarly the Bororo "year" is actually a dry and a wet season (*jorukau* and *butaukau*) character-ized by the relative presence/absence of rain.

There is, however, continuity across seasonal periods. The sun, moon, and particularly the stars have a regularity that allows them to be used as a standard for time observations and decisions, although always within the context of corroborating environmen-tal information. In fact, observations of the sun's position (with respect to its north-south peregrination), the moon's position and phases (watched on a nightly, monthly, and yearly scale), and the positions (and perhaps other characteristics, e.g., relative bright-ness) of the stars already characterize a system of multiple layers of observation and cross-referencing. As celestial phenomena with the most regular cycles, or greatest degree of continuity, the stars and sun are the most consistent and therefore the most practical entities with which to compare other temporally concerned obser-vations. It is this characteristic that, among other things, is being alluded to in the origin of the stars myth when the stars are described as beautiful: not only are they colorful and bright, but by coursing in ordered regularity, they consistently reiterate them-selves, expressing the essence of being for the Bororo, who see themselves as socially ordered relatives of the *aroe*, beings who exemplify order and identity.

Other celestial phenomena possess less regular cycles and greater discontinuity and can serve to mark off periods within the continuity of the more regular celestial movements. The moon, for example, is characterized by slightly irregular phases and monthly and yearly movement because its orbital plane is tilted 5° from that of the earth's, and by an inherent "wobble" in its motion. In addi-tion, neither the synodic nor sidereal periods of the moon can be factored evenly into one solar or tropical year, which greatly con-tributes to its discontinuity relative to the sun and stars. (A sidereal lunar month—the moon positioned with respect to the stars—is approximately 27.32 days, thirteen periods of which fall short some ten days of the solar year: $27.32 \times 13 = 355.16$; a synodic lunar month—the moon in reference to the sun—at about 29.53 days also falls short: $29.53 \times 12 = 354.36$; a solar or tropical year can be estimated at 365.24 days.) Planets, shooting stars, and per-haps even comets, while exhibiting possible continuities of their own, are relatively discontinuous with respect to the sun and stars and can be used to mark off periods within the continuity of the more regular bodies and events. Alternatively, these bodies may be so discontinuous as to serve no practical time-reckoning function, but rather as omens for divinatory purposes. One other prominent nocturnal celestial feature, the Milky Way, can also be observed in a continuous cycle.

The Milky Way

Several expressions in Bororo are used to name the Milky Way: (I)Kuieje-doge Erugudu ("the ash—or light/luster—of the stars"), Ipare Erugudu ("the ash—or light/luster—of the youths"), or Ipare Eguru ("the tears of the youths"). All of these terms are references to the origin of stars myth.

Informants commented upon the "interesting movement" of the Milky Way, which, with hand gestures, they show to be a sort of flip-flop motion.[6] This is a rather apt description, since the Milky Way appears as an ellipse that intersects the celestial sphere in a lopsided fashion near its poles. Throughout the course of the night or year its shape may stretch across the very center of the sky, may be barely visible low along the horizon, or may cut diagonally across a portion of the sky. Unfortunately, how accurately this movement was observed by the Bororo and to what use it was put has not yet been fully detailed.

As is common among indigenous South Americans, from whose latitude the Milky Way's light and dark patches are particularly prominent, the Bororo recognize certain dark areas as "constellations."[7] These include Pari, a rhea—an ostrichlike bird—whose head is the Coalsack and whose neck (Pari Itoru) and body follow behind it. Oddly, the rhea's thigh, Pari Bopona, is seen in α and β Centauri, while either its foot or footprint (Pari Burea) is the Southern Cross. As can be appreciated from figure 7.2, this results in the bird's leg and foot extending alongside its neck and head. Informants describe the celestial figure of this large, flightless bird to be either sleeping or running; when confronted with the apparent incongruity of these descriptions, they agree that it is strange but are otherwise unperturbed. The Eastern Timbira also see a rhea in the Milky Way, apparently identical or similar to the Bororo version: "The Milky Way with its dark spots is interpreted as an ostrich . . . whose head lies below the southern cross" (Nimuendajú 1946:233). Nimuendajú reports that the Apinayé also recognize a rhea in the Milky Way, although its location is not given (1967:140).

A black mortar and pestle (Kaia, Kaibore) are also observed, described variously as near Scorpius or extending from Sirius (one of whose names in the literature is Kaibore). One informant also explicitly commented upon a Pari Kigadurewu or "White Rhea" in the Milky Way's lighter areas, a phenomenon that would correspond to Urton's "Light Cloud constellations" (Urton 1981b:111). It is said to resemble the black rhea, but I could obtain no precise identification or location for it.

Very likely more use is (or was) made of the Milky Way than I have been able to ascertain. The Bororo do not seem, however, to utilize a scheme of Milky Way constellations similar to that of the Quechua Indians described by Urton (1981a and b); in the Andean community of Misminay, black animal constellations are closely observed and related to life cycles and behavior patterns of their terrestrial counterparts. Considering that one Bororo term for the stars is Kiege Barege (birds/mammals), and that the origin of the stars is mythically related to the origin of game animals, it is plausible that a similar system among the Bororo may have functioned among observations of star-to-star constellations.

The Planets

Although falling categorically within the general classification of "star," several planets are observed and named by the Bororo and may serve in a somewhat complicated system of "morning star" observations and marked time periods of the dawn and predawn hours.

The Bororo have gained some notoriety in the literature for their ability to see Venus, the next-brightest regular feature of the sky after the sun and moon, in broad daylight (e.g., *EBI*:285; Lévi-Strauss 1969:231, note 14). This feat, however, though impressive, is not as remarkable as it may first appear, and the Bororo are not alone in their ability to make diurnal Venus sightings, as such observations have been recorded among the Pawnee and Quechua Indians.[8] Astronomers A. F. Aveni (1980:83) and A. P. Norton (1964) confirm the possibility of day time Venus sightings. To quote the latter, Venus, "brightest of the planets, sometimes seen in broad daylight, may even cast a shadow" (1964:33). In fact its brightness changes, with "greatest brilliancy during [its] crescent stage—as an evening star about a month after, or as a morning star before, greatest elongation [from the sun], which at maximum is 47°"

(Norton 1964:33). Venus's brightness also varies within a longer time cycle. "The maximum magnitude (–4.4) occurs about every eight years, when Venus is in perihelion near the end of December and south of the Celestial equator as a morning star, therefore more favourably situated for southern observers; she is then twelve times brighter than Sirius [which is the brightest star]" (Norton 1964:33).

Day time observations of Venus, therefore, depend upon a number of factors: the viewing conditions (clarity of the sky), its position with respect to the sun and the earth, some prior knowledge as to its position, and of course keenness of vision. Ability to view Venus under these conditions may or may not indicate a profound knowledge of Venus's cycles, such as those described above by Norton; even prior knowledge of the planet's position could be achieved by recalling its elongation from the sun on the previous evening's sighting (when an evening star) or the same day's morning sighting (when a morning star).[9]

In general the Bororo seem aware that the evening and morning appearances of Venus are manifestations of the same celestial body. Some informants explicitly related that it is. But informants uniformly refer to it by different names in these positions (data that coincide with Chamberlain's Pawnee material). Venus as evening star (its position when visible during my fieldwork) is specifically and consistently referred to as Orowaribo Kajijewu, "that which is/rises over the large water," referring to the Paraguay River to the west of the central area of Eastern Bororo occupation. Another term for Venus, Jekurireu, "the large face," was also given by informants, but the term applies to Venus when in the east, as morning star. At least three other names were given for Venus: Ari Reaiwu, Barogwa Tabowu, and Tuwagowu. The first two of these are positional references (to be discussed in more detail below), while the third may pertain to relative brightness, since Tuwagowu is the name applied to Sirius and one other bright star never identified but said to rise "over the house of Apiborege," that is, southeast.

Given their developed powers of observation, as well as their obvious interest in the night sky, it is difficult to imagine that other planets visible to the naked eye (e.g., Mercury, Mars, Jupiter, and Saturn) are unrecognized by the Bororo. We have some data for at least two of these. Mars is called Bika Joku, "the eye of the *anu-branco* (bird)" (*EBI*:611). *Bika* is the onomotopeic name for the bird that utters this call, which is a good omen for hunting.

Another call of the same bird, *cijiji*, is also used as a hunting omen. Whether or not the planet also serves in this capacity is not discussed in the *Enciclopédia Bororo*, nor was I able to collaborate or extend this information during my work in Garças village.

Jupiter was in the constellation of Scorpius during my field study and was identified by two informants as Barogwa Jeiba. This term is one of three terms that specifically refer to a "morning star" (*barogwa* is "dawn"): Barogwa Jeiba, Barogwa Tabowu, and Barogwa Kododu. Barogwa Jeiba can be glossed as "lord of the dawn," Barogwa Tabowu connotes "with the dawn," and Barogwa Kododu is "increase—or full—dawn." The last expression can be compared with the Bororo *barogwadodu* (table 5.6), which denotes the time just before sunrise. Based upon these glosses and the placement of these terms in the sequences of star names presented in table 7.2, these expressions suggest a series of observed celestial entities appearing and named in the sequence given above (Barogwa Jeiba, Barogwa Tabowu, Barogwa Kododu). That such a series of observations is made becomes likely in light of the traditional pattern of the "callers that guard the night" (see chapter 5), which involves a sequence of men making announcements and giving instructions at intervals during the predawn to sunrise period. While perhaps any bright star if appropriately positioned at dawn may serve to indicate the moment for a caller to perform, it seems significant in this regard that (a) planets—other than Venus—are generally not designated by nomenclature common to the stars in spite of their presence, and (b) two of the three "morning star" designations are explicitly linked to planets.[10] It is primarily the planets therefore, as opposed to bright stars, that are used in the series of morning star observations, which themselves correlate to the sequence of dawn callers who act as "guards of the night." The morning star names are likely spatiotemporal positional references that are applied to the appropriate celestial entity—particularly planet—when it is in the right place at the right time. This is similar to data that Williamson reports for the Zuni. "Sometimes . . . the demands of certain ceremonies related to Morning Star [Venus] require the appearance of a morning star when Venus is an evening star or not visible. The Zuni then substitute any other convenient planet or bright star" (1984:49). That the planets would be especially prominent in this regard is related to their degree of relative discontinuity as observed among the more continuous flow/patterning of the stars. Perhaps somewhat anomalous to the Bororo, the planets, while very obvious, do not quite fit into the normal scheme of stellar patterns and the naming of stars.[11]

It is not likely that the Bororo were cognizant of the specific cycles of the different planets in terms of periods of counted days. Nevertheless, awareness of their presence and their interplay with well-recognized stars and their regular patterns and cycles of movement may have inspired the Bororo to use planetary appearances in certain locations for intermittent calibrations within the framework of their other stellar observations.

The expression Ari Reaiwu, "that which accompanies the moon," falls along the same lines as the morning star designations. It is specifically applied to Venus, although as with the morning star designations it may be applicable to other planets and even to bright stars (cf. *EB*I:611) in the appropriate position.[12] Both the moon and planets move with respect to the relatively fixed background of stars but are confined within a band of constellations we refer to as the zodiac (ecliptic). Hence it is likely that the moon would be accompanied during some parts of its journey by a planet (an occurrence referred to in Western astronomy as "conjunction"). With its regular appearances as morning and evening star, Venus is the most likely planet to be in frequent conjunction with the moon. Observation of the moon with respect to planets and stars also suggests Bororo attention to sidereal lunar periodicity, an interest prominent in Inca calendrics (Zuidema 1977, 1983).

The stars, fixed in orderly patterns of time and space, are given proper names, in this respect similar to the Bororo themselves who inherit proper names based upon the structural location—localized social group—of their birth. The planets, however, as relatively unfixed in space and time, receive appellations with a spatiotemporal reference. In fact Venus, known for its regular eastern and western appearances, is also marked with proper names, while Mars is given a name that refers specifically to a bird whose call is a divinatory device, i.e., characterized by discontinuity with respect to the regular flow of time.

Counterplay between the regularity/continuity of the stars and the irregularity/discontinuity of the planets affords particular value for prognostication, as indicated by the Mars example. In Bororo mythology, Meri decrees that the Bororo—after having forced the culture hero ingloriously into the sky—must do without his direct counsel and depend rather on signs they might perceive around them. Discontinuous movement and positions within a framework of continuity—including the stars and the specifically alluded to

144

sun—provide the substance of such signs. Even the moon's monthly reappearance in crescent form is observed for indications relevant to weather prediction (see chapter 5).

Although the stars exist in orderly patterns and move with regularity both throughout the year and yearly, corresponding environmental phenomena can nevertheless vary from year to year. The two serve as different layers of time that are observed and compared with each other. Social time is yet another layer, and an attempt is made to synchronize these layers at the heliacal rise of the Pleiades in June, when male youths are initiated into adulthood. The relatively discontinuous movement of the planets among the stars, at the same time fixed within the ecliptic band and possessing periodicities of their own, serves as yet another layer of temporal indicators. Amidst the various temporal layerings that can be recognized (e.g., ecological cycles, social cycles, the sun, moon, stars, and planets), a series of analogies can be constructed reflecting the relationship of the continuous and discontinuous:

> continuous : discontinuous : : sun : moon : : stars : planets : :
> cosmic (astronomical) time : ecological and social time.

It is the difference between the analogs, and their interplay, that produces meaning and measure for the Bororo and almost certainly for other native Brazilian groups as well.

Shooting Stars and Comets

Perceived by the Bororo as too irregular in appearance to serve as yet another layer of temporal reckoning, shooting stars or meteors and comets are left, in their extreme discontinuity, with only a prognosticatory function (that is, as omens).

Aroe Kodu is the expression applied to a shooting star or meteor. It literally connotes "flight of the soul" and is perceived as a bad omen. One interpretation of its occurrence is that a malicious spirit (*bope*) is stealing someone's soul. Traditionally a *bari* shaman is called upon to interpret the event. During my stay in Garças village, the observation of some of the most spectacular shooting stars I have ever witnessed produced little or no response from the villagers; however, it should also be noted that the period of observation of most of these coincided with a period when the village lacked a resident *bari*.

Another category of shooting or moving star is called (I)Kuieje Kodu, "flight of the star." Although informants placed it in contrast to the Aroe Kodu, none were ever specifically identified, and so it is not clear upon what the contrast between the two is based.

One informant further contrasted the two categories above with what he claimed was a recent phenomenon, one he called a "walking star" (*estrela andando* in Portuguese). It was my informant's claim that it is not a real "star," but man-made. When such a phenomenon was pointed out, these "walking stars" actually had two different appearances: one was a steady, regular movement of a single point of light, most probably an orbiting satellite. The other was also a single point of light, but with erratic movement that could unexpectedly appear or disappear. Neither of these phenomena are accompanied by perceivable sound. Although both types would occasionally arouse comment, they were unaccompanied by any relevant activity.

Comets are called (I)Kuieje Ukigureu in Bororo ("tailed star," *EBI*:612). Unfortunately, little else is known about Bororo observation of and reaction to this infrequent phenomenon.

The Toribugu Myth: Analysis with Respect to an Astronomical Code

Lévi-Strauss has been a pioneer in demonstrating the presence and significance of astronomical coding in myths through analysis revealed in his *Mythologiques* series. His key myth, a version of the Toribugu myth, supplies examples of such a coding, and as our knowledge of Bororo astronomy has been advanced since Lévi-Strauss originally presented his analysis, further investigation into the astronomical coding of the Toribugu myth is warranted.

In *The Raw and the Cooked*, Lévi-Strauss is concerned with an opposition between the constellations of Corvus and Orion that relates to their roles as seasonal referents as perceived in the Northern and Southern hemispheres and in Old and New World mythology. Among the Bororo and in the Toribugu myth, Lévi-Strauss identifies the mythical figure of Jerigigiatugo (Toribugu) with the constellation Corvus Jerigigi (1969:228; see also Colbacchini and Albisetti 1942:219). In doing so, Lévi-Strauss rejects data presented by the *Enciclopédia Bororo* identifying the constellation of Jerigigi with a part of the constellation of Orion (*EBI*:612; illustration, 613).[13] He also notes the confusion in identifying different types of turtles in the Mato Grosso area, since the Portuguese terms *jabuti* and *cágado*, normally used to distinguish between an aquatic turtle and land tortoise, respectively, are commonly interchanged, leading to possible confusions or "transferences" in the identifications of turtles and turtle constellations.

In the case of Bororo turtle constellation identifications, the situation is further complicated as no less than four such constellations exist. Textual and field research reveal two Jerigigi and two Upe constellations (see Appendixes A and B and figure 7.1). For Jerigigi, Rigel and four neighboring stars (one actually of Orion, the other three of the constellation Eridanus) are given as one possibility, and Corvus as another. Upe has as identifications parts of Scorpius and alternatively the head of the constellation Hydra. That all of these identifications are coherent is apparent when recourse is made to the actual celestial locations of these constellations. At about 5^h right ascension the Orion Jerigigi is followed in approximately four hours by the Hydra Upe (right ascension approximately 8.5^h) which is then followed in four hours by Corvus Jerigigi (right ascension approximately 12.5^h), itself followed in about four hours by Scorpius Upe (right ascension 16^h).[14] All of these constellations are within 30° of north-south arc of each other, centering over the celestial equator. This pattern is too systematic to be explained away by coincidence or to negate by claiming erroneous identifications based mainly upon time-depth justification. It is apparent that there is significance to the Bororo turtle constellation scheme, although it is not evident what the significance might be. That turtles are a marked category in Bororo classification is also suggested in Crocker's work (1985:62–63), where it is reported that the turtles *jerigigi* and *upe* are prohibited from the diets of parents of a newborn child, although these two species are "not endowed or subject to the metonymic logic of the [other] foods tabooed during pregnancy," with the exception of "alligators" (*Caiman* sp.).[15]

As constellations alternating in four-hour intervals, the turtles produce the effect of bracketing or ordering nightly and seasonal time. For example, in early June, sunset may be followed by the observation of all four turtle constellations in the sky: Scorpius Upe has just risen and Corvus Jerigigi is high in the east, while Hydra Upe is high in the west and Orion Jerigigi is about to set. By the end of the tropical night, however, all of the turtles are effectively gone from the sky: Scorpius Upe has just set, and Orion Jerigigi is about to rise. With some leeway for the differences—minimized in the tropics—between the seasonal length of daylight and night time, this pattern will reverse itself in early December, when at sunset virtually no part of the turtle constellations will be visible, but following the rise of Orion Jerigigi shortly thereafter, all of the turtles will make their appearance before sunrise. Just before sunrise they will be spread across the sky in a manner analogous to their positions at sunset in early June.

Returning to a discussion of Toribugu and his association with an underlying astronomical code, besides Jerigigiatugo he is also known as Tugiga Tabowu, which can be translated as "he who has his antler" or "the antlered" (*EBI*:1265). This name is an obvious reference to the transformation of the hero into an antlered *atubo* deer in order to take revenge upon his father. The name also bears resemblance to the star Tugiga Kiwu (*tugiga* is "his antler"), itself probably part of the Bororo Atubo constellation. The hero of the myth is therefore associated with another constellation. Although neither the star nor the constellation were identified while in Garças village, Tugiga Kiwu was described as a reddish star that rises over the house of Paiwoe (i.e., south of east). These characteristics are met by β Ceti, and I identify Cetus as the Atubo constellation, which occupies a section of the sky otherwise relatively clear of identified Bororo constellations. This identification has the additional significance of locating Atubo (right ascension approximately 1.5^h) in opposition to Corvus Jerigigi (approximately 12.5^h right ascension), while both are centered about 20° to the south of the celestial equator and therefore pass very near zenith in the Bororo area. Both also rise "over the house of Paiwoe," the clan to which Toribugu (also called Jerigigiatugo or Tugiga Tabowu) belongs. They are spaced about twelve hours apart and achieve prominence overhead half a year apart (for example, Corvus Jerigigi is in the zenith at midnight towards the end of the rainy season in March and April, while Cetus Atubo achieves the same position in October or at the beginning of the rains).

Lévi-Strauss had made one other astronomical identification with respect to the Toribugu myth, this time involving the Pleiades. When the hero of the myth transforms himself into the large, antlered *atubo* and attacks his father, the latter is impaled and tossed into a lagoon where he is consumed by piranha, while his liver and lungs float to the surface and become water plants. Lévi-Strauss presents a set of myths with similar segments, in some of which there is a relation between floating organs, aquatic plants, and the Pleiades (1969:243–45). The incident in the Toribugu

148

myth therefore may also be a code reference to the Pleiades star cluster and presumably some portion of their cycle.

Briefly, the astronomical coding latent in the Toribugu myth as advanced by Lévi-Strauss includes an identification of the internal organs of the hero's father with the Pleiades (1969:243), while the hero himself is related to the constellation Corvus Jerigigi, significant because the hero is associated with wind and heavy rains (i.e., the rainy season), and because according to Lévi-Strauss's postulation, the Bororo associate Corvus with the rainy season (1969:229).

Given the present state of our knowledge, it is possible to elaborate beyond these preliminary suggestions. First, the name of the hero links him to more than one constellation: as Jerigigiatugo he is related to both Corvus and Orion (each called Jerigigi), and by this identification to a scheme of Bororo turtle constellations whose significance is not yet completely clear. In addition, as Tugiga Tabowu the hero is related to the Atubo constellation or Cetus. This information needs to be put into perspective with respect to the myth's diachronic sequence.

Each myth version begins with the Bororo still resident in the main village, i.e., not yet involved in dry season trekking. However, the version included in chapter 2 begins with the hero's mother collecting a wild tuber said by informants to be available only during or immediately prior to the dry season. Another version begins with women collecting palm for the penis sheaths to be presented to boys upon their initiation, which must occur with the heliacal rise of the Pleiades in June. The myth, therefore, begins at a time when the rains have already ceased, but before the first heliacal rise of the Pleiades, which signals the initiation of youths and the commencement of trekking; the time is probably late April or May. The hero's attempts to locate his people after his separate wanderings include several explicit references to the dry season, including the availability of certain foods and the shifting campsites of his fellow villagers. His reunion with the village is accompanied by wind and rains, an almost certain reference to the returning rainy season. The informant who supplied the detailed account in chapter 2 commented at the end of his narration that the incidents occurred at the time we were then in, late April. While this is most likely a reference specifically to the myth's beginning, it may also refer to the myth's final episode: after the winds and rains that accompany Toribugu's reappearance, there is an unspecified period of village residence, a likely correspondence to the rainy season. Finally, the fateful deer hunt is likely to occur at the end of the rainy season after fawns born at the beginning of the rains have matured enough to allow adult deer more mobility. The myth therefore appears to start and finish at roughly the same time of year—during the transition from rainy to dry season—and to encompass a year's time.

Although Lévi-Strauss allows a single astronomical referent to imply a specific temporal period, simply relating a constellation to a certain time of year may obscure rather than clarify the relevant native concepts. For example, although Corvus Jerigigi rises heliacally (with the sun) at the beginning of the rainy season (October), it is observed rising in the evenings in May and is therefore quite prominent in the night sky of the dry season. Cetus Atubo is characterized by a cycle just opposite to that of Corvus Jerigigi, while Orion Jerigigi heliacally rises in June but is prominent overhead at midnight in December and as a result of its proximity to the Pleiades has a cycle that in general conforms to that of this important star cluster (see table 7.1).

To interpret these astronomical identifications within the context of the Toribugu myth, when the myth begins, near the first heliacal rise of the Pleiades (since palm is already being prepared for the male initiation), the hero's position subordinate to his father is illustrated by the precedence of the Pleiades—related in the myth's final episodes to his father—over Orion Jerigigi in the sky (the former is closely followed by the latter). A season later the heliacal rise of Corvus Jerigigi coincides with the beginning of the rains in October and with the hero's return to the village—this time no longer subordinate to his father nor in spatial proximity to him, indicated by their separate abodes in the village and reflected in the celestial distance separating Corvus Jerigigi and the Pleiades. By the end of the rains, Cetus Atubo is rising heliacally, illustrative of the hero's dominance over his father who as the Pleiades follows some four hours behind, not visible at all in the night sky during this period.

This interpretation of the astronomical data with respect to the myth sequence correlates well with the interpretations of the myth presented in chapter 2. That is, the seasonal references in the myth, substantiated by the astronomical code, indicate that the myth action transpires during the course of one year, beginning and ending near the time of the heliacal rise of the Pleiades, the final stage of male initiation. The myth details the maturation of a male Bororo individual (and by extension males collectively) from boyhood to adult, a transition traditionally related to the course of one year that culminated in the imposition of the penis sheaths on the youths (*ipare eno o badodu*) and the transformation of the boys into cultured adults via the mediation of fire during the Akiri-doge Ewure Kowudu ceremony. Thus the calendric significance of the period of the heliacal rise of the Pleiades as emphasized in the myth is particularly appropriate.[16]

Interpreted in this manner, the Toribugu myth is drawn even closer to the origin of the stars myth, in that both relate the annual cycle of natural, ecological time to the period of social maturation. Clearly the Bororo are concerned with synchronizing and superimposing different temporal cycles and thereby integrating themselves within the cosmos. In addition, as the Toribugu myth also details (1) the general cultural development of the Bororo through their acquisition of rattles essential to ritual; (2) the complex of animals associated with retribution killing for a deceased performed by a member of the opposite moiety; and (3) control over fire, the emphasis on the period of transition from rainy to dry season is also appropriate, as the heliacal rise of the Pleiades at this time also signals the end of the funerary period and the period of most significant Bororo ritual.

In order to better promote social production and reproduction, Bororo society attempts to integrate its social space with social time and to integrate social space-time with cosmic space-time. Table 7.3 details some of the overlapping and intermeshing layers of temporal cycles of the Bororo calendar.[17] The yearly cycle reflects and is analogous to the various temporal cycles of which the Bororo are aware, all conforming to a single model. The human cycle of growth, maturation, reproduction, and death and cosmic cycles expressed through the movements and representations of the *aroe* spirits are integrated within the annual calendar. This attempt at integration is seen in correspondences between certain celestial and Bororo social processes:

> (1) The major east-west village axis and the directionality of the daily movement of celestial entities (particularly the sun);
>
> (2) The reversal of the principal east-to-west movement by the moon, perceived as "rising" in the west, as well as the apparent slipping eastward of the sun and moon with respect to the stars, and ceremonial processions of actors proceeding from west-to-east into the dance plaza;

Table 7.3
Partial Depiction of the Bororo Calendar

Months	Sun	Pleiades	Climate	Residence	Agriculture	Ecology	Ceremony
June	21 Solstice	1st Heliacal rise	*DRY* / *JOKURU*	*TREKU* / *MAGRU*	Clear gardens	*Jatobá* fruit (*Bokwado*)	*Akiri-doge Ewure Kowudu* (Male initiation, end of funeral)
July						*Manai* flower: parakeet young	
August	4 Zenith	Overhead at dawn	Strong winds			*Manu guru oko* flower: fish arrive	Training of new initiands begins
September	21 Equinox	60° in west at dawn	Light rains	*MAIN VILLAGE*	Burning fields	*Ema oko* flower: rains	(Funerary period begins)
October		45° in west at dawn	*RAINS* / *BUTAOKU*		Planting	*FISH*	*AROE IN VILLAGE*
November	12 Nadir						
December	21 Solstice	Rise at dusk					
January					*HARVEST*	Piki fruit (*eko*)	*Kuiada paru*: Green corn ceremony
February	1 Zenith					Cashew fruit (*jatugo*)	
March	22 Equinox						
April		Set at dusk	Light rains		Begin to clear gardens	*Kuoga* flower: cold	*Mano* races (when no funeral)
May	10 Nadir	Not visible	Dry				

(3) The north-south-north movement of the sun over the course of the year, and the north-to-south or south-to-north movement of males in the village over the span of the life course, as well as the direction of all intermoiety exchanges;

(4) At 15° S. Lat. the fact that the sun is observed for the greater part of the year in the northern part of the sky, and the structural location of the hereditary chiefs in the northern (Exerae) moiety;

(5) The sun's daily movement when north of its zenith passages (i.e., for most of the year) is observed as counter-clockwise, and this is likewise the main direction of movement in all Bororo ceremonies that include circular dance patterns; and the corollary of the above, the sun's less frequent clockwise motion, and the occasional clockwise reversal of otherwise counterclockwise dance movements; and

(6) The observance of the circular disc of the sun, the sun's annual "circle" or cycle, and the circularity of the village and in general the recursivity of all social space and time.

These observations suggest that the Bororo are concerned with actively replicating their social world after what they perceive in the cosmos around them, which in turn is re-replicated from their social realities. Astronomy therefore has metaphoric relevance to society since society can be seen as an assembly of parts in relation to each other, producing and reproducing itself, as the various celestial entities repeat themselves over space and time. Bororo society offers a prime example: the social groups are ideally structured in a synchronic arrangement composing village organization, undergoing the diachronic periodicity of natural and social life courses. The nature of the relationship between astronomy and society among the Bororo is more than metaphor, however: it is structural, in that each is defined with respect to the other; and it is processual, in that each is used to actively replicate or transform the other.

Eight

Structure and Process in Bororo Society

For the Bororo, village organization is patterned by their social structure and orients the inhabitants in both space and time. Organizing features of the social system common to all Bororo villages include two moieties—Exerae in the north and Tugarege in the south—established by a major east-west axis, four localized clans and their subdivisions within each moiety, and "upper" and "lower" village halves formed by a secondary north-south axis. The central men's house is positioned along this axis, crosscutting the primary moieties. In that all things observed in the Bororo universe pertain to one or another of the localized social groups, Bororo village organization relates the society via its underlying organizational principles with the rest of the cosmos. A basic comprehension of this fact is fundamental for approaching any investigation of Bororo culture.

Chapter 3 presents various models of the Bororo village, ranging from a simplified scheme through idealized patterns to the layout of a contemporary village. As these deal principally with spatial components of Bororo social organization, they present mainly the static aspects of Bororo society. Perception of village and social organization from the additional perspective of (social) time yields a more dynamic and accurate depiction of the society.

Male spatial occupancy is specifically related to social development. Men live first in the natal house (that of the mother and mother's name group/subclan/clan to which they pertain), from which they traditionally move to occupy the men's house at the center of the village plaza immediately following their initiation into adulthood. Afterwards, marriage and uxorilocal residency locates them in the house of their wife and wife's parents, so that over time Bororo males shift in habitation from village periphery to village center and back to periphery again, and from one moiety to the other. Since the moieties are predicated by the east-west village axis, male life-course movement is directionally north-to-south or south-to-north, depending upon the moiety of their birth.

This movement of Bororo males is paralleled by movement within the category of *iorubodare* relations, which encompass not only marriage and affinal relations but traditionally extend beyond affinally related households to incorporate relations at the structural level between clans, subclans, and name groups. These relations are fundamental for the exchange of goods and services across moiety lines and result in a complex of dynamics that are conceived of by the Bororo as lines or paths (*utawara*) that crisscross village space, weaving together the village's social components. Such dynamics, not readily apparent in the static diagrams of the spatial organization of Bororo society, illustrate that a grasp of Bororo village and social organization requires the perspective of both space and time.

The integration of process with the static aspects of Bororo social and village structure is indicated in many ways. In the outline of the village residential periphery, for example, three of the four quarters of the village are characterized by two clans each. The southwest quadrant in the Tugarege moiety, however, is characterized by a reduplication of clans and ideally encompasses groups from four clans.

Whether or not four clan groups are represented in this quarter in each village, this quadrant is always marked by some reduplication.[1] Reduplication within the clan organization introduces a dynamic principle at the most basic level of village structure. This "dynamic principle" is a factoring process, since the usual clans (or major social units) per quadrant become four, a total that in itself is a factor (2×4) of the complete set of Bororo clans. The importance here is not the specific mathematics as much as the dynamic process revealed in the village structure.

The spatial structure of Bororo village organization is directly linked with time in the system of dawn callers (chapter 5), men who alert the village to the approach of day. Structurally located along the Tugarege side of the village, these five men function sequentially in space-time, proceeding from west to east as predawn and full dawn advance towards the rise of the sun over the eastern horizon.[2] The significance of these men's positions and their function is reiterated through the placement and responsibility of the last of the sequence, Meriri Baru, in the men's house. As the easternmost guard of the night, Meriri Baru makes his announcement immediately before sunrise; he guards not only the night and "entrance" of the day but the entrance of the village as well, since his structured position is directly adjacent to the eastern

155

end of the primary village axis. He is likewise positioned closest to the Tugarege door in the *baimanagejewu*, the men's house, and also acts as guard of that entrance. Thus the Bororo are using the space-time patterning of social structure as a premise for social function, or vice versa.

I use the scheme of guards of the night and its space-time relativity as a model to hypothesize a more structured set of age classes for the Bororo than has hitherto been suggested. Based upon data presented by Zarko Levak and the *Enciclopédia Bororo* (see chapter 4), I suggest that the Bororo had a set of eight age classes, structurally positioned within the Tugarege moiety—as in the case of the guards of the night—with only one class's name pertaining to an Exerae clan, the Baadajebage Xebegiwuge at the western base of the village adjacent to the principal axis. While no direct evidence as yet details a sequential system of age-class function, the pattern of night guards suggests that the eight age classes may have served in a west-to-east sequence to order Bororo males spatiotemporally, a juxtaposition with their north-south/south-north spatial shifts already described.

Data from other central Brazilian groups (e.g., a five-year period between initiations for the eight age-sets of the Shavante, and a forty-year cycle of localized age classes among the Timbira) contribute to this hypothesis in that the Bororo eight-class system may have organized village males in five-year intervals within a forty-year cycle, in structured positions running from west to east (counterclockwise) along the village circumference principally within Tugarege space. The Bororo were able to mark an annual period analogous to our solar year as evidenced by their attention to heliacal stellar phenomena and so could also have maintained the regularity of such a multiyear system (as do the Shavante), especially since much of the actual "counting" in such a scheme could have been tallied among positioned social groups of the village pattern. Boys were chosen for initiation based upon their physical development as opposed to age in counted years. The span of approximately five years between initiations has the advantages over yearly initiations of promoting social cohesion by gathering a large group of boys and of conserving village energy and other resources. A flexible five-year cycle of initiation, marked specifically by eight localized groups, would encompass the average forty-year active span of a male villager's life.

Bororo village orientation centers upon its principal east-west axis, which is based upon the sun and its daily path. Significantly, in the Bororo heartland area (the Rio São Lourenço and its tributaries) terrestrial water also flows predominantly from east to west. Therefore the village plan is in accord with and channels the flow of cosmic forces as they are perceived in solar movement and in the run of terrestrial water. This accord with cosmic power is graphically represented in village space-time by the placement and function of the *aije rea* (the path of the *aije*) and *aije muga* (the plaza of the *aije*), features that extend westward along the major axis past the village plaza and the residences along its circumference. These two features are used during the heightened ceremonialism of the funerary period, including the final male initiation rites. Bororo males representing the *aroe* enter village space from these features, and they are particularly significant for the activities and entry of the *aije-doge*, aquatic *aroe* who represent male and spiritual power.

The *aije* function exclusively in male initiation and in the final phase of the funeral, marking the transition both of boys to manhood and of mortal being (*boe*) to spirit (*aroe*). These beings embody the link of men with *aroe* by ushering boys into manhood and the concomitant duty/ability to represent *aroe* in ceremony, and by ushering the soul of the departed mortal *boe* into the spirit world of the *aroe*. The *aije* represent the antithetical relationship of the *aroe*—beings connected with structure and identity—with respect to transformations in states of being.

Thus *aije* are active when social process most threatens to reduce the orderliness of society to chaos, such as when a member of society dies, and when boys mature into sexually active adults capable of social reproduction both physically and ceremonially. When drawn by a native informant (see figure 3.2), the village with its *aije rea* and *aije muga* extension takes on a phallic image, illustrative of Bororo conceptions of power. It is male penetration of the female that joins the sexes as well as the categories of *bope* (transformation, process) and *aroe* (identity, structure) and results in the growth of new life. The *aije rea* and *aije muga*, extensions of the village and positioned along its axis, penetrate the cosmic domains of sky/earth/water, upper world and underworld, society and nature, mortality and spirituality. It is by the penetration of these domains that power flows, and both power and penetration are traits associated with adult males. Consequently, the *aije* cult is ideally maintained as privileged or secret among Bororo men; viewing of the *aije* by uninitiated boys and all females is considered extremely dangerous and potentially lethal.

157

Dynamism in the "static" aspects of village organization also flows along a historical sociopolitical process mapped out on the village plan: the movement of the two original chiefs proceeds from southernmost positions to west and east extremes (see figure 8.1). Birimodo (Aroroe Xobugiwuge), one of the original Bororo chiefs, is not represented in the night guards scheme although he is related to it: he is credited with instructing the Bororo on how to tell time and specifically with organizing the night callers system. When he ceded his chiefly powers to his father Bakorokudu (Baadajebage Xebegiwuge), he became Bakororo, chief of the village of the dead at the western extreme of the world. His counterpart Akaruyo Boroge (Apiborege Xebegiwuge), who is part of the night guards scheme, likewise ceded his powers to his father Akaruyo Bokodori (Baadajebage Xobugiwuge) and became Itubore, chief of the village of the dead at the eastern extreme of the world.

Sociopolitical positioning is also related to natural time via directionality. That is, Birimodo, original culture chief, is related to night and west: west, *meributu*, where the sun sets spatially, temporally introducing the night. Birimodo's powers, ceded to Bakorokudu at the western extreme of the village, include primacy in displays and rituals that take place in the village, linking the west with inside. The other original culture chief, Akaruyo Boroge, is a member of the night guards who announce the coming of day, and he appropriately shifts his position to the east, *merirutu*, where the sunrise begins actual day time. Akaruyo Bokodori, his father and recipient of the original chief's powers, is structurally positioned in the easternmost village section and operates over functions occurring outside village space, linking the east with the outside. In the *baimanagejewu* or men's house, all four hereditary chiefs, that is, the two original chiefs and the two Baadajebage to whom the chiefly powers were ceded, occupy central positions (see figure 3.6). Although the authority of these hereditary chiefs is limited—particularly that of Birimodo and Akaruyo Boroge who ceded their powers away—they nevertheless integrate aspects of social, political, and ceremonial power within themselves. In their centralized location in the men's house, which is itself centralized within the village, these men occupy the intersection of cosmic axes: the horizontal east-west axis along which flows celestial power and terrestrial water; the secondary, horizontal north-south axis, which divides the village into "upper" and "lower" halves; and a vertical axis epitomized by the central pillar of the men's house, which pierces the layers of earth, underworld (although this con-

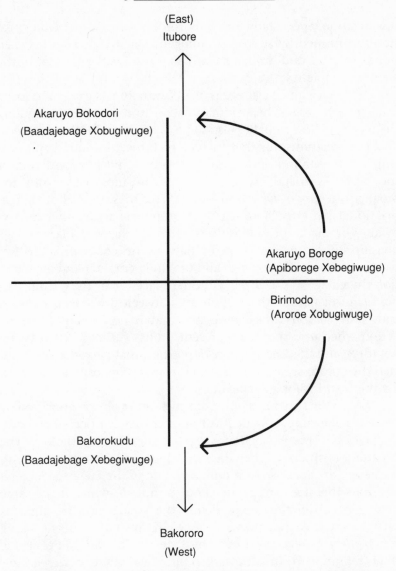

Fig. 8.1. Historical sociopolitical process in a Bororo village.

cept is not very well developed among the Bororo), and heaven. These four men are positioned around, and in a sense become, the "pivot of the four quarters" (Wheatley 1971), by position and function serving to centralize cultural, natural, and cosmic forces.

The foregoing discussion prompts a reconsideration of Lévi-Strauss's question, "Do dual organizations exist?" (Lévi-Strauss 1963a). In his essay, Lévi-Strauss prefers to view the dyadic structures of the Bororo and other societies as special types of triadic

organization. Specifically for the Bororo, he favors the triadic organization formed by supposed endogamic marriage rules between
upper, middle, and lower subclans as preeminent over that of the
exogamic moieties.³

The Exerae and Tugarege moieties function as exogamic social
units, continuing to be a primary factor in mate selection among
the Bororo. These moieties also serve as the basis for the *iorubodare*
alliances, relationships that include reciprocal initiation sponsor-
ship, representation of *aroe* spirit "totems," and representation of
the dead. Marriage unions are also encompassed within the
broader category of *iorubodare* ties. Besides these crucial dual organizational patterns, Bororo culture is replete with other binary,
dyadic, or diametric oppositions, such as the secondary village
division into upper and lower halves; the concentric dualism
between sacred village center and profane perimeter and by extension the village as socialized, cultured space versus the encompassing realm of nature; the dichotomy between dry season trekking
and rainy season village residence that is accompanied by the
period when *aroe* spirits are present (rains) versus when they are
not (dry); and the *aroe* and *bope* opposition that pervades all life. In
fact, the Bororo seem to exhibit an unusual propensity for organizing their world along dyadic lines.

The dyadic structures of Bororo society are always animated by
process. For example, figure 8.1 illustrates the historical, sociopolitical process of Bororo society as explained in their mythology. The
structural positions of the chiefs Birimodo and Akaruyo Boroge in
the village are at the southernmost section of the Tugarege moiety,
positions that are contiguous—and so united—while at the same
time their distinction helps define the village north-south axis
(that is, an axis that passes between them, but also one along
which the Tugarege and Exerae moieties can be said to lie). These
chiefs relinquished their powers to their relatives (considered their
fathers) Bakorokudu and Akaruyo Bokodori, respectively. Bakorokudu and Akaruyo Bokodori are located in opposition at west and
east extremes of the Exerae moiety; they uphold the north-south
axis by polarizing its oppositional high versus low criteria and
establish the important east-west axis that separates the moieties
and that is the crucial path of cosmic forces (a horizontal axis
mundi). The striking feature of figure 8.1 is that by their structural
positions the hereditary chiefs in fact form a triangle, with the
Baadajebage chiefs forming the base and Birimodo and Boroge at
the apex. This shape is formed only indirectly by the exchange of

spouses that constitutes Lévi-Strauss's triadic schemes; more directly it is based upon the exchange of political and ceremonial power.

The various processes involved do not cease there. Birimodo and Boroge, after ceding their powers, go on to become chiefs of the villages of the dead, located at the western and eastern extremes of the world. They thus reenforce the east-west axis mundi, aligning all hereditary chiefs along its course and creating yet another triadic structure, which is concentric in nature: village center is opposed to village periphery, and the entire village is opposed either to its encompassing natural realm or to the distant abode of the spirits. Concentrically, the feature that is furthest removed from the village—the realm of the spirits—is also the feature most closely related to the village center. Dyadic dichotomies act in opposition to form triadic structures that collapse or "implode" to become single units: the four hereditary chiefs, themselves structurally in diametric and triadic organizations, form a single "pivot" in the central confines of the men's house. The Exerae and Tugarege moieties are opposed and yet form a single whole society that is juxtaposed to "outside" or foreign societies. Sherente village organization as depicted by Nimuendajú (1942:16–23) similarly illustrates the relation between a binary, dual organization and a triadic social structure, by locating moieties in the northern and southern arcs of the village but opposing them in the eastern half of the village to clans incorporated from foreign tribes or "outsiders" who occupy the western ends of the open, horseshoe-shaped Sherente villages. One is opposed to two, and two is opposed to many, a conceptual formulation that is expressed in both Bororo social structural models and in their system of numeration. Dual organizations exist not as isolated structures, but rather as phases of the processes animating social organization.

The Sun and Spatiotemporal Mediation

The rights and responsibilities of chieftaincy given by the original Bororo chiefs to Bakorokudu and Akaruyo Bokodori include roles as ritual specialists crucial to the performance of certain ceremonies. These Baadajebage chiefs lead and organize activities that take place both inside and outside the village, plan and "construct" the village by choosing its location, and determine its layout and orientation. Chiefly power and cosmic power are linked by the structural positioning of the chiefs along an east-west axis, the path of cosmic flow, and are also evident in the social relationship between Bakorokudu and Meri (Sun), who pertain to the same clan.[4]

The sun in its regular daily and annual motion exemplifies both space and time, mediating both structure and process. Bororo and Gê circular villages reflect the spherical imagery of the celestial orb of the sun, as well as the temporal cyclicity of solar movement. The annual progression of time is recursive, observed to be the result of the sun's peregrination between northern and southern horizon extremes. Symbolically, the Bororo central men's house, with its cardinal orientation and its location within the circle of family houses, can be seen as representing the linear limits of solar movements: the corners of the men's house, extended intercardinally, are symbolic demarcations of the solstices (see figure 8.2). Furthermore, the interior of the men's house is divided into quadrants, as is the village as a whole, a spatial quartering that must have its analogy in temporal space. The quartering of temporal space is demonstrable diurnally with Bororo observations of sunrise (*merirutu*), noon (*meri baru oyadadu*), sunset (*meributu*), and midnight (*boexo oya*). Annually, important observations of the Pleiades are made on or near both solstices and equinoxes (see table 7.1) and suggest a quartering of the year. The Bororo village pattern with its central men's house is therefore a squaring of the circle, in demonstration of the observation that solar linear spatial movement orders the cyclicity of time (cf. Aveni 1980:223–31).

The sun's characterization in both its celestial and mythical aspects is that of a powerful entity controlling the night, related to life force, and possessing great stores of transformative power. Sun's orderliness, structured movement, and nurturance are opposed to his capriciousness and potential destructiveness. These oppositional traits of the sun can be compared with those related to the two major Bororo spirit categories of *aroe* and *bope*. The *aroe* are connected with order, identity, and structure; for Crocker they represent "immutable categorical form." The *bope* are identified with disorder, change, and process; again according to Crocker, they embody "the principles of organic transformation" (1985). The sun is able to incorporate both sets of traits within himself. The Bororo mark this distinction of the sun by recognizing Meri as an *aroe* but crediting him with being father of the *bope*. On the one hand, this is merely an extension of the Bororo rules of exogamy and matrilineality; on the other hand, the sun mediates or joins the two antithetical sets. Through their combination he is able to effect a complete and living system.

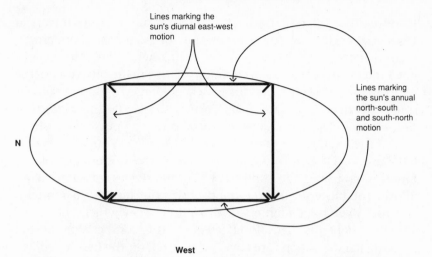

Fig. 8.2. The men's house and squaring the circle. Note: The oblong nature of the circle and the resulting longer east and west sides of the men's house are attempts to represent the longer period required for the sun to make its annual north-south-north journey. This method of representation is based on my assumption, as no Bororo informant ever explicitly expressed such a concept to me.

While the Bororo maintain a dichotomy between the different sets of traits of *aroe* and *bope*, they also recognize the combination of the elements in a dynamic interplay. Although society and nature are opposed in a concentric modeling of space within and beyond the village, with village center as most "cultured" and space outside of the village increasing in wildness with distance, the two domains are joined by the village's diametric organization, which links center to periphery. This link is effected via the main axis running through the village connecting it with the eastern and western villages of the dead at the world extremes, and via the *aroe*, who, as the essence of Bororo society and village structure, define its social categories. Although the *aroe* reside outside the village in "uncultured" space, they enter and are associated with the very center of the village. Nature is also organized within Bororo social structure, since the eight clans of the Bororo encompass all known entities of their world. This socialization of natural and cosmic phenomena makes them (at least conceptually) more accessible to the Bororo and contributes to Bororo harmony within the social and natural universes.

The striving for harmony is also evident in the attempted integration and synchronization of social and natural space-time. Village residency shifts with the seasons: the dry season, with relatively easily traversed trails and open terrain permits travel far from the village and the exploitation of resources abundant in regions inaccessible during the long rains, while the rainy season encourages more settled occupation of the main village and the performance of ceremonies for which the largest group possible is most effective. As discussed by Turner, the Gê-Bororo pattern of dry season trekking is crucially a social one, "supporting the structure of the relations of production" (1979a:177). After arguing that the basis of Gê-Bororo social structure is the dominance of the father-in-law over the son-in-law, Turner suggests that trekking affords the father-in-law the opportunity to exercise "meaningful control" over his daughters, a discipline upon which the social structure depends. This is effected by the composition of the trekking bands, which "are always organized on the basis of collective male groups" with the father-in-law taking his wife, daughters, and their husbands (regardless of the latter's other group affiliations) with him (Turner 1979a:177). This effectively substantiates the control of the male household head over the members of his household, a control otherwise threatened by the uxorilocal residence rule and its characteristic female core around which relatively transient males come and go.

While this pattern can be linked to a significant social process, its imposition along seasonal lines serves to more effectively integrate Gê-Bororo society with the encompassing realm of nature. Observant of seasonal cyclicity that affects the materials (e.g., faunal and floral resources) crucial to cultural production, the Bororo logically develop seasonal activities crucial to their sociocultural reproduction. This entails dry season treks associated with male-dominated groups and production activities of the hunt, and rainy season village occupation associated with female-centered uxorilocal households and female-linked production activities such as agriculture and local gathering.

It is evident that the Bororo are interested in effecting an integration between social and natural space-time, as exemplified by the ceremony of Akiri-doge Ewure Kowudu. When the Pleiades are rising, boys become men in the final rites of their initiation, mortal beings become spirit beings as the souls of the deceased are accepted in the villages of the dead, the spirit beings (*aroe*) themselves leave the physical world to return to their distant abode, and members of society leave the social space of the village to infiltrate and inhabit nature during their months of trekking.

164

Nine

A Fuller Comprehension of Indigenous Space-Time Constructs

For the Bororo and other native Brazilians, ideas and knowledge of the dynamic interplay of antithetical natural and social domains are achieved through keen observation of the environment and a heightened sensitivity on all sensory levels to its messages. This approach is systematic in that it is constantly and continually applied. Two principal means by which the Bororo, and by extension other native Brazilians, organize their observation-based knowledge are through the techniques I call "layering" and "sequencing."

Layering

The technique of layering information involves the observation of synchronous events and/or coincident structures whose different sets of data are related to each other. In this process it is the overlapping of the sets that yields precise identity and information, giving a more complete picture than viewing the separate events or structures singly, much the way an impressionist painter applies colors and shapes, allowing the viewer's gaze to meld these into the painting's forms.

In social organization there is an obvious presence of the layering principle. That a Bororo's identity is established by his or her name itself implies knowledge of the individual's name group, subclan, clan, and moiety, information that amplifies the specific knowledge inherent in the person's name. Additionally, the social identity of each Bororo is also linked to his/her set of *iorubodare* relations, other ritual relations in which he/she may be involved, the different degrees and types of friendships associated with him/her, and his/her membership and role in a *roça* group (a cooperative farming group that shares the labor and products of a common field or garden plot). Status considerations that center principally upon the person's knowledge of tradition, active role in ceremony, and family size and constituency are also significant to a Bororo's social identity. All of these separate, though often interrelated, bits of information form a composite by which people identify themselves and each other (cf. Zuidema 1964, 1986:83–84).

Layers organizing concepts and information can also be described for the concentric model of village-centered space, in which the core of the village—men's house and dance plaza—is the most cultured space, with less culture and more nature characterizing spatial layers further away from the village. Some South American groups such as the Suya (Seeger 1981) and Barasana (C. Hugh-Jones 1979) demonstrate this organization particularly well. Many cultures also describe a layered universe, dividing the earth and upper world and in some cases the underworld into separate levels; indigenous Mesoamerican cosmology is especially noteworthy in this regard. For the Bororo, the sky is divided into layers, but there is some discrepancy in the specifics of the system. Colbacchini and Albisetti (1942:111) list ten denominations for specific levels or types of sky (see Appendix A, Baru entries), but it is not clear if these are conceived of in layers or describe different perceptions of sky manifestations. The *Enciclopédia Bororo*, however, is clear in specifying three levels of sky—white nearest the horizon, red above this, and blue the highest—that describe both physical and metaphysical aspects of the firmament (see Appendix A; *EBI*:772–77).

In planting, concurrent observations regarding the time of day, phase of moon, and season are all considerations. The collection of wild plant stuffs require these and occasionally additional cues for the greatest success. In native palm working, palm shoots are sought just before full moon when the shoots are said to open, thereby eliminating their usefulness for basketry purposes. The steps required to prepare shoots for use as weaving materials and the atmospheric conditions under which they are woven are related to day and seasonal time (Blatt-Fabian 1985). Fishing requires detailed observations of the environment including seasonal time as indicated by the stars and meteorological patterns, as well as floral growth and the blooming of flowers, the phase of the moon, and day and night time, for optimum success.

There is a qualitative difference between layers that organize Bororo social identity and those that concentrically organize space or the layered sky: in the former the layers overlap and are to some degree coincident, while in the latter the layers are exclusive of each other, although their edges may be blurred. Bororo concepts of space-time and their time-reckoning practices are characterized by both types of layers. Layers exclusive of each other involve distinctions between day and night or between the seasons. However, temporal reckoning within these categories includes the perspectives of overlap and interrelation.

The application of the technique of layering, particularly with respect to temporal reckoning, is of extreme significance in indigenous life patterns. Whereas one observation may yield only moderately useful, accurate, or precise information, multiple observations made between corresponding sets of data result in highly useful and more precise information. This relationship is schematically presented below, in a situation in which five distinct temporal layers are being cross-referenced; line lengths correspond roughly to lengths of time.

Plant
Month
Time of day
Season
Star

The five layers could correspond to a point in time in the cycle of a specific plant being observed in a particular month at a certain time of day during one of the seasons and during the annual cycle of an observed star or constellation. Any single observation among the five could produce useful information, but combining the information derived from all five observations would yield the most significant indication for a particular activity. Such information can be put directly to practical use: while a contemporary hunter may decide by calendar date the appropriate period to hunt, a native Brazilian will be observing several environmental indicators. The use of a single codified calendar date may result in the desired end, but it also may not, regardless of the technical skill of the hunter. In the native case, game is secured by combining the hunter's skill in the chase with his observations and knowledge of these temporal and other environmental factors.

The world-famous bow hunter and outdoorsman Fred Bear relates a relevant anecdote (1976). For several years he returned in late September and early October to the same river area in Canada to hunt grizzly, which in that season hunt spawning salmon before hibernating for the winter. Although Bear's trips were made at the same calendar period, he found the ecological system at slightly different stages each year. One year he missed most of the bear activity when he arrived too early and had to leave before the salmon run (and relevant grizzly activity), which peaked around 5 October. The following year, to allow for this possibility, he arrived later, only to find that the whole run was already over by his arrival on 6 October. With the Bororo, although the blooming of specific flowers indicates the arrival of fish up the rivers and smaller watercourses, their keen observations of other indicators lead them to successful fishing even if fish arrive prior to the flowers' bloom.

Sequencing

Sets of data are observed, organized, and recalled in sequences. Bororo sequencing tends to be nonnumeric; although the elements of a sequence could be counted, they generally are not, as it is not usually the number of items between two points that holds interest for the Bororo but rather the order of the items and the items themselves.

When asked to describe village social organization, the Bororo list the specific social groupings by name, giving the various name groups, subclans, and clans that compose the two moieties by which their society is organized. Invariably this listing begins in the west, at *ba paru*, the base of the village, and proceeds sequentially to the east, each village half given in this manner (as was described in chapter 3, Bororo men tend to list the moiety opposite to their own first).[1] One cannot inquire as to the "fifth" or "eleventh" name group mentioned; rather one would have to name the group or give reference to a name group on either side of the name group in question in order to find out its name. Bororo clans are perceived in sequence. These clans own such "property" as proper names, rituals, songs, and perhaps even specific myths. Since certain myths (such as those recounting the exploits of culture heroes) and rituals can best be appreciated sequentially, there may be a relationship between clan sequence, myth sequence, and sequences of space-time and calendar. In the Toribugu myth, for example, the relationship between Toribugu and his father, and their respective structural locations on the village circle, can be linked not only to the diachronic and synchronic sequences of the myth, but to specific constellations and their diachronic and synchronic relationships as well. The sequence of clans is a memorized scheme that completely and effectively organizes village space.

Traditional rules and laws then govern the relations between the groupings so organized.

Myths are memorized sequences of events, within which may be more specifically noteworthy sequences: the star list given in the Toribugu myth, for example. Such sequences can be used to refer to time, as do the rising stars named by Toribugu; to space and topography—although also intimating a time dimension—as do versions of a myth describing a journey of exploration by the Bokodori Exerae clan in which geographical features are given names (*EB*II:#4; Colbacchini and Albisetti 1942:244–45; Wilbert and Simoneau 1983:#27 and #28); and to space-time, as in the excursion of the Meri-doge described in chapter 6. These sequences may be significant recordings of sociohistoric proceedings, or ways to group meaningful data for recall and application.

Distances traveled by the Bororo are generally gauged by named points along the way, not by quantitative measurement. Similarly, Seeger reports that "to take a long hunting-fishing-gathering trip with some [Gê-speaking] Suya is to be introduced to their history, their geography, and their perception of space outside the village. Place names are considered an important part of a person's knowledge, and children are taken on long trips by their relatives . . . so that they will learn to identify the locations and learn the oral history attached to particular spots" (1981:75; see also 76–77). While on occasion a temporal referent may also be given for distance traversed, such a referent is immediately indicative of a qualitative measurement to those familiar with the area in question. Myths, songs, and rituals are characterized by extensive lists of animal species, place names, people, and activities, meaningful sequences that are nevertheless dependent upon intimate knowledge of the entire cultural system for comprehension of their highly contextual significance.

Time sequencing helps to structure observations and activities. The heliacal rise of the Pleiades marks the entry of boys into manhood, the new soul into the spirit world, and the trekking of groups out from the village. It is preceded by the cessation of rains and followed by the blooming of certain flowers and the run of fish in local waterways. Daily, monthly, seasonal, and annual rounds are constructed of sequences of events, often coupled with their places of occurrence, in ways that give meaning and measure to life. Such natural cycles are related to the human life course as the Bororo attempt to make sense of their world and the human condition within it.

Continuity and Discontinuity

All points on the arc of a circle are equal in that all are equidistant from the circle's center. Bororo residences and social groups, arranged as they are in a circular pattern, present an impression of social equality. A listing of the specific name groups that comprise the village circumference, however, immediately establishes an order and implies ranking, whether or not the Bororo have an ordinal nomenclature to express it. There is a name group that is first and one that is last. Goody claims that the idea of hierarchy in a list is so compelling that "extraordinary steps have to be taken to avoid the implications of higher and lower, first and last, with their associations of differential power or responsibility" (1977:130). He suggests that one way around this problem is to compose the list in the form of a circle, and he cites the example of the Round Table, "to avoid the linear hierarchy implicit in the list as part of a figurative table and the seating plan as part of a physical one" (1977:132). Obviously the Bororo have similar ends in mind with the circular arrangement of their social groups.

The village, patterned by cosmological concepts, has an "upper" (*xobugiwu*) portion in the east, and a "lower" (*xebegiwu*) portion in the west, terms that again could imply a hierarchical system. The specifics of social ordering that are also present, however, do not support such an interpretation. Since the moiety lists are always given beginning in the west, at the base of the village, those social units first in order sequentially are "lowest" in terms of the cosmological description of the area they occupy. Furthermore, these "lower" groups are apparently privileged over their eastern or "upper" counterparts, in that the western plaza immediately open to them is the focus of most village activity, including the temporary burial of deceased villagers, most ceremonies performed outside the men's house, the congregation of the men in the evening, and announcements. Occupants of the "lower" western houses therefore (mostly women and children, since men are usually participating in the activity that occurs in the plaza) have easier access to the proceedings enacted at the "center" of the village.[2] For the Bororo then, the terms "upper" and "lower," while descriptive of an ideal topographic/cosmological feature and applicable as such to the village social units, cannot be taken as associated in any simple fashion with relative degrees of social order. Nor is there an observable functional social order corresponding to the west-to-east listing of the social groups: those in the west do not enjoy a comprehensive social preeminence over those in the east.

Nevertheless, Bororo society is characterized by different systems of ranking, and these at times do relate to an individual's "structured" identity, that is, to his/her name and the localized social group to which he/she belongs. (Since my data in this respect deal exclusively with males, I employ only the male pronoun here.) Hereditary village chiefs pertain to the Baadajebage clans positioned at the western and eastern extremes of Exerae space. For the Bororo it seems, both first and last positions are ranked as first, since these chiefs bracket the sequence of Exerae social groups (this is loosely speaking; only one of the two detailed descriptions of the village included in chapter 3 lists either of the chieftain name groups in the exact end position, and then only one of the name groups is so positioned). While their structured positions on the village circle may not be completely indicative of their social status, however, another patterning of social structure, the men's house organization, plots both chiefs at the center pole of the *baimanagejewu*. They share the space and the distinction of its central location with the two original Bororo chiefs, Birimodo and Akaruyo Boroge who, rather than being at the extremes of their moiety on the village circumference, are at its midpoint.

Revealed in neither the village circumference nor the men's house organization and yet related via their names to both are the "chiefs" of each clan, men who inherit a position of prominence in their clan through the name group into which they are born and through the designation of the name which they are given. The location of certain positions of higher status among the social groups structured in the circular village plan mark an otherwise continuous organization with certain discontinuities. While higher and lower status is recognized among the Bororo, actual authority over the village rests in no single pair of hands: even the hereditary chiefs, who preside over certain rituals and village functions, do not give orders, nor can they alone make decisions by which the village must abide. Decision-making power lies with the village elders, men of consummate traditional knowledge and recognized status who are the de facto organizers and often performers of ceremonies and other village activities. These men and the heredity-based positions give dimension to the sociopolitical organization, as do other positions such as that of shaman. As discontinuities marking a continuous pattern, they animate as much as they disjoin. Rather than disrupting the inherent meaning in Bororo social structure, they create meaning in the order: in Bateson's words (1980), they are a "difference that makes a differ-

171

ence." Whereas the circular village pattern equilibrates Bororo society by deemphasizing rank as naturally associated with a listing of social groups, marked positions along the circular structure reintroduce social differentiation and hierarchy.[3]

An analogous situation exists with respect to time reckoning. Without marking, the flow of time would be so uniform as to be meaningless. This situation never arises, as both natural and social factors contribute in making meaningful periodicities within the flow of time. Night changes to day, the new moon swells to full, the cloudless sky darkens and rains come; a person is born, grows to puberty, reproduces, and dies. In dying, a Bororo becomes *aroe*, his/her soul part of the underlying structure of the cosmos by which nature and society are joined, antithetical but interrelated, complementary domains. The flow of time goes on. Stars that rise and set with clocklike regularity repeat their patterned movements annually; periods of disappearance and reappearance contribute to marking off this annual cycle. Beyond the year, this continuity is punctuated by the relative discontinuities of the planets in an otherwise starry sky. With periodicities of their own, the planets course through the constellations we describe as the ecliptic band, which all observant stargazers recognize in their own way. By intersecting the annual flow of time and movement of the sun with celestial cycles beyond a year, they contribute to marking off a longer progression of time in increasingly large cycles.[4]

Without a developed system of utile numerics, the Bororo and most other native Brazilian groups are without an overt system of computation-based cycles. But by combining keen observations, structured cosmology, and a heightened intuitive sense, they are cognizant of intermeshing cycles and demonstrate this knowledge through their synchronization of social and natural space-time. To recognize the appearances of Venus in the east (as morning star) and in the west (as evening star) as manifestations of the same celestial body—which several Bororo informants attested to—can serve as the beginning of a fairly sophisticated temporal system.

Consistent observation of the reappearance of Venus in the east (Jekurireu, in Bororo) would have resulted in noticing its repositioning at regular intervals (eight solar years or five Venus years) among the stars of the same constellation at the same time of year. The number five is also the number of guards of the night who function specifically in the predawn and dawn hours to awaken the village. These men use observations of the "morning stars" as partial indicators for the timing of their calls, perhaps sug-

Table 9.1

Eightfold Division of the Year, Latitude 17°–18°S

Date	Sun Reference	Interval, in Days
June 21	Solstice	44
August 4	Zenith	48
September 21	Autumnal Equinox	52
November 12	Anti-Zenith	39
December 21	Solstice	42
February 1	Zenith	49
March 22	Vernal Equinox	49
May 10	Anti-Zenith	42
	Solstice	

gesting more than a coincidental link with a number significant in the Venus cycle. It is also tempting to hypothesize that the number eight that occurs in Bororo social structure in the amount of clans and in the number of age classes somehow corresponds to the tallied recognition of the Venus cycle.

Alternatively, the number eight may relate to a natural yearly division. As pointed out to me by anthropologist Billie Jean Isbell, the latitude of the Bororo heartland (17°–18° S) is coincidentally characterized by solar zenith passages and antizenith or nadir crossings, which are interspersed between the solstices and equinoxes in such a way as to result in eight nearly equal periods of the year (see table 9.1; discussion of this principle and a table of computations was originally presented by Isbell in a New York Academy of Sciences conference and publication: see Isbell 1982). Since traditional patterns of time reckoning have been irreversibly altered by influences from neo-Brazilian culture, it is impossible to determine from on-site observations today if the Bororo were ever consciously noting such an eight-period year. They certainly possessed the observational ability, and the layout of their village along the cardinal directions and their awareness today of solar horizon extremes indicate their knowledge of solstices and equinoxes. The zenith passage is noticeable with the use of any gnomonlike device, and once established, the anti-zenith dates are already at least implied.[5]

The hypothetical relevance of numbers observed in astronomical cycles and their correspondence with numbers inherent in social structure is quite feasible. Native societies that exist in constant interaction with the natural environment not only attempt to socialize their environment through processes such as domestication, the selection of pertinent metaphors in folklore, and the development of cosmologies; they also recognize both culture and nature as interacting parts of a whole that encompasses both. This encompassing whole is related to the boundless—diachronically at least, due to the constant motion and repetition that characterize it—canopy of overarching sky whose periodicities so affect its observers. Periodicities, continuities marked by intermittent discontinuities, and the structure of process are most effectively approached by recognizing discrete units and by naming these units.

Although the Bororo do not habitually make detailed temporal calculations, they can and do count when necessary in both calendric and noncalendric contexts. Furthermore, the paradigmatic village pattern can be and is used to structure and codify their world, and this includes time-related matters. Specifically in this regard I have presented sets of data on "time-factored" and "time-factoring" (to use Marshack's terms; 1972) systems that are ordered by their localized settings in the village plan. The data on the system of callers who guard the night and the age classes demonstrate the indigenous use of the Bororo village in structuring and reckoning space-time. The relatively sophisticated Bororo astronomical observations, such as the series of turtle constellations and the Pleiades calendar, can be and are used to reckon time, marking both nightly and annual periods. These observations are combined with observations of the natural environment (e.g., faunal and floral cycles, meteorological phenomena) and of the positions of sun and moon, the whole of which is brought back into the social realm.

Precise and Systematic Knowledge

After detailing and analyzing the specifics of Andean astronomy, Urton concludes, "Observations on the astronomical system in the community of Misminay call for a complete reassessment of our present notions of astronomy and cosmology (i.e., of the nature and status of precise knowledge) in the Peruvian Andes" (1981b:196). In like manner, after a detailed investigation of Bororo concepts of space and time, I find it equally necessary to reassess the level of precise and systematic knowledge in Bororo culture, and by extension in that of other lowland South American cultures.

In chapter 1, some opinions on native Brazilian time reckoning of noted Brazilian anthropologist Herbert Baldus were summarized; this scholar emphasized the apparent deficiencies and impre-cisions of the systems in question. Leach expresses similar attitudes towards what he refers to as systems of "primitive time," claiming that the various cyclical time-marking schemes characteristic of primitive time reckoning (such as day and moon counts and sea-sonal checkpoints) are generally carried on in an imprecise fashion (1954:115–20). Leach does recognize, however, that the signifi-cance and viability of time thinking is contextual (1954:126), and herein lies part of the problem in evaluating native Brazilian sys-tems of time. That is, we must more fully understand the contexts of native time reckoning.

To begin with, Bororo precision in areas other than time must be appreciated. Their attention to detail in the manufacture of bas-kets and other traditional artifacts and in their ritual regalia and somatic decorations is profound and involves skills trained since childhood. These skills are complemented by a well-developed ability to aim a bow and arrow and firearms, and to gauge lengths, heights, and distances. For example, in the construction of the house in which my wife and I were to live, several Bororo men who were working on the project went off separately to cut and carry the required posts and poles for the various uprights, cross-pieces, and roof supports. When the pieces were brought back, each rela-tive type, even though several men may have brought them in, corresponded almost exactly in height or length. Such visual aids as a man's height and reach, as well as the length of an axe handle (although none of these measurements are "standardized" between individuals), were used in this project, which demonstrates the ability of Bororo men to accurately measure materials with a con-siderable degree of precision. As an instrument for measuring, the naked eye is not to be demeaned or underrated, a position also taken by Aaboe and Solla Price. "In the pre-telescopic era there is, in fact, a curious paradox that even a well-graduated device for measuring celestial angles and coordinates is hardly a match for the naked and unaided eye judiciously applied to that class of esti-mation for which it is best suited" (1964:2).

An extension of this ability and concern for precision in a time-related aspect has already been related: the tendency for Bororo to correct my attempts to indicate solar positions by the native method of pointing the outstretched hand. Bororo truly aimed their hands in this practice. I have also already described how individuals could and did point out the locations of solar horizon extremes as seen from the village (although no artificial horizon markers are used, and natural features were minimal). While I was not able to measure the accuracy of these indications with a surveyor's transit, my personal observations over the course of our stay in the village verified the essential correspondence between the pointed-to directions and the location of the sun at the appropriate times of year. There was also the expressed knowledge of the seasonal meteorological conditions relevant to these solar locations. It seems obvious that the Bororo were capable of significant degrees of precision and accuracy in their time reckoning; this knowledge would have been particularly useful when added to their knowledge of the location and variety of faunal and floral species, since as Cook reports, every Bororo knew "when and where and how to obtain . . . about everything edible in his environment" (1908:60).

It must be admitted, however, that in certain contexts, Bororo time reckoning did appear to be imprecise. This especially occurs when one attempts to fix a period in the past, for instance to find out when a particular event may have transpired. Maybury-Lewis reports similar characteristics among the Shavante. After detailing the Shavante forty-year age-set cycle of eight age-sets with five-year intervals between initiations, and the possibility for using this scheme to specify activities within forty-year time intervals, Maybury-Lewis comments that such use of the system virtually never occurred, and that, in fact, time calculations were frequently "wildly inaccurate" (1974:155). Maybury-Lewis observes that rather than being interested in the calculation of periods of time or in when past events happened, the Shavante are interested in seniority, an interest quite adequately fulfilled by the age-set system. Furthermore, he adds, the sequence within this system can be used as a reference for other events that occurred in the past. In an analogous fashion, the sequence of Bororo localized social units in the village is applied beyond its immediate function of ordering inhabited space.

As with the Shavante, the Bororo are not generally concerned with counted time measurements. This predilection is undoubtedly what led the Salesians to report the Bororo inability to count past a couple of days. But a distinction is necessary between predilection and ability. The Bororo and other native groups effectively utilize sequences and synchronized temporal layers for precise use of and reference to time when desired. However, if and when an exact count should be necessary, tally counting can be easily and accurately performed. Such tally counting can be used in both temporal and nontemporal contexts, even without a developed numerical system. For example, after helping several Bororo men to bag and stack a portion of harvested rice, I was interested when one man counted up the bags in Portuguese; I then challenged him to count them in Bororo, knowing that beyond *mito* as "one" and *pobe* as "two" Bororo numbers become rather cumbersome.[6] To my surprise the man quickly and simply ticked the bags off on his fingers and toes, arriving at the same sum as he had in Portuguese (although he had no discrete term with which he could express in Bororo the tallied quantity of sacks, he did have a concrete notion of how many there were, using either counting system). Tally counting can also be used for calendric purposes where a specific number of days have significance. This is done not only by the Bororo but among the Shavante: "the elders were keeping track of the initiation ceremonies by making a notch for every day in a ceremonial pole erected at one end of the village" (Maybury-Lewis 1965:215).

Bororo temporal precision is arrived at through consistent astronomical and environmental observations and a trained accuracy of observation technique. While their interest does not lie in measuring the length of time between events, they effectively use their temporal knowledge by synchronizing layers of sequentially organized time. Thus I do not agree with Leach's claim that unless "long-term seasonal variations are correlated with a system of counting moons or days, no true calendar system exists. For without such counting prediction of forthcoming events is only possible in the vaguest terms" (1950:248) As I have demonstrated, consistent observations of astronomical and other ecological events yield sequences that can be effectively used in place of counting. With recognition of the repetition or cyclicity of these sequences in time, actual predictions are possible, such as predicting the availability of fish after observing the bloom of a flower known to occur contemporaneously, or knowing when a certain star will make its heliacal appearance based upon the position of other stars in the sky. If an exact count of days is required or desired, tally counting can be used to more accurately fix the time. But is this precise knowledge systematized over time in any effective way? Lacking writing, is there any scheme by which the Bororo can codify and store their temporal notations?

The paradigmatic Bororo village pattern of localized social groups (lineages/name groups, subclans, clans) serves such a function. These corporate social groups own sets of names, decorations, spirit representations, and *aroe* "totems," while all faunal and floral species are divided up and pertain to specific clans. This notation and classification of knowledge has already been described in the preceding chapters to include temporal elements. The callers who "guard the night" are related through their structural spatial sequence in the Tugarege moiety to the temporal sequence of their duties. Likewise, the pseudo-system of eight Bororo age classes is also spatially organized primarily along the Tugarege moiety.[7] Thus the temporal periods of predawn to sunrise and the effective adult life span of forty years (which I have suggested was encompassed by the age-class system based upon Gê comparative material) are systematized along Bororo village space.

Also, each moiety may be related to a particular season, for example as reported by Nimuendajú for the rainy season moieties of the Eastern Timbira (1946:84–86) in which the eastern moiety is related to the dry season, and the western to the rainy season. Of greater concern is how the various social groups may have related to specific temporal periods of the year. The system used to relate this information is complex, and must be extracted from clues found embedded in myths and in the lists of clan-related names and plant and animal "totems" (partial lists of these clan-related "totems" can be found in *EBI*:438; Colbacchini and Albisetti 1942:31–33; Viertler 1976, and Crocker 1985:335–38). As regards mythic texts, the Toribugu myth, which I interpret as encompassing a year's length of time, may give some indication as to the relation of myth, time, and social space. Astronomical time has already been related to the myth's diachronic structure. The annual period this entails may be expressed by the entire circular village layout, connecting Toribugu's father, as a Baadajeba Xebegiwu in the west part of Exerae moiety space, with Toribugu's structural location at the western end of Tugarege moiety space (see figure 9.1). Tugiga Kiwu or β Ceti was described by an informant as "a red star which rises over the house of Paiwoe" and has already been linked in the preceding chapter with Toribugu. This star not only rises over the house of Paiwoe but does so at nightfall in mid-October with the onset of rains; it also rises heliacally in April with the cessation of the rains. This star provides important evidence therefore of the relationship between the rainy season and the Tugarege moiety, since both its temporal and spatial periodicities bracket these subsets of Bororo space-time. Location of the sun as a "totem" of the Exerae complements the coupling of Tugarege and rains with the relationship of Exerae and the dry sea-

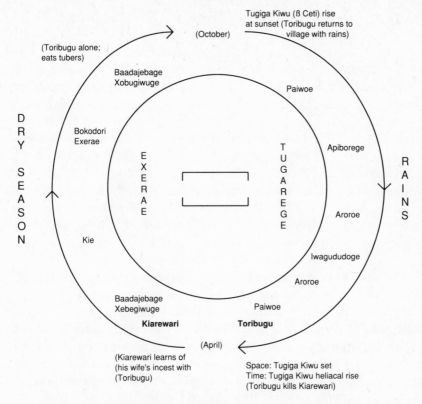

Fig. 9.1. The annual cycle on the village circle: the Toribugu myth

son. Temporal directionality can be expressed on the spatial village map as beginning at the west with Toribugu's father's clan, proceeding clockwise around the village through the two seasons, and ending at Toribugu's position. As was evident in the system of night guards, time that is mapped onto village space begins as does the social space itself, in the west at the base or "beginning" of the village (*ba paru*).[8]

The Bororo village, as a sequence and list of specifically located corporate groups, technically functions as a list associated with literate systems as defined by Goody; according to Goody, a list is a "catalogue, consisting of a row or series of names, figures, words" (1977:80). Lévi-Strauss reports that in 1936 the chief of Kejara village could summon the men to their places on the plaza by a roll call (1975:240). Z. Levak also refers to the roll call when he lists the Bororo lineages: "I started with Badajebage Chebegiwuge because this is the order followed by the chief in calling out clan members for the evening meeting on the village plaza" (1971:120). Such a roll call, which was rarely used during my field stay, would consistently reenforce the list of Bororo social groups.

In addition, the Bororo village pattern also resembles what Goody defines as a table: "an arrangement of numbers, words or terms of any kind, in a definite and compact form, so as to exhibit some set of facts, or relations in a distinct and comprehensive way, for convenience of study, reference, or calculation" (1977:54). In fact, the Bororo village pattern entails both main functions credited by Goody to writing systems: (1) information storage, and (2) shifting language from the aural to the visual domain (1977:78). I am not suggesting that the Bororo village pattern be considered a system of writing, but that as a notational system it can be described as fulfilling the two main functions of writing, and that, furthermore, its format specifically resembles devices such as lists and tables that are associated with writing systems.

Goody's claim that such classificatorial systems as tables, lists, formulas, and recipes are present far more and are much more important in literate than in nonliterate societies, and his over-stressing of literacy as a causal factor in the origin of rational and scientific thought has already been quesioned by Zuidema (1982:422–23).[9] According to Zuidema, the Andean cultures, as seen through Inca culture and its capital, Cuzco, "had a well-developed interest in rational thought and empirical verification and various means of using intricate tables and lists [even though] the culture did not have writing" (1982a:423). Incaic exact and systematic knowledge was recorded and stored in *quipus*, knotted strings, and in the Cuzco *ceque* system, a sort of imaginary or geographical *quipu*, with 328 shrines organized along forty-one lines, like so many knotted strings.

Andean interest in exact and systematic knowledge, Zuidema attests, was motivated not by an interest in measurements but rather by such moral and abstract concepts as "sin," "health," and "order" (1982a:425). Grappling with these issues led the Incas to explore the "boundaries of knowledge," so much so that the "abstract system that they developed then helped them in the solution of practical problems" (Zuidema 1982a:425) The Bororo initially may also have been more interested in moral and abstract concepts in arranging and codifying the village pattern. Basic to the village organization is the underlying system of *aroe*, the spirit beings related to identity and categorization. It is according to the classification and ordering of these beings and their inherent characteristics that Bororo clans are structured, as is all clan "property."

The village, therefore, systematizes social knowledge such as the names and arrangement of social groups, the relationship between these groups (e.g., moiety exogamy, and the *iorubodare* ties between specific subclans and name groups), and the relationship to these social groups of corporate goods (personal names, ritual regalia, spirit representations, decorative motifs, and plant and animal entities). Among the basic concerns represented in this system is that of order on social, ecological, and cosmic scales.

It is perhaps through this concern for order that time elements were also incorporated within the basic village plan: the village is ordered and paradigmatic not only with respect to its internal elements (i.e., the respective positions of the social groups) but also with respect to the larger realm of the cosmos through its essentially cardinal orientation. In that the principal axis runs east-west and is specifically related to the sun, temporal concerns are inherent in the system. Once the village was patterned according to more abstract concerns, it could also be used as a referral system for such practical matters as where, when, and what to hunt, fish, gather, plant, and harvest. Determination of the exact details of how these practical concerns are met via village organization and its essential quality as a list and table is hampered by the setting and changing life-style of the contemporary Bororo. Nevertheless, since the information contained within the structure of the Bororo village is shared by each member of the culture, the village layout can be spoken of as a notational system allowing cultural knowledge to be accumulated, learned, passed on, and innovated upon in ways to serve the productive and reproductive activities of the society.

It is not likely that the Bororo were alone in their concerns or in their solutions to them. Other indigenous South American societies certainly had ways of systematizing the precise knowledge through which their cultures were organized and by which they effectively pursued their productive and reproductive activities.

Ten

An End and a Beginning

Solomon Grundy,
Born on a Monday,
Christened on Tuesday,
Married on Wednesday,
Took ill on Thursday,
Worse on Friday,
Died on Saturday,
Buried on Sunday.
This is the end
Of Solomon Grundy.
—*The Real Mother Goose*, 1916

The Mother Goose nursery rhyme "Solomon Grundy" relates the life course of a man to the days of the week. More than nonsensical children's babble, it demonstrates recognition of the essential sameness between the passage of a week and the human life course: both are a linear progression in time. Disregarding the difference in their respective durations, both periods of time are bounded by a beginning and an end and are marked by a metered sequence that orders the space between those points. Therefore the two temporal sequences are directly analogous; when correlated to each other, the days of the week become the phases of a human life. What strikes one as dissimilar between the two periods of time is that the days of the week repeat themselves indefinitely. This recursive element seems to be missing from the week's analog, the life course, for after the death and burial of Solomon Grundy, the man's life course really has come to an end. Or has it?

All of the Bororo data and principles (see, e.g., Lehman 1985:26) concerning space-time are encompassed within a single, theoretical model (fig. 10.1). The model can be stated as a process, beginning at a given point (P_0) within a domain of bounded space (S, S') and proceeding from that point, will return to its point of origin after reaching the boundary of the domain (a restatement of the paradigm stated in chapter 1). A paradox accompanies the model, however: either the most interior point, P_0, is considered the fundamental entity from which the larger space, S/S', is defined, or the

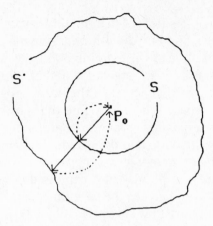

Fig. 10.1. Model of Bororo data and principles

larger space may be considered primary, with its interior points defined relevant to it. This paradox accounts for many inconsistencies in the perception and description of culturally determined domains of bounded space, e.g., space-time. Therefore while the model defines and organizes the static and dynamic elements of Bororo culture and society, apparent contradictions between these elements and their relationships are possible and to some degree to be expected.

Although the nursery rhyme quoted above and the culture that produced it are unknown to the Bororo, their concepts of time are directly comparable to the poem's underlying concepts. For the Bororo, day and night time, the synodic (and possibly sidereal) lunar month, the seasons as they comprise the year, periods beyond the year, and the human life course are all marked by named sequences that refer to phases within each time context and that order the space between the beginning and end points of each respective period. At the end of each period the sequence repeats itself. As sequenced periods of linear temporal progression, the various time contexts reckoned by the Bororo are analogous to each other and can be and are correlated, while an attempt is also made to synchronize different periods or levels of time.

It is essential to acknowledge time as the domain of relations within temporal space. Time is technically a "space," and therefore not only are different periods of time analogous but time and space as well. The techniques of sequencing, layering, and marking discontinuities within continuous frameworks that characterize Bororo space-time reckoning are all defined by the single abstract model given above. Sequences determine lines of linear progressions in space-time, and any discontinuities marked within a continuous frame can serve as the defining points of such lines. What I have described as "layers" are the different boundaries of the recursive mechanisms that act upon the linear progressions in the context of Bororo space-time and define the subsets of the entire domain. The encompassing nature of the domain of space-time, the necessity of recursivity, and the paradox of defining the primitive element of the domain as postulated above inspire the numerous beginning and end points—also expressed as "openings" and "closings"—in Bororo-perceived space-time, as well as diverse directions of flow and flow-reversals. All of these elements are characteristic of Bororo and other native Brazilian domains of space-time and must to some extent be present in any culture's space-time system. They also account for Bororo perceptions of interrelationships between stellar objects and movement, natural cycles, and social organization and social action.

Does the existence of a culturally defined bounded space, and the return to the point of origin of a given process within this space, necessarily indicate that the given culture perceives only up to and within that bounded space? Do the Bororo, who recognize in the return of the Pleiades to the dawn sky the completion and beginning of cycles of time, while having no formalized count of years, perceive time as cyclical to the exclusion of time as a progression? Clearly not: the Bororo are acutely aware of the development and growth of human individuals, of flora and fauna, and of their "place" in history as they know it, witnessing the dramatic changes and cultural upheavals brought on by their increasing contact with outsiders and the impact of Brazil's rapidly developing society. The problem, therefore, is not one of perception but of naming. For example, within the domain of numbers, the set of nonnegative integers increases lineally from 0 to 1 to 2 to 3 to infinity. As no finite organism can have a distinct name for each point of this domain, the issue of enumeration of the points on the line is a problem for all societies. For all finite organisms, as for all cultures, a recursive mechanism must be introduced into the counting system. Our own system of enumeration is based upon the unit of ten (0, 1, 2, . . . 9) and its repetition, although greater quantities are specifically named. The Bororo, on the other hand, have discrete terms for one (*mito*) and two (*pobe*), and it is after this that their recursive mechanism manifests itself: three is essentially two plus one. However, the Bororo have no difficulty in perceiving

184

increasing quantity; even large quantities can be counted by using tallies based on the vigesimal system of fingers and toes.

In Western culture we name the days of the week and number fifty-two weeks in a year, ten years in a decade, ten decades in a century, and so on. We can count our time backwards and forwards and declare that today is the nth day in the mth year. Clearly the Bororo are not as concerned as we with enumeration of the progression of time but rather emphasize the recursive elements. Even the human life course is a cycle, since society is collectively reproduced through successive generations.

Among the Bororo, recursivity of the human life course is given greater overt emphasis than in Western culture through the institutions of naming and the *aroe maiwu*, in which a man chosen to portray the deceased during funeral proceedings afterwards continues to ritually occupy the deceased's genealogical position. In the myth of Toribugu, after killing his father Toribugu assumes his father's identity and possessions. Here the son's identity as his father is also descriptive of the *aroe maiwu* institution in that only a man from the moiety opposite to that of the deceased can fulfill this role. With moiety exogamy prescribed, Bororo children belong to the moiety of their mother, and so men of one moiety are collectively sons of the men of the other moiety, and vice versa. In naming also, not only society as a whole but individuals are "recycled" with the name groups bestowing names from their corporate holdings on generation after generation of Bororo. By applying their space-time paradigm to its farthest social extension, so long as the *aroe maiwu* and naming institutions are maintained, the Bororo have ensured themselves social continuity and the identification of past with present and future. Had Solomon Grundy been Bororo, his life course would recycle along with the days of the week—or rather with the year.

Geographical and cosmic space are also domains upon which the Bororo paradigm of lineality and cyclicity is logically applied. In chapter 3, concentric and diametric models of Bororo geographical, cosmic, and social space are discussed, the two models being not only complementary but interdependent. Innermost village space, including the men's house and dance plaza(s), is strongly related to society and culture and the realm of the sacred. The village periphery, while still cultural space, is considered closer to nature and more secular than the village center. Outside the village is natural, relatively uncultured, and wild space. However, the movement of men out from and back into the village center links

185

these different zones. Furthermore, the very outermost regions, associated in myth with the *aroe*, are brought in direct relationship with the village center since these spirit beings are the very essence of Bororo society and culture. The entities themselves arrive in the village during the important ceremonialism of the funerary/rainy season period and are otherwise symbolically present in the ordered clan locations and corporate "holdings" (e.g., proper names, decorative and utile possessions and designs, etc.) that constitute personal and group identity.

The east-west directionality is of key importance for the Bororo and is marked by the main village axis, itself predicated by the diurnal path of the sun, and secondarily by the local flow of terrestrial water. By rising in the east and setting in the west, the sun as perceived by the Bororo traverses the entire domain of space-time, but its spatiotemporal progress is no less cyclical; rather it is paradigmatically cyclical in repeating its daily course. The secondary north-south village axis is also predicated by solar cyclicity following the sun's annual peregrination between northern and southern extremes. Thus they perceive that the sun's movement east-west and north-south underlies both concentric and diametric models of space. On the ground the link between these models is made, as discussed in chapter 3, by the location of east and west villages of the dead, by their chiefs Itubore and Bakororo, by the relations between these chiefs with the hereditary Baadajebage chiefs and the original Tugarege chiefs Akaruyo Boroge and Birimodo, and by the respective sets of powers controlled by these chiefs that stress a linkage of west with center and east with periphery.

Among the Eastern Timbira, it has already been observed that a similar connection between concentric and diametric models is made, although the specifics are reversed: center is linked with east and periphery with west. Furthermore, in the Eastern Timbira case east is considered "upper" space and west "lower," similar to the Bororo world view, with each direction related to age-class moieties.

In his paper "Dual Opposition, Hierarchy and Value," Turner (1984) gives a detailed theoretical treatment of moiety structures. According to Turner, the essential function of the moiety structure characteristic throughout central Brazil is the generalization of the "regulation and collective standardization of the relationship between wife's parents and daughter's husband, defined within the context of uxorilocal residence . . . with its associated connotations of dominance and subordination, and its projection from the level of the extended family household to that of the community as a whole" (1984: 357). Ultimately, for Turner, the binary form of the moiety structure is an outgrowth of the hierarchy between contrastive relationships and is functional in character, serving "as a means of controlling the process of social (re-)production" (1984: 365). In central Brazil the extended family is generated by transformations of family relations in a pattern that itself has a dual form: (1) "a pair of contrasted relationship categories" (i.e., those of intra- and cross-family ties), and (2) "successive generations of actors [that] . . . become identified or aligned with one of these categories in contrast to the other" (Turner 1984: 361). Finally, each society can be identified with its own weighting of these transformations, a process that yields a "symmetrical expression of an asymmetrical pattern" (Turner 1984: 361).

Turner specifically compares Eastern Timbira society with the Kayapó, both of whom have moiety organizations associated with the east and west hemispheres of circular villages. As mentioned, among the Eastern Timbira the eastern age-class moiety is considered upper, and the western lower. Among the Kayapó the situation is reversed, and it is the western age moiety that is upper, and the east lower. Further associations among the Kayapó moieties are east as root or base, and west as tip or top. This shift in conception of upper/lower between the two societies is related to two considerations: the obvious element of temporal process that proceeds from east to west as predicated by the sun's diurnal movement, and differential weighting of the two principal stages of the life course, that is, association with one's natal family and association with one's family of procreation (Turner 1984:346–53).

Invoking the space-time model illustrated and defined above for the Bororo, we can readily state that one domain of time is analogous to another: the earlier part of the day, associated with the east, is related to the natal family phase of the life course, whereas the west and later day time is associated with the stage of one's family of procreation. Among the Eastern Timbira, strong ties are maintained with one's natal family throughout life, and therefore the weighting of this first phase of the life cycle is expressed in the conception of east as upper. Kayapó males, however, largely sever ties with their natal families in favor of strengthening extended family ties in their uxorilocal residences, and this weighting of the later phase of the life course is reflected both in the growth symbolism expressed in their concepts of east as the root and west as the tip of a growing organism and in the designation of west as upper and east as lower. Further comparison between the two cultures reveals that whereas among the Eastern Timbira "each pair of moieties encodes a simple relationship of complementary opposition," among the Kayapó "the moieties cannot be contrasted with each other as simple embodiments of the contrasting terms of an opposition" but rather take a more complex and "recursive" form in a sequence of negations and affirmations in their relationships (Turner 1984:354). Turner thus defines the Kayapó system as one of "irreversible alternation" from one set of relations to another (replicating as well the ties between families at different phases of the life course), and the Eastern Timbira as having social processes taking place in a pattern of "reversible alternation" (1984:356).

Turner's model and discussion incorporates elements of both space and time and is theoretically applicable to specifics of Bororo space-time. Although the Bororo hold the east-west solar direction-ality as fundamental and conceive of east as upper and west as lower, neither the temporal progression nor the apparent weight-ing of directionality indicated by the terms "upper" and "lower" can be readily applied to Bororo moiety structure, which in con-trast to Eastern Timbira and Kayapó moiety structures comprises the northern and southern halves of the village. Other features of the respective moiety systems also differ, most significantly the fact that Bororo moieties are localized both on the village perime-ter in extended family houses and in the village center within the men's house; also among the Bororo, relations between the moi-eties are characterized by prescriptive reciprocity, in general con-trast to the Northern Gê.

Growth and progression, exemplified by the sun's diurnal east-west journey, is replicated in the moiety structures of the Northern Gê by localized east and west social groups. The Kayapó emphasize this relationship by referring to the east as root and the west as tip. Northern Gê society is also characterized by displacement in the family structure of the wife's brother by the sister's husband, a uni-directional flow of men in the village. These factors highlight the irreversible, asymmetrical character of social and cosmic space-time. In Bororo villages, however, localization of the moieties in the northern and southern halves of the village has the effect of neutralizing the east-west flow and inherent asymmetry. Con-comitantly, the prescriptive reciprocity between the moieties, including marriage, nullifies the unidirectional displacement of males by favoring the exchange of sisters (perhaps appropriately conceived of as women exchanging brothers). This system is so consistently adhered to that men of the Exerae moiety refer to older men of the Tugarege classificatorily as *iogwa*, "father," and to older men within their own moiety as *iedaga*, "grandfather"; the Tugarege apply the same terms, respectively, to older Tugarege and Exerae men (cf. Colbacchini and Albisetti 1942:43). The Bororo need to balance the irreversible replacement of men from the households as they are matrilineal: theirs is a real need to retain men, even while losing them, to perform the crucial tasks of socialization required of them within their clans. Even the Gê asymmetrical loading of the father-in-law/son-in-law relationship that occurs through male displacement is reduced in the Bororo system.

Asymmetry is potentially present in the Bororo system through the subclan system of "upper," "middle," and "lower" clan divisions. However, Levi-Strauss's contention (e.g., 1963a, b) that these divisions served as intermoiety endogamous units has not been borne out by further research. Quite to the contrary, the *utawara* ("roads") that crisscross the village linking subclans in *iorubodare* relations do so irrespective of "upper," "middle," and "lower" denominations, which prove themselves to be designations conforming to the perceived geographical conditions of Bororo territory with east as up and west as down, and are socially nonfunctional.

There is, of course, hierarchy within the Bororo system, as has been described in preceding chapters. The contemporary hereditary chiefs, for example, are Baadajebage of the Exerae moiety. Prescriptively, certain Baadajebage subclans also have the right to marry within other Exerae subclans: one subclan each of the Baadajebage Xobugiwuge and Baadajebage Xebegiwuge can unite matrimonially with a subclan of the Bokodori Exerae and of the Kie, respectively (cf. *EB*I:449). This results in an apparent asymmetry north to south, as opposed to the east-west asymmetry of the Northern Gê. But again this asymmetry is contradicted: on the one hand, by the reversal of the north-south positioning of the moieties on the village circumference within the men's house where the Exerae occupy the south and the Tugarege the north, symbolically (at least) reducing the north-over-south hierarchy; and on the other hand by the cultural fact that the contemporary hereditary chiefs owe their powers to the original Bororo chiefs, both of whom were Tugarege. Furthermore, these Tugarege chiefs, Boroge and Birimodo, became the chiefs of the eastern and western villages of the dead, respectively, with the result of evening out the north-south asymmetry. In addition, the placement of men within the men's house reserves the central position around the middle supporting post not only for the two hereditary chiefs Akaruyo Bokodori and Bakorokudu but for their predecessors Boroge and Birimodo, as well. This positioning has the effect of creating a concentric hierarchy as opposed to a diametric one, but certain features within Bororo society, such as the structural location of these men on the village periphery and the de facto occupation of the center of the men's house by all acting "cultural chiefs," serve yet again to reduce this apparent hierarchy. Even the sequencing of Bororo social units along the village circumference and the implied hierarchy that might normally apply in such a list is nullified to some extent by literally rounding out the sequence into a circle on the ground and by redistributing the men from this order within the men's house.

Perhaps the Bororo system can best be described as one of "complementary symmetry" characterized by binary opposition between the moieties but with a tendency to reduce the differentiation between these oppositions. For example, the Baadajebage of the Exerae moiety are the "constructors of the village," a responsibility that effectively emphasizes their relation to the spatial domain: the selection of terrain suitable for a village and the layout of the actual village plan. Among the Tugarege, on the other hand, at least two examples of temporal emphasis have been determined ethnographically: the system of night guards who make dawn announcements to awaken the village, and the pseudo-age classes that were found to be localized (with one exception) along Tugarege village space. Also, Crocker brings important data to light concerning Bororo cosmology, spirit essences, and shamans: he interprets the Bororo as relating *bope* spirits with the Exerae moiety and *aroe* spirits with the Tugarege (1985:198–99). This at first appears to contradict the initial binary characterization, since the *aroe* are associated with identity and "structure," themes represented in the duties of the Baadajebage (Exerae) in ordering the village plan, while the *bope* are associated with organic transformation and "process," themes more evident in the Tugarege relationship with time. But the fact that these spirit essences may be related to the moieties as Crocker states is accompanied by a significant corollary: shamans of the *bope*, the *bari*, should be members of the Tugarege, while the *aroe etawarare*, shaman of the *aroe*, should be of the Exerae (Crocker 1985:198–99), a principle analogous to that which allows only male Tugarege to portray the Exerae clans' totemic *aroe*, and vice versa.

The above binary oppositions are themselves internally mediated and neutralized. If the Tugarege are associated principally with predawn and/or night time, then we might suggest that the Exerae are associated with day time. Additionally, certain elements favor a relationship between the Tugarege and the rainy season: the astronomical and cultural details referred to above stemming from my interpretation of the Toribugu myth; the categorical association proposed by Crocker between the Tugarege moiety and the *aroe* who have a preference for water and appear collectively in the village during the rainy season; the possession of certain natural substances of the rainy season by social groups of the Tugarege, such as the *mano* plant; and the *mano* races, which are run only during the rains. The Exerae, on the other hand, have a more direct relationship with the dry season through the presence of Meri, Sun, as an Exerae *aroe*, and the fact that spatially the north is associated with the sun during the months of the dry season, as the celestial orb reaches its northern extreme at that time.

The symmetrical complementarity between north and south is maintained to replicate and recreate the basic relationships that serve as the font of social production and reproduction, as well as to replicate what the Bororo perceive as fundamental in the cosmos around them. A Bororo male is born to parents of opposite moieties and belongs to that of his mother. He will learn the knowledge of his clan from his name-giving *iedaga*, an older male of his clan but will be trained in other cultural knowledge by his father and his *iorubodare*, both men of the opposite moiety. While subordinate to these men, he will also have the responsibility of representing his *iorubodare* in death as the *aroe maiwu*, so that he becomes his *iorubodare* after the latter's death. A Bororo is therefore socialized through his relation with both *iedaga* and *iorubodare*, although the latter is more significant in terms of a boy's wider social role. This process itself is socialized through the institution of the men's house: centrally located in the village at the social and cosmological core of society, the men's house reverses the north-south directionality of the moieties at the same time that it serves as the levering device to move men from north to south or south to north, that is, from their unsocialized boyhood to their socialized adult status. This institution and process replicates the cosmic process of the annual movement of *meri*, the sun, north to south and back to north and the effects this natural cycle has upon the alternation of the seasons, as well as on the production, reproduction, and growth of natural species.

Social relations within Bororo society express the mediations, directionality, reciprocity and complementarity that are logical applications of the Bororo paradigm of space-time within the social domain. The Bororo socialize time by relating the life cycle, particularly the adult, male aspect of it, to the annual cycle. At the heliacal rise of the Pleiades, the initiation of new adult males is completed, and funerary proceedings are brought to a close. It is the beginning and end of both the year and the human (social) life course. Following the Pleiades rise villagers embark upon dry season trekking, when training of new male initiands is begun. For society, then, it is a time of primal socialization, when society trains its new members in the fundamentals of being properly "human." Group residence at this time is outside of the village in "wild," uncultured space, although the ordered village plan is replicated in the arrangement of camp space. Also during this period foodstuffs are mostly from "wild" sources, when the agricultural calendar is at rest, being past harvest and before planting, while food is prepared in the makeshift camps, again outside of cultured village space.

By late September or early October increasing atmospheric pressure and gathering thunderheads announce the coming rains. Groups return to the village and prepare for planting and their period of village residency. During the rainy season people are in the village, and plants are in the ground. Society matures with its domesticates: human, faunal, and floral. Even though wild food products are still hunted and gathered, they are now mostly prepared and eaten in the village. After several months the crops and society as a whole ripen: from January onwards maize and other agricultural products are harvested; the fruit from the fields can be compared to both the maturing young adults and to the physical birth of new babies.[1] By the end of the rains in May both the harvest and society are in states of advancing old age, a period of some ambivalence. It is the dried corn of this time that can best be stored and ground into flour, but the abundance of the season's domesticated food is also coming to an end; likewise with human old age, the accumulated knowledge and social relations of the elderly are accompanied by increased prestige as well as increasing physical infirmities. Death follows, but new life as well. The synchronization of different domains of space-time serves to help the Bororo maintain a sense of control—not over nature, but over themselves with respect to nature.

During the rainy season when the Bororo inhabit their main villages, the ancestral and totemic *aroe* also make their arrival and appearances within the cultured social space of the village. No known ceremony is performed for either the arrival or the departure of these beings en masse, but their presence is obvious at, and essentially limited to, both major and minor ceremonies of the funerary cycle. That the funeral cycle should comprise the greater part of village residency and the rainy season might seem contradictory, as this is also precisely the time of societal maturation. However, noting the Bororo propensity for devising and neutralizing asymmetries, it is consistent that the period of greatest growth and socialization should occur within the rubric of the attention and respect given the dead. After all, death delivers a human being into the realm of the *aroe*, the structural essence of Bororo culture and society. It is the *aroe* who must preside over such crucial life stages as initiation and ascendancy to the status of hereditary chief, rites of passage that occur beneath the canopy of the funeral cycle. It perhaps would be more appropriate to designate this period of heightened ceremonial activity by other than the "funeral cycle," except that the Bororo themselves adhere to this conceptualization. Sadly, the precise relationship between the various rites of passage, the funeral cycle, and their placement within the year and longer time periods is not likely ever to be known, as contemporary village life begins increasingly (and to an extent necessarily) to function in rhythm with the pulse of the encompassing national culture.

The multidirectionality, reversals, and neutralizations that characterize Bororo space-time are fully consistent within the culturally conceived paradigm of this domain. Furthermore, the Bororo apply their understanding of the paradoxical relationship between interior points and the boundary of bounded space rather broadly within their culture. Perceiving the whole of encompassing space-time as the outermost border of the domain in which they exist, the Bororo both replicate what they perceive as natural processes and order within their society, and project onto those natural processes and order explanations consistent with their own social theory. Celestial observations serve as bases for social action and themselves become replications of social relations. The *aroe* define society and are themselves defined by society.

Greater socialization for the Bororo means greater knowledge of and involvement with these ancestral, totemic beings whose pattern of relations serves as the paradigm for village social organization. The *aroe* link society with nature, not only by coming from their distant abodes into the dance plaza and men's house and thereby mediating "wild" and "cultured" spaces, but through the system of clan "ownership" of certain natural species. While faunal and floral species may pertain to specific clans, however, they are never completely socialized, as they do not build and occupy that quintessential domain of culture and society, the village. The concepts embodied within the dichotomies of *aroe* and *bope* (e.g., structure and process, society and nature) underlie all Bororo ideas of power, aesthetics, production, and reproduction. The dynamic interplay of these categories produces cosmic power and force. On the social scale, the knowledge and ability to interact successfully with this dynamism is what yields social power.

Appendix A

Significant Celestial Phenomena

Abbreviations used for data sources:
RBF: Rondon and Barbosa de Faría 1948
CA: Colbacchini and Albisetti 1942
EBI: *Enciclopédia Bororo* I
F: Fieldwork by the author, 1982–83
Star identifications were aided by referring to Bourge and Vignand 1976, Gaposchkin n.d., Menzel 1964, Mourão 1982 and n.d., and Norton 1964.

1. *Aiepa*
   Identification: β Centauri.
   Source: RBF
   Remarks: This word does not appear in *EBI*, nor was I able to confirm the identification during fieldwork.

2. *Akiri-doge*; other names: *Okire-doge, Ikuie*
   Identification: the Pleiades; leaves/flowers of the *anjiko*, and "white down."
   Source: RBF, CA, *EBI*, F
   Remarks: The most well-known and significant stellar entity for the Bororo: its position is used to tell the hours of the night and the seasons of the year; its heliacal rise (mid-June) serves as announcer for the Akiri-doge Ewure Kowudu ceremony relevant to the dry season and the initiation of boys.

3. *Ari*
   Identification: Moon, the celestial body; the period of a synodical lunation; and a culture hero and *aroe*, brother to Meri, sun.
   Source: RBF, CA, *EBI*, F
   Remarks: Both the moon's phases and position are significant for telling time; used to indicate appropriate activities—particularly planting and gathering—as well as for weather predictions.

4. *Ari Reaiwu*
   Identification: Venus; other planets and stars; "that which follows the moon."
   Source: *EBI*, F
   Remarks: *EBI* has it as any star or planet that appears to accompany the moon. One of my informants related this name specifically to Venus when it is in the east (as morning star).

5. *Aroe Kodu*
   Identification: meteor, shooting star; "flight of the soul."
   Source: RBF, *EBI*, F
   Remarks: It is generally perceived as a bad omen, said to be the sign that a malicious spirit (*bope*) is stealing someone's soul. A *bari* shaman is called upon to interpret the occurrence. Cf. (I)Kuieje Kodu, below.

6. *Atubo*
   Identification: Cetus (?); a large, antlered deer.
   Source: F
   Remarks: This constellation was never identified in the field. However, the star Tugiga Kiwu was described as a red star rising just south of east, and refers to the antler of Atubo. I identify the star as β Ceti (Diphda) and the constellation as Cetus. See chapter 7 for details on the identification.

7. *Ba Paru Kadoda Jebage*
   Identification: stars in Ursa Major; "those which cut the west of the village."
   Source: *EBI*
   Remarks: Ba Paru, "base" or "beginning of the village," is the westernmost part of the village. Although I could not confirm this identification, it may be that the setting of this constellation helped orient the village.

8. *Barogwa Jeiba*
   Identification: Jupiter, or other planet/bright star; "lord of the dawn."
   Source: F
   Remarks: Jupiter can serve as only a tentative identification; it was related by two informants when Jupiter was in Scorpius (May 1983). It may also have referred to an object "in the southern sky at dawn." With the next two entries it was part of a series of observations immediately preceding dawn; my suggestion as to their order is (1) Barogwa Jeiba, (2) Barogwa Tabowu, (3) Barogwa Kododu. See chapter 5 for more details.

9. *Barogwa Kododu*
   Identification: (bright star/planet); "increase of dawn."
   Source: F
   Remarks: Compare with *barogwadodu*, "full or end of dawn."
   See entry #8 above and chapter 5 for details.

10. *Barogwa Tabowu*
    Identification: Venus (as morning star); "with the dawn."
    Source: *EBI*, F
    Remarks: *EBI* has this as any star/planet that appears at the break of day, while two of my informants gave this name for Venus when in the east. See entry #8 above and chapter 5 for details.

11. *Baru*
    Identification: the sky.
    Source: RBF, CA, *EBI*, F
    Remarks: The Bororo indicate with this word both the physical sky and the abode of certain spirits (*bope, maereboe*), in which they recognize certain layers: see #15–#17 below.

12. *Baru Bekurureu*
    Identification: "resinous sky" (?).
    Source: CA
    Remarks: I could not confirm this; one informant wondered if what was meant was *baru ekureu*, "yellow sky," but could give no explanation for either.

13. *Baru Ikajareu*
    Identification: "sky that has the canoe mouth" (?).
    Source: CA
    Remarks: No further information.

14. *Baru Kagorireu*
    Identification: "violet sky" (?).
    Source: CA
    Remarks: No further information.

15. *Baru Kawarureu*
    Identification: "blue sky."
    Source: CA, *EBI*
    Remarks: *EBI* describes this as the highest level of sky in a cosmology that recognizes three colored levels, blue the highest, then red, and white the lowest (see #16 and #17 below, and *EBI*:772-77 for details). Contemporary villagers would neither confirm nor deny this scheme.

16. *Baru Kigadureu*
    Identification: "white sky."

Source: CA, *EBI*
Remarks: The lowest sky level according to *EBI*.
17. *Baru Kujagureu*
Identification: "red sky."
Source: CA, *EBI*, F
Remarks: *EBI* has this as the middle sky. One of my informants commented that *baru kujagu*, red sky, was an omen that signified human blood or war.
18. *Baru Otto-Urugureu*
Identification: "sky that has the luminous extremity" (?).
Source: CA
Remarks: One informant translated this as "the glowing reddish sky" (*lustroso de vermelho* in Portuguese) but had no other comments.
19. *Baru Pegareu*
Identification: "bad sky."
Source: CA
Remarks: This could be descriptive of a general category characterized by a sky covered with heavy, glowering clouds.
20. *Baru Pobo-Berereu*
Identification: "sky with boiling water."
Source: CA
Remarks: Perhaps referring to clouds resembling boiling water, as suggested by one Garças informant.
21. *Baru Toriga Oyareu*
Identification: "sky that resembles the cuts made at the funeral"
Source: F
Remarks: Such a sky is either streaked with clouds or has rents in the cloud cover, resembling the many cuts Bororo self-inflict during funerals.
22. *Baru Xoreu*
Identification: "black sky."
Source: CA
Remarks: Translation is good; no other data available.
23. *Baxe Iware Reuge (Baxe Iwara Eruge, Baxe iware arege)*
Identification: Orion's belt (δ, ϵ, and ζ Orionis).
Source: RBF, CA, *EBI*, F
Remarks: Etymology unclear; *baxe* (sometimes *maxe*) is generic for "heron" but can also mean "mosquito." *EBI* further glosses *iwara* as "ramrod," connoting something straight and hard; *eruge* is glossed as "to make fire."

24. *Bika Joku*
    Identification: Mars; "eye of the *anubranco*."
    Source: *EBI*
    Remarks: *EBI* gives this as being "red like the eye of the *anubranco* bird" and specifically identifies Mars, which was not confirmed during my fieldwork. The word *bika* is the onomatopoeic name for the bird, one of whose calls is *bika*, the other *cijiji*, both being essentially good omens for the hunt.

25. *Boeiga Biagarewu*
    Identification: ε, ξ, e, f Centauri; "the lesser rifle."
    Source: *EBI*, F
    Remarks: There is some discrepancy as to the identification of the "lesser" and "greater" rifles (cf. *EBI*:612–13), although the same stars are involved. The distinction between the firearms as perceived by the Bororo is that of a rifle and shotgun.

26. *Boeiga Kurirewu*
    Identification: γ, τ, G, σ, δ, ρ Centauri; "the greater rifle."
    Source: *EBI*, F
    Remarks: Same as those for Boeiga Biagarewu, above.

27. *Boiga*
    Identification: α Canis Minoris (Procyon); "rifle, bow."
    Source: RBF
    Remarks: Unconfirmed during my fieldwork.

28. *Bokodori Jari Paru Kado Jebage (Bokodori Jari Paru Kajeje Wuge)*
    Identification: α Eridani (Achernar), β Ceti (Diphda), and γ Pegasi (or possibly α Andromedae, Alpheratz).
    Source: (RBF), *EBI*, F
    Remarks: The etymology refers to the hunting of the *bokodori* or giant armadillo, describing either the holes made near the burrow or the hunters around it waiting to catch the animal. Different sources give either three, four, or five stars for this constellation. The positive identification I made was with an informant at 1:30 A.M. in mid-June 1983, when the three stars named were just rising evenly spaced and parallel to the horizon. One informant compared the hunters waiting for the *bokodori* to these stars waiting for the sun. RBF has Bocodori Jari Paro Cado Xobagui as the constellation Centaurus.

29. *Ikoro*
    Identification: a term for morning star.
    Source: *EBI*
    Remarks: This was not confirmed during my fieldwork; *EBI* suggests that it is used primarily in songs.

30. *Ikuie*
    Identification: the Pleiades; referring to brightness.
    Source: F
    Remarks: (I)Kuieje-doge is one denomination for all the stars (see #31 below), and the Pleiades may therefore be marked as "the" star (see #2 above).

31. *(I)Kuieje-doge*
    Identification: the stars; "the possessor of the cord."
    Source: RBF, CA, *EBI*, F
    Remarks: This and other names used to designate the stars (Ipare, Kiege Barege) are references to the origin of stars myth (see chapter 7). The stars as a set are said to pertain to the Apiborege clan.

32. *(I)Kuieje-doge Erugudu*
    Identification: the Milky Way; "ash/luster of the stars."
    Source: *EBI*, F
    Remarks: Informants comment upon its "interesting movement." It seems closely observed considering the importance of certain of its black areas as constellations and the significant stars/constellations in its proximity (see also Ipare Eguru, Ipare Erugudu).

33. *(I)Kuieje Kodu*
    Identification: ?; "flight of the star."
    Source: F
    Remarks: This was contrasted with Aroe Kodu, but no identification was made; a third category of moving star, *estrela andando* (Portuguese), is described as man-made and was applied to satellites and some other unidentifiable phenomena.

34. *(I)Kuieje Kujagureu*
    Identification: ?; "red star."
    Source: F
    Remarks: Although mentioned by different informants, no identification was ever achieved.

35. *(I)Kuieje Kurireu*
    Identification: Venus; "the great star."
    Source: *EBI*
    Remarks: This expression was not used by Garças informants.

36. *(I)Kuieje Ukigareu*
    Identification: any comet; "the tailed star."
    Source: *EBI*
    Remarks: I was unable to confirm this identification.

37. *Ipare, Ipare Eta Mana Mage, Ipare Eta Vie Mage*
    Identification: all stars, the larger/brighter stars, and smaller/
    dimmer stars, respectively; "youths," "older brothers," and
    "younger siblings," respectively.
    Source: F
    Remarks: A reference to the origin of stars myth in which
    young children flee to the sky via a string and become the
    stars; *ipare erudu* can be used to refer to the rise (*erudu*) of stars
    in general (see (I)Kuieje-doge, and Kiege Barege).

38. *Ipare Eguru, Ipare Erugudu*
    Identification: the Milky Way; "tears of the youths," "ash/lus-
    ter of the youths."
    Source: F
    Remarks: Etymology that refers to the origin of stars myth (see
    (I)Kuieje-doge Erugudu, above).

39. *Jekurirewu*
    Identification: Venus (in the east); "the large face."
    Source: *EBI*, F
    Remarks: Although *EBI* does not distinguish this for Venus's
    eastern appearance, my informants were consistent in naming
    Venus in the west Orowaribo Kajijewu, while some recognized
    both eastern and western manifestations as the same celestial
    body. Other names for Venus include Ari Reaiwu, Barogwa
    Tabowu, and Tuwagowu (see specific entries). The Bororo are re-
    ported to have been able to make day time Venus sightings
    (*EBI*:285).

40. *Jerigigi*
    Identification: Rigel (β Orionis)—head—with τ Orionis and β,
    ψ, λ Eridani; alternatively Corvus; a land tortoise.
    Source: CA, *EBI*, F
    Remarks: There is some confusion with respect to this and
    other turtle/tortoise constellations, complicated by the lack of
    standard application in the Bororo area of the Portuguese terms
    jabuti and *cágado* that normally distinguish a terrestrial turtle
    from an aquatic one. Although references in the literature and
    my own fieldwork yield no less than two Jerigigi and two Upe
    (the aquatic turtle; see below), all are acceptable identifications
    and comprise a scheme of constellations four hours apart from
    each other, with an alternation between the species. Just why
    turtles should be so marked is as yet unclear (see chapter 7 for
    further discussion, and figure 7.1).

41. *Jure*

Identification: rainbow, "anaconda" (Portuguese *sucuri*).

Source: RBF, CA, *EBI*, F

Remarks: *Jure* is also a dance, referred to in the myth of Toribugu.

42. *Kaia*

Identification: a black constellation in the Milky Way; the "mortar" of a mortar and pestle.

Source: *EBI*, F

Remarks: One informant showed this as the black spot next to Scorpius's tail; another said that it was "above" the Southern Cross (see Kaibore, below).

43. *Kaibore*

Identification: a black spot in the Milky Way; the "pestle" of a mortar and pestle.

Source: *EBI*, F

Remarks: The same identifications apply as for those of Kaia, above. Additionally, RBF names Caibore as a star of the constellation of Canis Major (Sirius?) and defines it as "mortar." A convincing mortar and pestle can in fact be seen extending from Sirius as black patches in the Milky Way.

44. *Ke*

Identification: α, β, γ, δ Ursa Majoris; a Bororo headdress.

Source: F

Remarks: The bowl of the Big Dipper was said to be the headdress, *ke,* of the culture hero Bakororo although *EBI* lists no such headdress.

45. *Kiege Barege*

Identification: all the stars; *kiege:* birds, *barege:* mammals/animals.

Source: F

Remarks: A note in volume II of the *Enciclopédia Bororo* (p. 1009) glosses *kiege barege* as *aves animais* in Portuguese, or simply *aves*, "birds"; it suggests that the term is specifically applied to the macaws. However, my informants used it for the stars as a group and appeared to apply a much broader gloss to the term, a usage corresponding to the same expression as it applies to a genre of Bororo song in which a great variety of birds and animals are named (e.g., CA:387–88).

46. *Kudoro*

Identification: the constellation Delphinus; "hyacinthine macaw."

Source: *EBI*, F (RBF, CA)
Remarks: This is the largest of the macaws, quite rare in the Bororo area today. RBF gives Cudoro as Algol (β Persei). CA gives Kudoro as part of the constellation Pavo.

47. *Kudoroe Eto-iagareu*
Identification: Dark zones caused at sunset or sunrise by luminous bands extending upwards from the horizon; "tail of the hyacinthine macaw."
Source: *EBI*
Remarks: Also called Meri Urugu ("sun's splendor").

48. *Kunorireu*
Identification: ?; a parrot (*EBI*: *papagaio-campeiro* in Portuguese).
Source: *EBI*
Remarks: I was unable to confirm this identification; *EBI* does not give the stars to which this parrot-shaped constellation corresponds in Western astronomy.

49. *Marido, Marido Imedu, Marido Aredu*
Identification: Corona Borealis as Marido and/or Marido Imedu, Corona Australis as Marido Aredu; a large "wheel" of buriti palm and other materials, paired as "male" and "female."
Source: *EBI*, F
Remarks: The Marido wheels are used for important ceremonies during the funeral, carried atop the heads of a pair of performers, one man supporting the weight of each wheel. Imedu = male = larger, Aredu = female = smaller.

50. *Meri*
Identification: Sun the celestial body; period of daylight; and a culture hero and spirit entity, older brother of Ari, Moon.
Source: RBF, CA, *EBI*, F
Remarks: The sun's position is used to tell day time, and its yearly movement is related to the seasons. The sun's movement forms the basis for the east-west axis of the village and is fundamental for Bororo concepts of space-time.

51. *Okire-doge*
Identification: Pleiades.
Source: F
Remarks: Probably used in special recitations, as Akiri-doge is the common designation for this important star cluster (see also Ikuie, above).

52. *(O)Koge Joku*
Identification: Aldebaran (α Tauri); "eye of the *dourado* fish."
Source: RBF, *EBI*, F

Remarks: Aldebaran as the eye of a fish can be perceived as part of a larger fish constellation whose head is the Hyades, but no Garças informant described it in this way.

53. *Orowaribo Kajijewu*
Identification: Venus, in the west; "that which is/rises over the great water (Paraguai River)."
Source: F
Remarks: This term is applied exclusively to Venus as evening star. Some informants described it as the star that rises and sets only in the west, others recognized it as the same body that appeared in the east as morning star, although maintaining the naming distinction. Other names for Venus include Ari Reaiwu, Barogwa Tabowu, (I)Kuieje Kurireu, Jekurirewu, Tuwagowu. Orowaribo Kajijewu is the only stellar body on which I have data as pertaining to a clan other than Apiborege, and that is to the Baadajebage Xebegiwuge.

54. *Otoe Ira Reuge*
Identification: ?; *otoe* is the plural of *oto*, an edible, nondomesticated plant.
Source: F
Remarks: A group of stars said to be in the shape of a leaf of the *oto* plant, whose fruit is purported to be available all year.

55. *Pari*
Identification: a large formation in the Milky Way composed of several black areas and stars, the head being the Coalsack; "rhea."
Source: *EBI*, F
Remarks: One of the most popular Bororo constellations, it is seen as either running or sitting and sleeping, with its leg and foot up on its shoulder (see #56–#58 below).

56. *Pari Bopona*
Identification: α and β Centauri; "thigh of the rhea."
Source: *EBI*, F
Remarks: These stars cross the rhea's neck and are well known to all Garças villagers.

57. *Pari Burea (Pari Burea-doge)*
Identification: The Southern Cross, α, β, γ, δ Crucis; "track/footprint/foot of the rhea."
Source: RBF, CA, *EBI*, F
Remarks: The Southern Cross is one of the best-known and most watched constellations; informants said that it (along with Akiri-doge, the Pleiades) was used to tell the hours of the

night, and one informant claimed that Pari Burea was "where the stars begin," although the statement was never clarified (see figure 7.6).

58. *Pari Itoru*

Identification: a long, thin, black area "beneath" the Coalsack, the rhea's head; "neck of the rhea."

Source: F

Remarks: This feature is crossed by Pari Bopona, α and β Centauri (see figure 7.6).

59. *Pari Kigadurewu*

Identification: an unidentified light area of the Milky Way; "white rhea."

Source: F

Remarks: This was said to be "below" the black Pari constellation but was never specifically identified.

60. *Piodudu Kudorurewu*

Identification: ?; "dark blue hummingbird."

Source: F

Remarks: I was unable to identify this star/constellation during my fieldwork; it may be significant that in some versions of the origin of stars myth it is a hummingbird who finally achieves tying the cord by which the Bororo children ascend to the sky. A hummingbird also helps Toribugu in some versions of his saga.

61. *Pobogo, Pobogo Aredu, Pobogo Imedu*

Identification: Aredu: ϕ, σ, τ, ζ Sagittarii, the female of this small deer species; Imedu: δ, γ, ϵ, η Sagittarii, the male.

Source: *EBI*, F

Remarks: Fieldwork sessions revealed the positions of these two constellations reported but unidentified in *EBI*. These deer have physical and behavioral characteristics quite distinct from the *atubo*. In one version of the Bororo flood myth a male Bororo mates with a female *pobogo* to re-procreate his people.

62. *Tugiga Kiwu*

Identification: Diphda (β Ceti); *tugiga*: "his antler."

Source: F

Remarks: Tugiga Kiwu is described as a reddish star that rises over the house of Paiwoe, southeast, and I have given it the unverified identification above. Tugiga Tabowu is another name for Toribugu, and the Atubo constellation (Cetus) may be identified with this mythical hero who turns himself into an *atubo* deer in order to kill his father. See chapter 7 for details of the astronomical argument.

63. *Tuwagowu*

Identification: Sirius; meaning unclear.

Source: *EBI*, F

Remarks: The term may be applied to stars other than Sirius, although this identification was made by more than one informant.

64. *Upe*

Identification: π, σ, δ, β, ω (or ψ) Scorpii; or ζ, ρ, ε, δ, σ, η Hydrae (Hydra's head); a freshwater turtle.

Source: RBF, CA, *EBI*, F

Remarks: There are two Upe constellations depicting the freshwater turtle, as there are two Jerigigi or land tortoise constellations, all of which preserve the shapes of their respective terrestrial counterparts. The celestial turtles comprise a system of four constellations, each spaced four hours apart (see chapter 7). While *EBI* depicts Upe with Antares as head, my informants traced a slightly different configuration, but both may be accurate.

65. *Uwai*

Identification: two possibilities:

(a) α, ε, β, γ, δ Corvi, γ Hydrae, and α Virginis

(b) α, ε, β, γ, δ Corvi, γ Hydrae, and η, γ, α, κ Virginis; "cayman."

Source: RBF, CA, *EBI*, F

Remarks: While *EBI* describes Uwai as being near Orion (it is not specifically identified), RBF and CA both link it to Argo (once a large constellation now generally divided into smaller parts in Western astronomy), the latter specifically listing it as Canopus (α Carinae). Garças informants, however, gave a small and large version of Uwai, in yet a third location; there is possibly a system involved comparable to that of the turtle constellations.

Appendix B

Celestial Cross-Reference

Aldebaran (α Tauri): Okoge Joku
Algol (β Persei): Kudoro
Black Spots in the Milky Way: Pari, Kaia, Kaibore
Bright Star/Planet: Barogwa (Kododu)
Centaurus: Boeiga; α and β Centauri: Pari Bopona; Aiepa
Cetus: Atubo; β Ceti: Tugiga Kiwu
Coalsack: Pari (head)
Comet: Ikuieje Ukigareu
Corona Australis: Marido Aredu
Corona Borealis: Marido Imedu
Corvus: Jerigigi, Uwai
Delphinus: Kudoro
Hummingbird Constellation: Piodudu Kudorurewu
Hydra: Upe, Uwai
Jupiter: Barogwa Jeiba
Mars: Bika Joku
Meteor, Shooting Star: Aroe Kodu; cf. Ikuieje Kodu
Milky Way: Ikuieje-doge Erugudu, Ipare Eguru, Ipare Erugudu
Moon: Ari
Morning Star: Ikoro, Barogwa
Orion's Belt: Baxe Iware Reuge
Parrot Constellation: Kunorireu
Pavo: Kudoro
Pleiades: Akiri-doge, Okiri-doge, Ikuie
Procyon (α Canis Minoris): Boiga
Rainbow: Jure
Rigel (β Orionis; and neighboring stars): Jerigigi
Sagittarius: Pobogo
Scorpius: Upe

Sirius: Tuwagowu
Sky: Baru
Southern Cross: Pari Burea
Stars: Ikuieje-doge, Ipare, Kiege Barege
Stars in Corvus, Hydra, and Virgo: Uwai
Stars in Eridanus, Cetus, and Pegasus: Bokodori Jari Paru Kado
   Jebage
Sun: Meri
Sunlight Phenomenon: Kudoroe Eto-iagareu
Ursa Major: Ba Paru Kadoda Jebage, Ke
Venus: Ari Reaiwu, Barogwa Tabowu, Ikuieje Kurireu, Jekurireu,
   Orowaribo Kajijewu

Appendix C

Plant and Animal Species

The following list of plant and animal species mentioned in the text is based primarily upon published information as opposed to samples collected and/or identified by the author and must be considered tentative. Identifying Brazilian flora and fauna is further exacerbated by the proliferation of different names regionally applied to the same species. The absence of English denominations in the lists below reflects either the lack of exact species identification and/or the deficiency of such terms in the published literature. In the latter case, the Portuguese term can be and often is employed. Some of the references used in compiling this information include: Colbacchini and Albisetti 1942, Crocker 1985, Delforge 1945, *EBI* and II, Grzimek 1975, Guimarães 1969 and 1980, Meyer de Schauensee 1970, Mors and Rizzini 1966, Pio Corrêa 1909, Seeger 1981, Von Ihering 1968, and Walker et al. 1983.

Plants

Bororo	English	Portuguese	Latin
Akiri i	—	Angico (branco)	*Piptadenia colubrina* (or *Acacia angico*); Fabaceae (Leguminosae)
Anabo	(aquatic plants)	—	—
Apegirerewu i	—	Cinzeiro or Pau-terra	Genus *Qualea*; Vochysiaceae
Apido	—	Acuri	Genus *Attalea* or *Scheelea phalerata*;

Bororo	English	Portuguese	Latin
			Palmae (Arecaceae)
Api i	—	Sucupira	Genus *Ormosia, Cassiea, Bowdicha* or *Ferreirea;* Fabaceae (Leguminosae)
Bie i	Genipa(p)	Genipapeiro	*Genipa americana;* Rubiaceae
Boe yabutu iworeu	(grass)	—	Graminae (Poaceae)
Bokwado	—	Jatobá (da floresta) or Jutaí	Genus *Hymenaea;* Fabaceae (Leg.)
Eko	Piki	Piqui	*Caryocar brasiliensis;* Caryocaresae
Ema i	—	Ipê- or Piuva-roxa	*Tecoma impetiginosa;* Bignoniaceae
Jatugo	Cashew	Cajú	*Anacardium occidentale;* Anacardiaceae
Kiiri	(wild tuber)	(cará silvestre)	Dioscoreaceae
Kudo	(wild tuber)	(tubérculo silvestre)	—
Kudo i	—	(Timbó do cerrado)	Fabaceae (Leg.) or Sapindaceae
Kuoga, Ixegu i	—	Paratudo or Carobeira	*Tecoma caraiba;* Bignoniaceae
Makaworewu	(wild tuber)	(tubérculo silvestre)	—
Mana guru i	—	Aricá	—
Mana i	—	Lixeira, or Cajueiro bravo	*Curatella (americana);* Dilleniaceae
Mano	—	Caeté or Piripiri	Marantaceae
Marido	—	Buriti	*Mauritia (flexuosa* or *vinifera);* Palmae (Ar.)
Noido	—	Babaçu	*Orbignya (oleifera);* Palmae (Arecaceae)
Oko	(wild tuber)	(cará silvestre)	Dioscoreaceae
Oto	(wild tuber)	(cará silvestre)	Dioscoreaceae
Pobodori	(wild tuber)	(cará silvestre)	Dioscoreaceae
Powari gagurewu i or Adugi i	—	Paineira da floresta	Genus *Bombax;* Bombaceae
Rito	—	Tucum-do-cerrado	*Astrocaryum humile;* Palmea (Arecaceae)
Tara i	—	Angelim	Genus *Hymenolobium* or *Andira;* Fabaceae (Leg.)

Animals

Birds

Bororo	English	Portuguese	Latin
Aere	—	Urutau	Caprimulgidae or Nyctibiidae
Aogwa	Red-crested finch	Tico-tico-rei	*Coryphospingus cucullatus rubescens;* Fringillidae
Aroe Exeba	Harpy eagle	Gavião-real	*Thrasaetus harpyja* (or *Harpia harpyja*); Accipitridae
Barugi	(small hawk or falcon)	(pequeno gavião)	Accipitridae or Falconidae
Baxe	(generic designation for long-legged and -billed birds, e.g., herons)	(garça)	Order Ciconiiformes
Bika or Xijiji	Guira cuckoo	Anu-branco	*Guira guira;* Cuculidae
Enari	(woodpecker)	(pica-pau)	Picidae
Ino	(small bird)	—	—
Kadogare	Kingfisher	Martim-pescador	(*Ceryle americana*); Alcedinae
Kidoe	Parakeet	Periquito	Genus *Pyrrhura;* Psittacidae
Kudoro	Hyacinthine macaw	Araraúna	*Anodorhynchus hyacinthinus;* Psittacidae
Kudorurewu	(dark blue hummingbird)	(beija-flor)	Troquilidae
Kunorireu	(parrot)	Papagaio-campeiro	Psittacidae (sub-family Pioninae)
Kurugugwa	Chimango caracara	Gavião-caracaraí	*Milvago chimango;* Falconidae
Metugu	Pale-vented pigeon	Pomba, Pomba-pocaçu	*Columba cayennensis* (*sylvestris*); Columbidae
O	(stork or ibis)	(socó)	Family Ardeidae
Pari	Rhea	Ema	*Rhea americana;* Rheidae
Parigogo	Guan	Jaku	*Penelope* (*boliviana*); Cracidae
Piodudu	(hummingbird)	(beija-flor)	Troquilidae
Toroa	(large hawk or falcon)	(grande gavião)	Accipitridae or Falconidae

Bororo	English	Portuguese	Latin
Xibae	Red macaw	Araracanga	*Ara chloroptera;* Psittacidae
Xiwaje	Turkey vulture	Urubu-caçador	*Cathartes aura (ruficollis);* Cathartidae
Xururu	Sooty-fronted spinetail	Crispim	*Synallaxia frontalis frontalis;* Furnariidae

Mammals

Bororo	English	Portuguese	Latin
Adugo	Jaguar	Onça pintada	*Panthera onca;* Felidae
Aigo	Puma, Cougar	Onça parda, Suçuarana	*Felis concolor;* Felidae
Aipobureu	Ocelot	Jaguatirica	*Felis pardalis;* Felidae
Atubo	Marsh deer	Veado-galheiro	*Odocoileus* or *Dorcelaphus dichotomus;* Cervidae
Bakure	(monkey)	(macaco branco)	Genus *Aotus;* Cebidae
Bokodori	Giant armadillo	Tatu canastra	*Priodontes giganteus;* Dasypodidae
Buke	Giant anteater	Tamanduá bandeira	*Myrmecophaga tridactyla;* Myrmecophagidae
Ive	Porcupine	Ouriço	Genus *Coendou (insidiosus);* Erethizontidae
Jugo	White-lipped peccary	Queixada	*Tayassu pecari* (or *T. albirostris*); Tayassuidae
Jui	Collared peccary	Caititu	*Tayassu tajacu;* Tayassuidae
Juko	(capuchin monkey)	(macaco)	Genus *Cebus;* Cebidae
Ki	Tapir	Anta	*Tapirus terrestris;* Tapiridae
Koda koda	(tree squirrel)	Caxinguelé, Serelepe	Genus *Sciurus;* Sciuridae
Kudobu	Coati	Quati	*Nasua nasua;* Procyonidae
Mea	Agouti	Cutia	*Dasyprocta aguti, D. azarae;* Dasyproctidae or Caviidae
Okwa	(foxlike animal)	Lobinho	(*Canis thous*); Canidae

Bororo	English	Portuguese	Latin
Pai	Howler monkey	Bugio	Genus *Alouatta*; Cebidae
Pobogo	Brocket deer	Guaçuete, Veado-pardo	*Mazama americana;* Cervidae

Reptiles

Bororo	English	Portuguese	Latin
Arao	(large, blue lizard)	(grande lagartixa azulada)	Order Squamata, sub-order Sauria
Jerigigi	(land tortoise)	(cágado or jabuti)	*Testudo* (*tabulata*); Testudinidae
Jure	Anaconda	Sucuri	*Eunectes murinus;* Boidae
Kukaga	(small lizard)	Lagartixa cabeça-de-pau	Squamata, suborder Sauria
Upe	(river turtle)	(tartaruga aquatica)	Chelidae
Uwai	Cayman	Jacaré	Genus *Caiman;* Alligatoridae

Miscellaneous

Bororo	English	Portuguese	Latin
Buiogo	Piranha	Piranha	Genus *Serrasalmus;* Serrasalmidae
Iyeragadu	(spider)	(aranha)	Order Araneae
Mamore	(giant grass-hopper)	Grande gafanhoto	*Acridium cristatum;* Acrididae
Okoge	(fish)	Dourado	Genus *Salminus;* Characidae

Notes

Chapter 1

1. See especially Aveni 1975, 1977, 1980, 1981, 1982; Aveni and Urton 1982; Aveni and Brotherston 1983; Krupp 1979; Williamson 1981; and Zuidema 1964, 1977, 1982a, 1982b, 1983.

2. For example, see Dumont 1976; S. Hugh-Jones 1979, 1982; Jara and Magaña 1980; Lévi-Strauss 1969, 1973; Magaña 1984; Magaña and Jara 1982; Reichel-Dolmatoff 1971; Urton 1980, 1981a, 1981b; Wilbert 1975; and Wilbert 1981.

3. However, the Bororo currently are making conscious efforts to halt what they themselves perceive as their demise. During my fieldwork an intervillage Bororo meeting took place in Garças village and the Meruri mission, gaining national news coverage. The meeting was the first of its kind for the Bororo, an attempt at consolidation among the villages in order to confront shared difficulties

4. Other relatively early writings on the Bororo include Waehneldt 1862; Koslowski (on the Western Bororo) 1895; Montanegro 1963:1–26; Frič and Radín 1906; Cook 1908; Rondon 1912; and Rondon and Barbosa de Faría 1948.

5. The Bororo are well represented in the anthropological literature, for example, having provided the base for many of Lévi-Strauss's theoretical formulations. Specific studies on the Bororo include the richness and extent of Bororo-derived toponyms (Drumond 1965) and botanic nomenclature (Hartmann 1967); the nature of the relationship of material culture to social organization (Dorta 1979); the Bororo concept of self (Viertler 1979); shamanic and spirit complexes (Crocker 1985); and especially their social organization (Crocker 1967; Z. Levak 1971; Viertler 1976).

6. A recent attempt at grasping native time concepts has been made by Turton and Ruggles (1978) for the Mursi of Ethiopia. These scholars reject the notion of investigating the concepts of time or time reckoning in a non-Western culture, preferring to study what they call "the measurement of duration," this preference based upon a presumed cultural loading of the concept of *time* that makes its use and investigation cross-cul-

turally nonproductive. However, I find their self-admittedly "cumbersome" phrase the "measurement of duration" even more problematic, as it immediately implies an operation—measuring—that by definition (measure: v.t., to compute, or ascertain the extent, quantity, dimensions, or capacity of, especially by a certain rule or standard) conjures up an image of calculations and figures not necessarily applicable to all cultures' reckoning of time. Given that by use of the word *time* we can only approximate another culture's concepts for a dimension that is perceived and marked in some way by all peoples, its use, and the constructive vagueness of the phrases "time concepts" and "time reckoning," seems to offer greater flexibility of application in a cross-cultural context than does the process of "measuring duration."

Chapter 2

1. *Api i* is Bororo for what is called in Portuguese the *sucupira* tree (family Fabaceae/Leguminoseae). As the story demonstrates, it is a wood of the hardest quality. It is fruit-bearing, is considered an excellent firewood when seasoned, and is used while still green for interior house uprights because of its strength and long-lasting quality. Oddly enough my informant did not refer to this as the name of the myth until the wood actually came into the tale (see note 36). The sucupira is regarded by the Gê-speaking Timbira as the "quintessence of strength and toughness" (Nimuendajú 1946:192) and is used by them to ward off fatigue and for medicinal purposes (Nimuendajú 1946:219). As in Bororo culture, the Timbira regard the sucupira as "the symbol of strength and resistance" (Nimuendajú 1946:236).

2. *Reruya* is the general Bororo term for "dance." *Iparereru* is literally "the dance of the youths" from *ipare* "youths," and *reru*, "dance." *Jure*, which my informant offered as another name for the dance, is Bororo for *sucuri* (Portuguese) or anaconda and is also the word for "rainbow." The dance has several parts to it, may have different versions as well, and is sometimes characterized by participating groups of different ages.

3. Toribugu, the protagonist of the myth, is of the Paiwoe clan and its Xoreu or Xebegiwu subdivision. He is also known as Jerigigiatugo, while *EBI* suggests that he is also called Baiporo, although this latter denomination was not in accord with my informant who uses this name (Baipore) for Toribugu's younger brother (note 38 below), while the two names are given as separate lineages (see figure 3.4). Another name for the hero, Tugiga Tabowu, will be discussed in chapter 7. Toribugu can be glossed as "the discoverer or lord of the mountain/stone" from *tori*, "hill, mountain, stone" and *bugu*, "discoverer." In Bororo custom, the first person to see or discover something had the right to claim it for his clan and thus became the lord or owner of it as well.

4. *Oko*, a wild edible tuber (unidentified) was described as ripe during *jorukau*, the dry season, thus fixing this segment of the myth with a calendrical reference. One informant related that flowers blooming on wild potatoes as early as the end of March (prior to the actual dry season) indicate their ripeness for eating.

5. This line was given in Portuguese, "A mãe confiou nesse filho," which can be taken to mean that the mother went too far in trusting her son, who was both audacious and insolent in this context. My appreciation to Silvia Caiuby Novães for her clarification of this line.

6. *Metotudawu*, in Portuguese "mingau de babaçu," is not glossed by other sources. Thick drinks of the nature of the *metotudawu*, a mixture of palm nuts and heart of palm with water, are relished refreshments of the Bororo. "Grandmother": my informant used the Portuguese *avó* to translate the Bororo *imarugo*, a term that can be used to address one's mother's mother, father's mother, father's sister, father's father's sister, or father's father's mother and in general older women of either consanguineal or affinal links (cf. Z. Levak 1971:12; Crocker 1985:53, 65). However, this is also the term by which a child will address the woman (generally a kinswoman of the same clan) who served as midwife upon his birth and who gave the child his name (cf. Z. Levak 1971:43–44; Crocker 1985:65), and thus may more properly be glossed in this instance as "godmother." Kikoroda is a name I have been unable to place with respect to clan membership, leaving this woman's actual relation to Toribugu unresolved. *Iyeragadu*, EBI: *ieragudu*, glossed simply as a large variety of spider. *Koda koda*: while my informant called it a little monkey (Portuguese *macaquinho*), EBI *kodo kodo* is glossed as *caxinguelê*, a squirrel (cf. von Ihering *Serelepe*). As a squirrel (rather than a monkey) the animal conforms to observed tropical squirrel behavior (Garber and Sussman 1984:140-43) which includes a preferred diet of large, hard-shelled fruits and certain palm nuts as particular favorites. *Awu-tu ewugeje:* I have as yet been unable to translate this line.

7. At this point in the narrative, my informant explained, the father wanted to kill his son out of jealousy.

8. *Powari gagurerewu i* (family Bombaceae) is also called *adugo i* or "jaguar tree" and is characterized by bark with deep "incisions." One Bororo myth describes Ari, Moon, as climbing this tree to escape a band of jaguars who, due to the thick, soft bark, are able to scale the tree successfully in pursuit; the incisions left by their claws forever mark the tree.

9. *Adugo do aki, adugo*: "jaguar," *do*: to do or make, *aki*: "you" (2d pers. sing.); together: "become a jaguar," or "you are a jaguar."

10. *Kudo i*, a hardwood of the cerrado. *EBI* describes it as a tree from which vines used to extract fish poison are taken.

11. *Parigogo*, Portuguese *jaku*, a fowl of the Cracidae family (cf. *EBI*, von Ihering). The plant itself is called *parigogo-doge etoyogarewu* (unidentified).

12. *Padarogwa rewure*, "something beautiful," from *padarogwa*, "beauty." While the harpy eagle is commonly called *aroe exeba*, it may also have other designations in the language used in myths and songs. Its feathers are used in many traditional headdresses and adornments.

13. *Kurugugwa*, a large falcon somewhat inferior in size to the harpy eagle, whose feathers are also important for traditional adornments. My informant called it *gavião menor*, the "lesser eagle," in deference to the harpy eagle.

14. In Bororo this plant is called *parigogo-doge etoyoga biagarewu*, literally the "smaller" or "lesser" of the variety named in note 11, above.

15. *Mamore*, a large grasshopper capable of noteworthy sustained flight, particularly prevalent in the Meruri area in January. There are two major varieties, one with a delicate purple shading on its underwings, the other with red underwings and darker in color overall. My informant described this *mamore* as of the red variety.

16. *Aroe*, natural, ancestral, totemic spirits who are the basis for Bororo social organization and in general for natural classification. *Aiyere aroe*, the lord of the rattle: *EBI*: *Aere-doge aroe*, from *aere* or *urutau* (Portuguese) bird. This *aroe* pertains to the Iwagududoge clan and is represented in ceremonies by men of the Kie and Bokodori Exerae clans. Von Ihering describes the urutau (Caprimulgideos fam., *Nyctibius* gen.) as a nocturnal bird also known as *mãe-da-lua* and *manda-lua* ("mother-of-the-moon" and "send-the-moon," respectively) and comments that this bird has "the most impressive nocturnal voice that was given us to hear in nature" (1968:723). *Aroe koe*, *EBI*: *Ekoe aroe*, from a variety of caterpillar or centipede. *Aroe joware*, no available information. *Aroe bakarai*, no available information. *Aroe bokomo-doge*, *EBI*: *bokomu-doge*, who pertain to the Baadajebage Xobugiwuge and are represented by men of Aroroe who chase people with sticks and hooks. *Aroe buregodure-wuge*, *EBI*: *buregodureuge*, pertaining to the Baadajebage Xebegiwuge and represented by Aroroe, who chase people and hit them with clubs. *Aroe paiku-doge*, no available information.

17. Toribugu addresses the jatobá (*bokwado i* in Bororo) as *iedaga*, Bororo for "grandfather" (father's father, mother's father) as well as for mother's brother; it is also the term used by a child for his/her name-giver.

18. Initially I had thought that the *aroe* were calling out the names of the stars as they rose, while Toribugu sat listening in the tree. This would be in keeping with other versions of the naming of stars myth or myth segment, in which a boy hiding in a tree learns the names of stars from

forest spirits. However, my informant was clear that it was Toribugu calling out the stars, answered by the *aroe*. The whistling language described here is still practiced by the Bororo, who communicate simple information quite effectively by this means through whistled syllables and tone variation.

19. *Kiyege barege erudu*, the "rising of the birds/stars." For details on this and other star terms see chapter 7 and Appendix A.

20. *(O)koge joku rutu*, the rise of Aldebaran, α Tauri.

21. *Bokodori jari paru kajeje-wuge erudu*, the rise of several stars that are compared to men who wait for the *bokodori* (giant armadillo) to leave its hole.

22. *Tugiga kiwu rutu*, a red star described as rising over the house of Paiwoe, or south of east as seen from the plaza. *Tugiga*, "his antler," is also part of one of Toribugu's names, Tugiga Tabowu.

23. *Tuwagowu rutu*, the rise of Sirius, α Canis majori.

24. *Jekurireu rutu*, the rise of Venus.

25. *Barogwa tabowu rutu*, "dawn" or "morning star" rises, from *barogwa*, dawn, and *tabowu*, "with" (?); applied to Venus and probably other planets in the appropriate position prior to sunrise. If the related star sequence has any practical calendric value as stated, then the rise of the Pleiades at this time would place it somewhere near mid-June. However, while a star sequence is indicative of such calendric usage, a specific myth-related sequence need not have literal application.

26. *Barogwa kudodu*, an observation made just prior to sunrise (cf. *EBI*: *barogwadodu*, "full or end of dawn").

27. *Tuberigara*, a rod or staff, probably with magical properties. My informant either did not know exactly what it was or, more likely, could not express it adequately in Portuguese.

28. *Ejerigiga: erigiga* is the heart, core, or hardest part of a tree (*EBI*). *Jerigi* is used generically for "firewood"; it is unclear whether the word used in the myth is used for just a general dry, dead wood or a specific type.

29. I have some difficulty with the meaning of this line.

30. The father seems to be using this line as an injunction against his son, as if saying it could bring about the desired results.

31. *Xiwaje* (*urubu-caçador* in Portuguese): von Ihering relates that this large vulture is differentiated at the subspecies level by either a red or orange head, lives in pairs rather than bands, is a masterful flyer able to coast or soar for particularly long periods of time without wing beats, and not only feeds off carion but hunts small prey such as lizards. My informant also made wing shape a distinguishing characteristic.

32. "Camp" is used for the Portuguese *campamento* my informant used here in the myth, as opposed to *aldeia*, "village," which is used at the

beginning and end of the myth. *Makaerewu/makaworewu,* no available information other than its being a wild, edible tuber. *Kiiri, EBI:* "a variety of *cará"* or yam (593). *Kudo, EBI:* "a variety of wild tuber" (593). *Pobodori, EBI:* "a variety of edible tuber of the forest" (593) whose leaves can be used as a "tobacco" (882). All were described by my informants as "wild potatoes" gathered and eaten during *jorukau,* the dry season.

33. *Imedu,* a term of address for any adult male, also applied to son or younger brother (cf. Z. Levak 1971:53).

34. *Imuga,* literally, "my mother." Z. Levak explains (1971:62) that a child may use this address for the woman who raised him/her, including a father's mother or father's sister (of the opposite moiety, and therefore not consanguineally related) when the child feels more at home with his paternal (affinal) relatives. At this point my informant commented upon the incongruity of this scene and the grandmother's actions (sitting with Toribugu on her lap) since, as he put it, "Toribugu was already initiated and sleeping in the men's house."

35. Toribugu is now addressing the old woman as "mother," as opposed to his earlier designation for her, *imarugo,* "grandmother" or "godmother." After using *campamento* again here, the informant briefly explained that it was *jorukau,* the dry season, meaning that the villagers were not inhabiting their semipermanent main village, but a temporary camp. The location of the old woman's shelter is problematic, depending upon her identity as a consanguineal or affinal relative of Toribugu. Even while on trek, the Bororo maintain the proper placement of their social groups in localized clan dwellings.

36. *Atubo,* defined by *EBI* as the *veado-galheiro,* Portuguese, is the largest variety of South American deer and is reported to actually turn upon and attack hunters when cornered. *Api ikiga,* also called *paro i (EBI)* or *parori ikiga,* although there may be some confusion as to the exact variety of tree referred to by the alternate terms. My informant was clear in his designation of the sucupira as the tree used by the hero. It was only at this point that my informant declared the title of the myth.

37. *Bakure : EBI:*214 elaborates upon this term as "a tactic of war and hunting that consists of encircling the objective with concentric circles of warriors."

38. Baipore, Toribugu's younger brother, was named only once by my informant; Baiporo is another name for Toribugu. *Anobo* is an aquatic plant unlisted in *EBI.* Upon mentioning it, my informant immediately referred to a myth he had given me on a previous occasion in which Ari, Moon, is defeated by Adugo, Jaguar, and is thrown into a marsh where he is consumed by piranha and also turns into water plants.

39. The Portuguese *aldeia* is used again here.

40. The woman had possibly noticed the signs where the antlers or sucupira branch had been. It was never specified if Toribugu's mother is one of the women, although such a reading is likely.

41. This final calendric reference was made at the very end of the account. Whether it refers to the calendar time at the end of the myth or to the myth's beginning is not clear; as there is an obvious time flow occurring during the tale, it cannot stand as a reference for the time of the myth in general. See relevant discussion in chapter 7.

42. For more discussion of these relationships see Fabian 1985 and Crocker 1979:283–93, esp. 292–93.

43. This conclusion is also reached by Terence Turner (1985) through his interpretation of the Kayapó (a Gê-speaking people) bird-nester myth. As Turner describes it, the youth left in the macaw nest cannot return with his relative (a sister's husband, in the Kayapó version) to his natal home in the village, because this would relegate him to the perpetual status of "fledgling." Although the relationships are different in the two myths, the Bororo bird-nester version is saying much the same thing: once a boy reaches a certain age, it is shameful for him to live (i.e., sleep) in the same abode as his mother and father (or mother's husband). In relating Toribugu's personal growth and maturation to that of males in general and to the development of certain aspects of culture, I am also presenting another theme that is similar to the results of Turner's myth analysis, which he identifies as a "fundamental principle" of Kayapó society. "The principle is: that control over the power of transformation develops as a corollary of the process of transformation itself. Becoming socialized, in other words, implies acquiring the power to replicate the process one has undergone, which is to socialize others" (1985:97).

44. Z. Levak reports (1971:195) that "when the decision for an initiation ceremony has been made, the men say, 'Let us cook the boys (*pawo ipare ekowu)'*." Although I and others have used the term "cook" to refer to the process of transforming boys into men, the more precise term from the Bororo perspective is almost certainly "roast": food roasted over a fire is characteristically hardened in the process, just as the boys are hardened by their initiation—hardness, as exemplified in the use of the sucupira branch by Toribugu, being the essential quality. The term "cook" in its broadest sense, "to prepare by heat," remains an applicable term. I am indebted to R. T. Zuidema for first bringing this point to my attention.

Chapter 3

1. See Bamberger 1971 for details of the adequacy of Kayapó ecological adjustment; these details can be extended to encompass the other Gê groups and the Bororo who occupy and exploit areas of similar ecology.

2. Hemming (1978: chap. 17) reports that seekers of gold on the upper reaches of the Paraguay River in the first half of the eighteenth century probably effected the first primary or direct contact between Bororo and Europeans/neo-Brazilians.

3. The cover of Manuela Carneiro da Cunha's *Os Mortos e Os Outros* (1978) provides an excellent color illustration of the spokes-of-a-wheel appearance of a Kraho village. Nimuendajú (1946:38, fig. 1) gives a drawing of similar appearance of a Canela village. The Canela and Kraho are both Eastern Timbira groups of the Northern Gê.

4. For more in-depth information regarding the Bororo village and social system, see *EB*I:428–75, *Boe e-wa* entry; Viertler 1976, in which several village models are presented; Z. Levak 1971, specifically 108–36; and Crocker 1967, 1985: esp. 26–37.

5. Subtleties of rhythm or cadence that normally might have characterized the recitation were not noted and were possibly obscured by my exchanges with the informants.

6. Among the Gê, the Eastern Timbira as described by Nimuendajú (1946) present the most dramatic example of layered social groups that crisscross the village and society. Nimuendajú originally detailed four localized moiety systems as functioning in a single Eastern Timbira village: matrilineal exogamous moieties (79–83), rainy season moieties (84–86), plaza moieties (87–90) and age moieties (90–92). In more recent research, Lave (1971, 1979) has criticized Nimuendajú's description of matrilineal exogamous moieties but has upheld the social complexity evident in the other localized and nonlocalized groupings of Eastern Timbira society.

7. In Garças village the two main support pillars on the north and south sides of the men's house each had the enlarged shape of a human hand painted upon them in white pigment (probably *noa*, a clay used in certain important *aroe* representations as body paint). No shapes were painted on the central pillar. Most men had no comment for what these hands represented, but one cultural chief explained that they were the mark of the *aije*, the powerful aquatic *aroe* who appear in the village from along the *aije muga* and *aije rea*, whirring the bullroarer, to preside over male initiation at the end of the funerary period and indicated that a funeral had been performed in the village.

8. The location of the four hereditary chiefs around the central pillar of the men's house, which itself occupies the most cultural and "sacred" space at the center of the village, appears to be a rather graphic representation of the concept "pivot of the four quarters" discussed by Wheatley (1979) with reference to the organization of ceremonial and urban centers.

9. For the Eastern Timbira, concentric and diametric concepts of organization are also combined, specifically through the function and

characteristics of the "rainy season moieties" (Nimuendajú 1946:84-86). In opposition to the Bororo scheme, however, the Eastern rainy season moiety is designated "people of the plaza," while the Western moiety is designated "people from without." A partial list of each of these moiety's characteristics follows.

People of the plaza	People from without
East	West
Sun	Moon
Day	Night
Dry season	Rainy season
Fire	Firewood
Earth	Water
Red	Black
Horizontal lines	Vertical lines

10. Many Gê societies also organize their villages or certain localized social groups within them with a sensitivity for cardinal directionality. Among the Northern Gê, the Eastern Timbira and the Suya have east-west moieties divided by a principal north-south axis, while the Apinayé have localized moieties in the north and south, emphasizing an east-west axis. The Sherente, a central Gê group, traditionally also have north and south moieties separated by an east-west axis that extends via an eastern road called the "path of the sun" (Nimuendajú 1942:16). All of the cultures traditionally construct circular villages, although the Sherente village form is attenuated into a half-moon or horseshoe shape (opening to the west). The dual structural organization of all of these societies and of the Bororo, while varying between an east-west or north-south principal axial orientation, seems to be expressing a shared, or at least similar, cosmological precept. Judging from the fact that either the moieties themselves or the axis separating them are related specifically to the sun (and moon) and its movement, this fundamental cosmological precept must be related in a basic manner to the observed movement and flow of cosmic force and power, as embodied particularly by the sun. Further data and discussion of this material are presented in subsequent chapters.

11. While it is premature to comment further on these structural similarities, they do encourage investigative comparisons on social organizational elements of societies in the Andes and central Brazil and of the area in between.

Chapter 4

1. At the Meruri mission in January of 1983, however, in at least one case a tribal elder sang over a newborn infant accompanied by ceremonial

rattles. Since all births to Garças women took place at the mission hospital during the fieldwork period, I was unable to observe traditional customs relevant to such occasions in the village.

2.   Crocker refers to the *imarugo* as a "generative mediator" in many myths, accomplishing "the passage of the hero from a deathlike sterility to an achievement of his vitality, thus reintegrating him into historical time," and cites the key myth of Lévi-Strauss (i.e., the Toribugu myth) as an example (1985:55).

3.   The repetition of actions three consecutive times seems to be important for proper performance in certain ritual contexts. Note for example Toribugu's three repetitions of the magical formulae that transform selected materials into the lifeless forms of certain birds and mammals.

4.   Z. Levak (1971:194) expresses the relationship between initiation and funeral in this way: "An initiation can only be held when there is a funeral ceremony. When the flesh of the dead person for whom the funeral ceremony is being held has decomposed, the child's brothers start to discuss whom to choose as his *yorubodare*; when the belongings of the deceased are burned, the boy is officially given to his *yorubodare*; when *marenaruye* (dirges) are sung, the sheath is put on the boy's penis."

5.   The relationship between the *aije* and male power is suggested in the phallic appearance of the *aije muga* and *aije rea* as they were drawn by a Bororo cultural chief in figure 3.1.

6.   The Pleiades are an important star group for so many cultures that it would be more surprising not to find them related to indigenous social time. Furthermore, specific correspondence with male initiation is not restricted to the Bororo: the complicated Barasana male initiation cycle is specifically linked in time and symbolism with the Pleiades (S. Hugh-Jones 1979), and the Gê-speaking Suya (Seeger 1981:64, 159) paint a design that is the Pleiades on the bottom of the lip plugs worn by initiated adult males.

7.   Among the Tapirapé, who are neighbors of the Bororo located on the western bank of the Araguaia River, Wagley (1983:101–14) reports age moieties—the "Bird Societies"—each with three age grades designated by bird names. These bird names do not apply to actual species, however, but are said to be "like" either white water birds or parrots. The use of names of legendary animals (or of beings like certain known species) is therefore a point of similarity between the age-ranking systems of the Bororo and those of the Tapirapé, while serving as additional support for the existence of the Bororo age classes.

8.   *Aroe* and *bope* receive the focused attention of Crocker in *Vital Souls* (1985). The complexities of the topic of Bororo spirit beliefs preclude thorough treatment here.

9.   Food exchange is also a more general means of expressing social relations in the village, but particularly during the funerary period communal hunts are undertaken in order to supply greater quantities of food—for human consumption and for the souls and spirits—and the products of any catch will be carried, in both their raw and cooked states, across the village along various lines of relations.

10. Subsequent Bororo chiefs who were granted rights to these powers have been men who exhibited a considerable depth of cultural knowledge and appropriate social comportment but were probably also those with rather specific ancestry within the Baadajebage name groups, or at least subclans, most loosely related to the original Baadajebage chiefs. In contemporary times, due to population decline, these conditions are somewhat relaxed.

11. Maybury-Lewis reports in his book *The Savage and the Innocent* that Shavante trekking occurred on occasion throughout the year, but this does not seem to have been the Bororo pattern. In addition, Maybury-Lewis describes the ability of Shavante trekking groups to remain in communication with each other by observing the telltale smoke from distant campfires and by closely scrutinizing human spoor they encounter while traveling. Hypothetically, such intergroup contact could enable a joint return to the main village if such a move were required (e.g., due to a death) but the existence of such contact does not mean that it would actually result in such a pattern. Trekking in itself was a highly significant social engagement (see Turner 1979a:175-78), while the character of dry season activities and resource availability is not conducive to supporting the type of activities more common to the rainy season. Unfortunately, no published description of Bororo trekking exists, and the Bororo do not currently trek in the traditional pattern, leaving some unresolved questions.

Chapter 5

1.   The positions of the guards of the night as they appear on the diagram are their structural positions, defined by the name group of their birth. Following the Bororo rules of moiety exogamy and uxorilocality, the men themselves would occupy houses in their wives' moieties on the Exerae side of the village, while the announcements were probably delivered from the center of the village.

2.   Similarly, the Shavante "make assignations by indicating a certain number of moons and the phase of the moon in which they wish to meet" (Maybury-Lewis 1974:155).

3.   Nimuendajú reports the same conceptualization of western moonrise among the Eastern Timbira (1946:84).

4. It is interesting to note that the list of months has a pattern of six/four; that is, the first six months begin with *"Ari,"* while the remaining four begin with *"No ari."* Besides estimating half the year, a period of six lunations is potentially significant for eclipse predictions (my appreciation goes to A. F. Aveni for this observation). Eclipses occur when the sun, earth, and moon are aligned, specifically at either new moon (potential solar eclipse) or full moon (potential lunar eclipse). However, due to an approximate 5° inclination of the moon's orbit relevant to the ecliptic (i.e., the plane of revolution of the earth about the sun), an eclipse can only occur when the moon is close to the nodes of its orbit, or the points of intersection of the moon's orbit and the ecliptic, which takes place at approximately six-month intervals. For a detailed discussion see Aveni 1980:67–82, esp. pp. 73–78.

5. Other than corn, the extent of indigenous cultivation and domesticated plant varieties before neo-Brazilian contact is largely undetermined for the Bororo. Cook (1908:60) describes some "little yellow corn" as "about the only thing [the Bororo] cultivate." Frič and Radín (1906:391–92) however, just two years earlier than Cook, refer to Bororo "plantations" in which both corn and manioc (probably of the sweet variety) were cultivated and which were supplemented by smaller house gardens. The *Enciclopédia Bororo* (*EBI*:754) pictures three different varieties of indigenous maize, distinguished by color: yellow, white, and purple.

6. Virtually no corn had been planted with the onset of rains before our visit, but no one could or would explain why it had not been, even though seed had been made available from FUNAI. While we lived in the village, however, a *bari* shaman, who is essential for the blessing of certain foods (including corn) before they can be safely eaten, moved to Garças village and coincidentally corn was being planted avidly with the onset of the next rainy season.

7. Nimuendajú reports such "intercalary" ceremonies for the Eastern Timbira, who observed alternations in years with performances related to initiation, and in those without.

Chapter 6

1. The Eastern Timbira Sun and Moon myth describes Sun as slaying Moon in anger, although the former regrets the act. Moon apparently, however, revives himself in this version (Nimuendajú 1946:244).

2. Apparently Meri's spirit animates the fish that is successfully caught by Ari; a similar technique is traditionally part of the *aroe etawarare* shaman's repertoire of abilities.

3. The north-south motion of the sun and moon is noted by the Bororo, who are able to point out the sun's extremes as seen from the vil-

lage of Garças, while also relating them to the appropriate seasons. Nimuendajú claims (1946:232) that the Eastern Timbira "know approximately where the sun rises and sets during the wet and dry seasons, but they do not empirically determine the solstice or use it in time reckoning." I find it difficult to accept that the Eastern Timbira did not determine the solar extremes, given other features of their culture.

Chapter 7

1. See Appendix C for animal nomenclature.

2. It is interesting to note that in both the Toribugu myth and the origin of stars myth the youths trapped in this dilemma use the sucupira tree to help resolve the conflict: Toribugu, by donning sucupira branches, becoming an antlered *atubo* deer, and impaling his father; and the youths of the stars origin myth by climbing away from their mothers via a cord tied to a sucupira tree in the sky. These similarities reenforce the interpretations of both myths as presented here, and the significance of the sucupira as symbolizing strength and hardness, and the relationship of these traits with maturation.

3. Figure 7.1 makes use of Sky Publishing Corporation's SC001 Constellation Chart, reproduced by permission. Lines linking the stars comprising Western constellations have been deleted, while those linking Bororo constellations have been added. Bororo astronomical terms are underlined.

4. To aid in the use of Appendix A, Appendix B lists astronomical bodies as known in Western astronomy with their Bororo counterparts.

5. In an earlier work (Fabian 1982:291–92) I analyzed two of the star sequences: versions C and D of table 7.2. The ability to make sense out of the order of the stars in each list has not been facilitated by fieldwork, as new versions and identifications have only added to the multiplicity of names and specific stellar groups and the relationship of these with empirically observable phenomena.

6. The most detailed treatment published to date of native South American beliefs with respect to the Milky Way, including illustrations of this apparent "flip-flop motion," is the work of Gary Urton (especially 1981b).

7. Dark formations in the Milky Way are classed by Urton as "Dark Cloud constellations" as translatable from the Quechua *yana phuyu* (1981b:109).

8. Von del Chamberlain, in his book on Pawnee astronomy, includes a letter from astronomer F. R. Moulton written in 1906 that relates in its first entry, on Venus, that "Good Eagle said he had seen

[Venus] while lying on his back near noon. This is a rather difficult feat for one who does not know precisely where to look, but it is by no means impossible" (1982:226). In the Andes, Urton also reports that the Quechua are able to make day time Venus sightings (1981b:166). It can be expected that other indigenous groups were capable of making similar observations of Venus in the day time, but that record of it has not always found its way into the published literature.

9.   Urton was told the "proper way" to make daytime Venus sightings by the Misminay Quechua. "The 'proper way' to look is by cupping the index finger into the base of the thumb to produce a tiny viewing slit. When the hand is held to the eye in this way, the amount of light entering the eye is greatly reduced and if one knows the exact position of Venus (and if it is in a crescent phase) the planet will be easily visible" (1981b:166).

10.   When designated Barogwa Jeiba by two informants, Jupiter was not currently appearing as a morning star.

11.   Urton also reports a class or classes of names applicable to the planets, representing data that he himself did not fully understand (1981b:166–67). It seems apparent that native South Americans perceived the planets as a special set of stars, but our comprehension of their beliefs is still lacking.

12.   Urton likewise notes that certain Quechua planetary designations are also applicable to bright (first magnitude) stars (1981b:167).

13.   Lévi-Strauss notes that Von den Steinen commented that the Bororo "were not always in agreement about the meaning of the constellations" (quoted 1969:228) and suggested a certain lack of stability in Bororo stellar nomenclature, which he demonstrates by citing names such as the Great Gun and Small Gun, that is, names of relatively recent influence. According to Lévi-Strauss, "the most recent [star names] are to be viewed with a certain degree of suspicion" (1969:229). The incidence of modern names among a stellar repertoire, however, neither necessarily reinforces nor denies the correctness of earlier constellation identifications as opposed to those made at a later time. Indeed, such appellations may indicate the robust state of a people's astronomy, reflecting other cultural changes.

14.   Right ascension is the system of celestial longitude used to measure the celestial sphere into twenty-four hour divisions, 0 hours (0^h) being at the vernal equinox on the celestial equator.

15.   Crocker suggests that both *jerigigi* and *upe* are in fact aquatic species, and that they obtain the marked distinction as taboo food for new parents through association with the "alligator," which is considered too

potent a food for such parents to consume. While Crocker's argument may be internally consistent, his identifications of both *jerigigi* and *upe* as aquatic species are questionable: in the constellations, Jerigigi is boxlike and similar to the terrestrial tortoise, while Upe has the long neck and general shape of the riverine turtle (e.g., *EBI*:613). Their marked state should be explained by reasons other than association with caymans.

16. In applying to mythology for astronomical content, it is not my intention to suggest that to have established such content is to claim a full rendering of the "meaning" of a myth. On the contrary, I agree with Lévi-Strauss's comment: "the astronomical context does not provide any absolute point of reference; we cannot claim to have interpreted the myths simply by relating them to this context" (1969:240). Neither, however, should the astronomical information in myths be overlooked for its fullest cultural contributions. Particularly in the realm of space-time can astronomy provide tools for greater cultural understanding. Lévi-Strauss describes the astronomical code in myth as being "drawn from a stable spatio-temporal whole, consisting, on the one hand, of the diachronic periodicity of the year and, on the other, of the synchronic arrangement of stars in the sky" (1969:240).

17. Compare this table with table 3 in Maybury-Lewis's *Akwe-Shavante* and with figure 3 of S. Hugh-Jones's *The Palm and the Pleiades*. The "Sun" category immediately below the Western calendar month designations is not meant to represent Bororo data, as Bororo observation or notation of all of these solar positions cannot be substantiated. Nevertheless, solar extremes are known, and knowledge of the equinoxes—as midway between—is therefore implied. Zenith positions (*baru aiadada*, "center of the sky") are also noted by the Bororo, although I did not specifically observe the marking of a solar zenith passage in Garças village.

Chapter 8

1. Zuidema (1982b) specifically relates the reduplicative southwestern quadrant (Cuntisuyu) of the Inca *ceque* system of Cuzco with considerations of a stellar- and sidereal lunar-based calendar scheme. Specifically, observations of the rise and set points of the Southern Cross bracket the southern section of the *ceque* system labeled by Zuidema IVB (including the double line IVA3a, c). The Cuzco data suggest further investigation into the principles by which the Bororo village is patterned and the positioning of localized social groups. It is not unlikely that, because solar observations are used to align the village, stellar observations might serve as factors in the placement of social groups. However, the coincidence of the data on Bororo village organization with that of certain Andean orga-

nization patterns, as in Cuzco, likewise suggests a further analysis of the factors behind the Andean reduplication patterns.

2.   Data on the system of callers who guard the night suggest a symbolic relationship between each caller and his function based upon the sets of clan "totems." For example, the last caller, Meriri Baru of the Paiwoe clan, tells people to color their bodies with urucu (or annatto; *nonogo*). Urucu pertains to the Paiwoe clan.

3.   Lévi-Strauss overstresses the significance of the endogamic marriage preferences between subclans (cf. *EBI*: Boe Ewa entry; Z. Levak 1971; and Crocker 1969b, 1978, and 1979), however, as well as the supposed hierarchic levels of the subclans. The reference to the latter as "upper," "middle," or "lower" actually refers most specifically to their conceptualized locations east to west, with east being "up" and west being "down." Furthermore, Lévi-Strauss particularly relates his discussion to details of marriage rules and preferences, leaving out important additional social and cultural material that could be brought to bear upon his central question. For more on these issues, see Maybury-Lewis's (1960) critique of Lévi-Strauss's article, and Lévi-Strauss's response (1960). In considering questions of dual organization it seems reasonable to extend the concept to encompass more than marriage regulations. In this regard I agree with Maybury-Lewis (1974, 1979a, 1979b), who suggests that the concept be extended so that any coherent set of cultural oppositions evident in cultural beliefs, institutions, and symbolism, and expressible by a dyadic model, be considered a dual organization. By all accounts, the Bororo are exemplary of either definition of dual organization.

4.   Sun is also perceived in social relations with the Gê people. Among the Apinayé, for example, the northern moiety is considered to be people of the Sun, and the southern moiety people of the Moon. Nimuendajú reports that the Apinayé "regard the Sun as their creator and the father of mankind, and to him they ascribe the dual organization and the localization of moieties" (1967:133).

Chapter 9

1.   Z. Levak contends, however, that the naming of lineages would proceed in a complete circle, rather than making two opposite semicircles (1971:123).

2.   For the Sherente, on the other hand, the clans located in the easternmost portion of the village seem to have a higher social ranking than the other clans, especially as opposed to the "foreign" clans located further to the west. The Sherente also deemphasize the importance of this spatially related social hierarchy by stressing additional prestige and power positions that are disassociated from clan positions. The eastern and west-

ern weighting for both Sherente and Bororo that does exist can be described as relating to the flow of solar and cosmic forces (east to west) and the integration of these forces within society.

3. Both of these ranking systems, that of clan chiefs based upon named identity, and men's house positioning, are characterized by some variance between their ideal pattern and actual practice. In the men's house, the central position is occupied by the village headmen, cultural chiefs with the greatest amount of traditional knowledge. Since hereditary chiefs may not even exist in a given village today, there is little or no conflict over the superimposition of two different hierarchy sets on the same space. As for clan "chiefs," Salesian data in the *Enciclopédia Bororo*, information gathered in Garças village, and early writings of Crocker substantiate hereditary name-based holders of these positions. However, contemporary observations also suggest that practical and demonstrated knowledge in *boe ero* (Bororo tradition) is rewarded by the village elders with recognition of increased status and de facto clan/subclan leadership. As Crocker has written about it, "The lineage which is ranked highest should provide the clan head. . . . These ranks . . . are completely fixed and unalterable. . . . In fact, though, the complex linear structure is greatly modified in practice to accord with the particular social, demographic and political situation in a given village" (1971:387). Crocker later writes, "There can be but one chief in any subclan, and Bororo constantly compare the ritual abilities and personal moralities of rivals for these positions. The fact that their incumbency is often temporary and the prestige hierarchy within the moiety ambiguous adds to the intensity of competition: the prize is never completely won" (1985:115). These differences in ideal and real patterns do not create difficulties within the contemporary context—indeed, they may have resulted because of it—because the small village populations of present day Bororo often lack representatives of the heredity-based positions.

4. In the New World the Maya are best known for their systems of interlocking cycles: the *tzol kin*, a 260-day cycle that combined 13 numerals with 20 named days; the *haab*, a 365-day "vague" year comprised of 18 months of 20 days (plus an additional 5); and the two intermeshed in a cycle that repeats itself every 52 years (see Aveni 1980 for a thorough treatment of Mesoamerican astronomy and calendrics). They were also aware of a 584-day Venus cycle (including periods of that planet's appearance as morning and evening star and its intermittent disappearances), and its intermeshing with the 365-day vague year every 8 solar years, or every 5 Venus years ($8 \times 365 = 2920 = 5 \times 584$).

5. The term "anti-zenith" was coined by R. Tom Zuidema in an effort to distinguish this phenomenon among the Inca from the more

technical "nadir" crossing of the sun, since the anti-zenith among the Inca was probably derived from calculations based upon solar zenith crossing. It was Zuidema's search for a location in Peru in which the year could be evenly segmented into eight parts according to major solar events (solstices, equinoxes, zenith and nadir positions) that led to the formulation of the computations presented at the New York Academy of Sciences meeting. For Incaic Peru, the location at which the eight-part year may be found centers significantly upon the Island of the Sun in Lake Titicaca.

6.   While tallying is a most effective way of counting, anyone involved in totaling quantities will eventually have use for naming those quantities and the figures that comprise them. (Note that the English verb "to count" comes from the Latin *computare*, which combines *com-*, together, and *putare*, to cleanse, prune, adjust, that is, the sense of counting or computing in making something neater, cleaner, better ordered.) The Bororo do have names for numbers, but only for one (*mito*) and two (*pobe*) are the terms discrete. Other numbers are unwieldy statements related to quantities expressed by digits upon the hands and feet, such as: 3, *ure pobe ma jewu metuya bokware* ("a pair of them and that one whose partner is lacking"); 5, *ure ikera awubodure* ("as many of them as my hand complete"); 10, *ikerako boejeke* ("my fingers all together in front") or *ikera pudogidu* ("one hand near the other"); 13, *ixare buture ivure boeyadadawuto pugeje* ("now the one on my foot that is in the middle again"); and 20, *ixare maka rema avure* ("now it is as many as there are with your feet"). (Numbers and translations are taken from Lounsbury 1978:761, and *EBI*:800.) For the Bororo, such numerics were adequate for recognizing the relation of celestial periodicities and natural diurnal and seasonal cycles, and for relating these intuitively and cosmologically with their own social cycles.

7.   Much of the hypothesized temporal system of Bororo age classes has been based upon the Shavante system as described by Maybury-Lewis (1974). It is interesting to note that the Shavante age-set system has been rigorously maintained over time, while that of the Bororo is vestigial. The Bororo, however, have maintained their system of localized social groups and the codification of knowledge that this system entails. Among the Gê, it is only the Sherente, close relatives of the Shavante, who have had localized clans reported (Nimuendajú 1942:16–23; although this claim has been questioned by Maybury-Lewis [1979b:232–33]). Sherente villages, like Bororo villages, are also oriented along a major east-west axis. The Shavante have preferred to emphasize the age-set system and deemphasize the localization of corporate units, and this shift away from spatial concerns is reflected in the lack of paradigmatic orientation of their villages, which have their horseshoe-shaped opening towards a source of water.

8.   Further analysis of both the Bororo culture in general and the Toribugu myth specifically is almost certain to complicate this space-time formulation. For example, some evidence may indicate that seasonality may not be directly related to the respective moieties but may rather span the moieties: one cultural elder claimed that *bubutu*, or rain, was associated with both Paiwoe and Bokodori Exerae clans, which might suggest that the eastern half of the village may have rainy season associations, implying also a relationship between the western half and the dry season. Such a situation would emphasize the secondary north-south village axis.

9.   Goody does, however, describe the "relationship between utterance and text, between oral and written discourse, [as] a complex, dialectical process" (1977:114). In attempting to deemphasize the dichotomy between the "savage" and the "domesticated" mind, he also observes that both magic and science, myth and history are present "not only in the same societies but in the same individuals" (1977:148).

Chapter 10

1.   While this comparison was never heard explicitly among the Bororo, neighboring groups, e.g., the Tapirapé, do specifically relate the annual maize cycle to the human life course (cf. Wagley 1983).

References

Aaboe, Åsger, and Derek J. de Solla Price
1964   Qualitative Measurement in Antiquity: The Derivation of Accu-
        rate Parameters from Crude but Crucial Observations. In
        L'Aventure de la Science 1:1–20, ed. Melanges Alexandre Koyre.
Abbeville, Claude d'
1963   *Histoire de la Mission des Pères Capucins en l'Isle de Maragnan et
        Terres Circonvoisins* (1614). Akademische Druck-u. Verlags-
        anstalt, Graz, Austria.
Actes du XLIIe Congrès International des Américanistes
1977   Vol. 2: Social Time and Social Space in Lowland South Ameri-
        can Societies, pp. 1–394 (1976). Paris.
Aveni, Anthony F.
1980   *Skywatchers of Ancient Mexico.* University of Texas Press, Austin.
1982   *Archaeoastronomy in the New World: American Primitive Astron-
        omy.* Cambridge University Press, Cambridge.
Aveni, Anthony F., ed.
1975   *Archaeoastronomy in Pre-Columbian America.* University of Texas
        Press, Austin.
1977   *Native American Astronomy.* University of Texas Press, Austin.
Aveni, A., and G. Brotherston, eds.
1983   *Calendars in Mesoamerica and Peru: Native American Computation
        of Time.* British Archaeological Reports no. S174, Oxford.
Aveni, A., and Gary Urton, eds.
1982   *Ethnoastronomy and Archaeoastronomy in the American Tropics.* In
        Annals of the New York Academy of Sciences 385. New York.
Bakhtin, M. M.
1981   *The Dialogic Imagination.* University of Texas Press, Austin.
Baldus, Herbert
1940   O Conceito do Tempo Entre os Indios do Brasil. In *Revista do
        Arquivo Municipal* 71:87–94. São Paulo.
Bamberger, J.
1971   The Adequacy of Kayapó Ecological Adjustment. In *Proceedings of
        the 38th Congress of Americanists* 3:373–79 (Stuttgart-Munich, 1968).

Bateson, Gregory
1980   *Mind and Nature*. Bantam, New York.
Bear, Fred
1976   *Fred Bear's Field Notes*. Doubleday, New York.
Birkhoff, Garrett, and Saunders MacLane
1965   *A Survey of Modern Algebra*. 3d ed. Macmillan, New York.
Blatt-Fabian, Surabela
1985   Basketry Knowledge and Weaving among Women of the East-
           ern Bororo of Mato Grosso, Brazil. Master's thesis, University of
           Illinois, Urbana-Champaign.
Bordignon Enawuréu, Mario
1987   Os Bororos na História do Centro Oeste Brasileiro 1716–1986.
           Missão Salesiana de Mato Grosso (CIMI/MT). Campo Grande,
           MS, Brazil.
Bourge, Pierre, and Michel Vignand
1976   Miniciel Austral: Carte Céleste Mobile. Bonnefoy, La Mênière,
           Paris.
Bruner, Edward M., ed.
1984   *Text, Play, and Story: The Construction and Reconstruction of Self
           and Society*. Proceedings of the American Ethnological Society,
           1983, Washington, D.C.
Carneiro da Cunha, Manuela
1978   *Os Mortos e os Outros*. Editora Hucitec, São Paulo.
Chamberlain, Von del
1982   *When Stars Came Down to Earth*. Ballena Press Anthropological
           Papers No. 26. Ballena, Los Altos, California.
Colbacchini, Antonio
1925   *I Bororos Orientali "Orari Mugudoge" del Mato Grosso (Brasile)*.
           Contributi Scientifici delle Missioni Salesiane del Venerabile
           Don Bosco, I. Torino, Italy.
Colbacchini, Antonio, and César Albisetti
1942   *Os Bororos Orientais*. São Paulo.
Cook, W. A.
1908   The Bororo Indians of Mato Grosso, Brazil. *Smithsonian Miscel-
           laneous Collections* 50 (1789):48–62, Washington, D.C.
Crocker, J. Christopher
1967   *Social Organization of the Eastern Bororo*. Ph.D. dissertation, De-
           partment of Social Relations, Harvard University, Cambridge.
1969a   Men's House Associates among the Eastern Bororo. In *South-
           western Journal of Anthropology* 25:236–60.
1969b   Reciprocity and Hierarchy among the Eastern Bororo. In *Man*
           4:44–58.

1971   The Dialectics of Bororo Social Reciprocity. In *Verhandlungen des XXVIII Internationalen Amerikanisten Kongress* (Proceedings of the 38th International Congress of Americanists), August 1965, pp. 389–91. Stuttgart.

1977   My Brother the Parrot. In *The Social Use of Metaphor*, ed. J. D. Sapir and J. C. Crocker, pp. 164–92. University of Pennsylvania, Philadelphia.

1978   Why Are the Bororo Matrilineal? In *Actes du XLII Congrès International de Américanistes* 2: 245–58.

1979   Selves and Alters Among the Eastern Bororo. In *Dialectical Societies*, ed. David Maybury-Lewis, pp. 249–300. Harvard University Press, Cambridge.

1983   Being and Essence: Totemic Representation Among the Eastern Bororo. In *The Power of Symbols*, ed. N. R. Crumrine and M. Halpin, pp. 154–73. University of British Columbia Press, Vancouver.

1985   *Vital Souls*. University of Arizona Press, Tucson.

Crowell, Janet I.

n.d.   Pedagogical Grammar of Bororo. Summer Institute of Linguistics.

Crowell, Thomas H.

n.d.   A Grammar of Bororo. Summer Institute of Linguistics.

Delforge, Henrique

1945   *Glossário dos Nomes Vulgares das Plantas do Herbário da Seção de Botânica*. Serviço de Documentação, Ministério da Agricultura, Rio de Janeiro.

Dorta, Sonia Ferraro

1979   Cultura Material e Organização Social: Algumas Inter-relações Entre os Bororo de Mato Grosso. *Revista do Museu Paulista*, Nova Série 26:235–46. Universidade de São Paulo, São Paulo.

Drumond, C.

1965   *Contribuição do Bororo à Toponímia Brasílica*. Instituto de Estudios Brasileiros, Universidade de São Paulo, São Paulo.

Dumont, Jean-Paul

1976   *Under the Rainbow*. University of Texas, Austin.

Enciclopédia Bororo (Cesar Albisetti and Angelo Venturelli)

1962   Vol. I: Vocabulários e Etnografia.

1964   Vol. II: Lendas e Antropônimos.

1976   Vol. III (part 1): Textos dos Cantos de Caça e Pesca. Museu Regional Dom Bosco, Campo Grande, Mato Grosso do Sul, Brazil.

Fabian, Stephen M.

1982   Ethnoastronomy of the Eastern Bororo Indians of Mato Grosso, Brazil. In *Ethnoastronomy and Archaeoastronomy in the American*

Tropics, ed. A. F. Aveni and G. Urton, pp. 283–302. New York Academy of Sciences, New York.

1983   Os Bororos Orientais Contemporâneos: Relatório Preliminar. In *Boletím Informativo,* ed. Missão Salesiana de Mato Grosso, pp. 41–50. Campo Grande, MS, Brazil.

1985   Life Through Death in the Bororo Funeral. Paper presented at American Anthropological Association annual meeting, Washington, D.C.

1987a   *Eastern Bororo Space-Time: Structure, Process and Precise Knowledge Among a Native Brazilian People.* Ph.D. dissertation, Department of Anthropology, University of Illinois, Urbana-Champaign.

1987b   Review of *Animal Myths and Metaphors in South America* by Gary Urton. *Western Folklore* 46:60–62.

Frič, V., and P. Radín

1906   Contributions to the Study of the Bororo Indians. *Journal of the Anthropological Institute of Great Britain and Ireland* 36:382–406.

Gaposchkin, Sergei

n.d.   The Visual Milky Way. Harvard Reprint #535, reprinted from *Vistas in Astronomy,* Volume 3 (Pergamon, New York). Harvard College Observatory, Cambridge.

Garber, Paul, and R. W. Sussman

1984   Ecological Distinctions Between Sympatric Species of *Saguinus* and *Sciurus. American Journal of Physical Anthropology* 65:135–46.

Geertz, Clifford

1974   *The Interpretation of Cultures.* Basic Books, New York.

Goody, Jack

1977   *The Domestication of the Savage Mind.* Cambridge University Press, Cambridge.

Grzimek, Bernard, ed.

1975   *Grzimek's Animal Life Encyclopedia.* Vol. 2, Insects; vol. 4, Fishes 1; vol. 5, Fishes 2 and Amphibia; vol. 6, Reptiles; vols. 10–14, Mammals 1–4. Litton World Trade Corp., Van Nostrand Reinhold, New York.

Guaman Poma de Ayala, Felipe

1936   *El Primer Nuevo Corónica y Buen Gobierno* (1615). Institut d'Ethnologie, Paris.

Guimarães Ferri, Mário

1969   *Plantas do Brasil: Espécies do Cerrado.* Editôra da Universidade de São Paulo, São Paulo.

1980   *Vegetação Brasileira.* In *Coleção Reconquista do Brasil,* Nova Série 26. Editora da Universidade de São Paulo, São Paulo.

Hanbury-Tenison, Robin

1973   *A Question of Survival for the Indians of Brazil.* Charles Scribner's Sons, New York.

Hartmann, Thekla

1964   Aculturação dos Bororo do São Lourenço—12 anos depois. MS on file, Museu Paulista, Universidade de São Paulo, São Paulo.

1967   *A Nomenclatura Botânica dos Bororo.* Instituto de Estudos Brasileiros, Universidade de São Paulo, São Paulo.

Hemming, John

1978   *Red Gold.* Harvard University Press, Cambridge.

Hugh-Jones, Christine

1979   *From the Milk River.* Cambridge University Press, Cambridge.

Hugh-Jones, Stephen

1979   *The Palm and the Pleiades.* Cambridge University Press, Cambridge.

1982   The Pleiades and Scorpius in Barasana Cosmology. In *Ethnoastronomy and Archaeoastronomy in the American Tropics*, ed. A. F. Aveni and G. Urton, pp.183–202. New York Academy of Sciences, New York.

Huxley, F.

1966   *Affable Savages.* Capricorn, New York.

Isbell, Billie Jean

1982   Culture Confronts Nature in the Dialectical World of the Tropics. In *Ethnoastronomy and Archaeoastronomy in the American Tropics*, ed. A. F. Aveni and G. Urton, pp. 353–63. New York Academy of Sciences, New York.

Jara, Fabiola, and E. Magaña

1980   The Jaguar Against the Wolf: Analysis of a Myth of the Kamayura Indians (Central Brazil). In *Boletín de Estudios Latinoamericanos y del Caribe.* No. 29, December, pp. 3–31. CEDLA, Amsterdam.

Koslowski, J.

1895   Algunos Datos Sobre los Indios Bororos. *Revista del Museu de La Plata* 6:373–412, La Plata.

Kozak, Vladimir

1963   Ritual of a Bororo Funeral. *Natural History Journal* 72 (1):38–49.

Krupp, E. C., ed.

1979   *In Search of Ancient Astronomies.* McGraw-Hill, New York.

Lakoff, George, and Mark Johnson

1980   *Metaphors We Live By.* University of Chicago Press, Chicago.

Lave, Jean

1971   Some suggestions for the Interpretation of Residence, Descent
            and Exogamy Among the Eastern Timbira. In *Proceedings of the
            38th International Congress of Americanists* 3:341–45 (Stuttgart-
            Munich, 1968).

1979   Cycles and Trends in Krikatí Naming Practices. In *Dialectical
            Societies*, ed. D. Maybury-Lewis, pp. 16–44. Harvard University
            Press, Cambridge.

Leach, E. R.

1950   Primitive Calendars. *Oceania* 20 (4):245–62.

1954   Primitive Time-Reckoning. In *A History of Technology* I:110–27,
            ed. C. Singer. Clarendon, Oxford.

Lehman, F. K.

1985   Cognition and Computation: On Being Sufficiently Abstract. In
            Directions in Cognitive Anthropology, ed. Janet W. D. Dougherty,
            pp. 19–48. University of Illinois Press, Urbana and Chicago.

Levak, Milena

1979–80   Motherhood by Death among the Bororo Indians of Brazil.
            Omega 10(4):323–34.

Levak, Zarko D.

1971   *Kinship System and Social Structure of the Bororo of Pobojari.* Ph.D.
            dissertation, Yale University, New Haven.

Lévi-Strauss, Claude

1936   Contribution a l'Étude de l'Organisation Social des Indíens
            Bororo. *Journal de la Socíeté des Amé. ricanistes* 28:269–304.

1960   On Manipulated Sociological Models. *Bijdragen tot de Taal-,
            Land-en Volkenkunde* 116:45–54.

1963a   Do Dual Organizations Exist? In *Structural Anthropology,* pp.
            132–66. Basic Books, New York.

1963b   Social Structures of Central and Eastern Brazil. In *Structural
            Anthropology,* pp. 120–31. Basic Books, New York.

1969   *The Raw and the Cooked.* Harper and Row, New York.

1973   *From Honey to Ashes.* Harper and Row, New York.

1975   *Tristes Tropiques.* Atheneum, New York.

1978   *The Origin of Table Manners.* Harper and Row, New York.

1981   *The Naked Man.* Harper and Row, New York.

Lounsbury, Floyd

1978   Maya Numeration, Computation, and Calendrical Astronomy.
            In *Dictionary of Scientific Biography.* Vol. 15, ed. C. C. Gillispie,
            pp. 759–818.

Magalhães, Basilio de

1919   Vocabulario da Lingua dos Bororos-Coroados do Estado de

Mato Grosso. *Revista do Instituto Historico e Geographico Brasileiro* (1918) 83:5–67.

Magaña, Edmundo
1984   Carib Tribal Astronomy. In *Social Science Information: Man and His Environment*, pp. 341–68. Sage, London.

Magaña, E., and F. Jara
1982   The Carib Sky. *Journal de la Société des Américanistes* 68: 105–32.

Manning, Frank E., ed.
1983   *The Celebration of Society*. Bowling Green University Popular Press, Bowling Green, Ohio.

Marshack, Alexander
1972   *The Roots of Civilization*. McGraw-Hill, New York.

Maybury-Lewis, David
1960   The Analysis of Dual Organizations: A Methodological Critique. In *Bijdragen tot de Taal-, Land-en Volkenkunde* 116:17–44.
1965   *The Savage and the Innocent*. Evans, London.
1974   *Akwe-Shavante Society*. Oxford University Press, New York.
1979a   Cultural Categories of the Central Gê. In *Dialectical Societies*, ed. D. Maybury-Lewis, pp. 218–46. Harvard University Press, Cambridge.

Maybury-Lewis, David, ed.
1979b   *Dialectical Societies*. Harvard University Press, Cambridge.

Menzel, Donald H.
1964   *A Field Guide to the Stars and Planets*. Houghton Mifflin, Boston.

Meyer de Schauensee, Rodolphe
1970   *A Guide to the Birds of South America*. Livingston, Wynnewood, Pennsylvania (for the Academy of Natural Sciences of Philadelphia).

Montanegro, O. P.
1963   Estructura e Rítmo na Sociedade Bororo. In *Boletin do Museu Nacional*, Antropologia, No. 22. Rio de Janeiro.

Mors, Walter B., and Carlos T. Rizzini
1966   *Useful Plants of Brazil*. Holden-Day, San Francisco.

Mourão, Ronaldo Rogério de Freitas
1982   *Atlas Celeste*. 4th ed. Editora Vozes, Petrópolis, Rio de Janeiro.
n.d.   Carta Celeste do Brasil. Livraria Francisco Alves.

Nimuendajú, Curt
1942   *The Serente*. Publications of the Frederick Webb Hodge Anniversary Publication Fund, 4. Southwest Museum, Los Angeles.
1946   *The Eastern Timbira*. Translated and edited by R. H. Lowie. In *University of California Publications in American Archaeology and Ethnology* 41. University of California Press, Berkeley.

1967   *The Apinayé.* In *Anthropological Publications.* Oosterhout N. B.,
            The Netherlands.

Norton, Arthur P.

1964   *A Star Atlas and Reference Handbook.* 15th ed. Sky Publishing,
            Cambridge.

Oliveira, J. Feliciano de

1913   The Cherentes of Central Brazil. In *18th International Congress of
            Americanists* (1912), pp. 391–96. London.

1913   The Cherentes: Linguistics, Numeration and Vocabulary. In
            18th International Congress of Americanists (1912), Appendix, pp.
            539–65. London.

Oosten, Jarich G.

1981   Filiation and Alliance in Three Bororo Myths. In *Current Issues
            in Anthropology : The Netherlands,* ed. Peter Kloos and Henri J. M.
            Claessen, pp. 200–214. Ministry of Education and Science, The
            Netherlands.

Parsons, Elsie Clews

1933   Hopi and Zuñi Ceremonialism. In *Memoirs of the American
            Anthropological Association,* No. 39. The American Anthropolog-
            ical Association, Menasha, Wisconsin.

Pio Corrêa, M.

1909   *Flora do Brazil: Algumas Plantas Uteis, suas Applicações e dis-
            tribuição Geográphica.* Diretoria Geral de Estatística, Typografia
            da Estatística, Rio de Janeiro.

Reichel-Dolmatoff, Gerardo

1971   *Amazonian Cosmos.* University of Chicago Press, Chicago.

Rivière, Gilles

1983   Quadripartition et Ideologie Dans les Communautes Aymaras
            de Carangas. *Bulletin du Institut Français des Etudes Andines*
            12(3–4):41–62.

Rondon, C. M. da S.

1912   Serviço de Proteção aos Indios e Localisação de Trabalhadores
            Nacionães. Oficio No. 644, Rio de Janeiro.

———, and J. Barbosa de Faría

1948   *Esboço Gramatical e Vocabulário da língua dos índios Borôro.*
            Conselho Nacional de Proteção aos Indios, no. 77, Rio de
            Janeiro.

Seeger, Anthony

1981   *Nature and Society in Central Brazil.* Harvard University Press,
            Cambridge.

Steward, J. H., ed.

1946   *Handbook of South American Indians,* volume 2. Smithsonian

Institution Bureau of American Ethnology, Bulletin 143. Washington, D.C.

Symposium: Recent Research in Central Brazil
1971   *Proceedings of the 38th International Congress of Americanists* 3:333–91 (Stuttgart-Munich, 1968).

Turner, Terence
1979a   The Gê and Bororo Societies as Dialectical Systems: A General Model. In *Dialectical Societies*, ed. D. Maybury-Lewis, pp. 147–78. Harvard University Press, Cambridge.
1979b   The Social Skin. In *Not Work Alone*, ed. Jeremy Cherfas and Roger Lewin, pp. 112–42. Temple Smith, London.
1984   Dual Opposition, Hierarchy, and Value: Moiety, Structure and Symbolic Polarity in Central Brazil and Elsewhere. In *Différences, Valeurs, Hiérarchie*, ed. Jean-Claude Galey, pp. 335–70. École des Hautes Études en Sciences Sociales, Paris.
1985   Animal Symbolism, Totemism, and the Structure of Myth. In *Animal Myths and Metaphors in South America*, ed. Gary Urton, pp. 49–106. University of Utah Press, Salt Lake City.

Turton, David, and Clive Ruggles
1978   Agreeing to Disagree: The Measurement of Duration in a Southwestern Ethiopian Community. *Current Anthropology*, 19(3): 585–600.

Urton, Gary
1980   Celestial Crosses: The Cruciform in Quechua Astronomy. *Journal of Latin American Lore* 6(1):87–110.
1981a   Animals and Astronomy in the Quechua Universe. In *Proceedings of the American Philosophical Society* 125(2):110–27. Philadelphia.
1981b   *At the Crossroads of the Earth and the Sky*. University of Texas Press, Austin.
1985   *Animal Myths and Metaphors in South America*. Salt Lake City: University of Utah Press.

Viertler, Renate
1976   As Aldeias Bororo. *Coleção Museu Paulista*, Serie de Etnologia, vol. 2. Universidade de São Paulo, São Paulo.
1978   O Estudo de Parentesco e as Práticas de Nominação Entre os Indios Bororo. In *Revista de Antropología* 21:61–68. Universidade de São Paulo, São Paulo.
1979   "A Noção de Pessoa Entre os Bororo." In *Boletin do Museu Nacional,* New Series no. 32, May, pp. 20–30. Rio de Janeiro.

Von den Steinen, Karl
1940   Entre os Aborígenes do Brasil Central (1894). In *Revista do Arquivo Municipal de São Paulo,* Nos. 34–58. São Paulo.

Von Ihering, Rodolpho
1968   *Dicionário dos Animáis do Brasil.* Editôra Universidade de
            Brasília, São Paulo.
Waehneldt, Rodolfo
1862   "Exploração da Provincia de Mato Grosso." In *Revista Trimensal
            do Instituto Histórico, Geográphico e Ethnográphico do Brasíl,* vol.
            27, part 1, pp. 193–229. Rio de Janeiro.
Wagley, Charles (1977)
1983   *Welcome of Tears.* Waveland Press, Prospect Heights, Ill.
Walker, Ernest, R. M. Nowak, and J. L. Paradiso
1983   *Mammals of the World.* Vols. 1 and 2. 4th ed. The Johns Hopkins
            University Press, Baltimore.
Wheatley, Paul
1971   *The Pivot of the Four Quarters.* Aldine, Chicago.
Wilbert, Johannes
1975   "Eschatology in a Participatory Universe: Destinies of the Soul
            among the Warao Indians of Venezuela." In *Dumbarton Oaks
            Conference on Death and the Afterlife in Pre-Columbian America,*
            ed. E.P. Benson, pp. 163–90. Washington, D.C.: Dumbarton Oaks.
1981   "Warao Cosmology and Yekuana Roundhouse Symbolism." In
            Journal of Latin American Lore 7(1):37–72.
Wilbert, Johannes, and Karin Simoneau, eds.
1983   *Folk Literature of the Bororo Indians.* UCLA Latin American Cen-
            ter Publications, University of California at Los Angeles.
Williamson, Ray A., ed.
1981   *Archaeoastronomy in the Americas.* Ballena Press Anthropological
            Papers No. 22. Los Altos.
1984   *Living the Sky: The Cosmos of the American Indian.* Houghton
            Mifflin, Boston.
Zuidema, R. Tom
1964   *The Ceque System of Cuzco.* E. J. Brill, Leiden.
1977   The Inca Calendar. In *Native American Astronomy,* ed. A. F.
            Aveni, pp. 219–59. University of Texas Press, Austin.
1981   Anthropology and Archaeoastronomy. In *Archaeoastronomy in
            the Americas,* ed. R. A. Williamson, pp. 29–31. Ballena Press
            Anthropological Papers, No. 22. Los Altos.
1982a   Bureaucracy and Systematic Knowledge in Andean Civilization.
            In *The Inca and Aztec States, 1400–1800,* ed. John D. Wirth, pp.
            419–58. Academic, New York.
1982b   Catachillay: The Role of the Pleiades and of the Southern Cross
            and Centauri in the Calendar of the Incas. In *Ethnoastronomy
            and Archaeoastronomy in the American Tropics,* ed. A.F. Aveni

and G. Urton, pp. 203–229. New York Academy of Sciences, New York.

1983   Towards a General Andean Star Calendar in Ancient Peru. In *Calendars in Mesoamerica and Peru: Native American Computations of Time*, ed. A. F. Aveni and G. Brotherston, pp. 235–62. *Proceedings of the 44th International Congress of Americanists*. B.A.R. International Series, 174. Oxford.

1986   *La Civilisation Inca au Cuzco.* Collège de France, Presses Universitaires de France, Paris.

Index